THOREAU'S AXE

Thoreau's Axe

DISTRACTION AND DISCIPLINE
IN AMERICAN CULTURE

CALEB SMITH

PRINCETON UNIVERSITY PRESS
PRINCETON & OXFORD

Published by Princeton University Press
41 William Street, Princeton, New Jersey 08540
99 Banbury Road, Oxford OX2 6JX

press.princeton.edu

All Rights Reserved

First paperback printing, 2024
Paperback ISBN 9780691256023
Cloth ISBN 9780691214771
ISBN (e-book) 9780691215280

British Library Cataloging-in-Publication Data is available

Editorial: Anne Savarese and James Collier
Production Editorial: Mark Bellis
Jacket/Cover Design: Katie Osborne
Production: Erin Suydam
Publicity: Alyssa Sanford and Carmen Jimenez
Copyeditor: Lachlan Brooks

Jacket/Cover Credit: Illustration, grass snake (Natrix natrix) from *Bilder-Atlas zur wissenschaftlich-populären Naturgeschichte der Amphibien in ihren sämmtlichen Hauptformen* by Leopold Joseph Fitzinger. Photo credit © Purix Verlag Volker Christen / Bridgeman Images

This book has been composed in Arno

For the river pride.

CONTENTS

Introduction: Distraction and the
Disciplines of Attention   1

PART I. FROM THE DEVIL TO DISTRACTION   29

1 "Wandring or distraction" (Thomas Clayton)   35

2 "Satan had hidden the very object from my mind"
  (Jarena Lee)   39

3 "Hundreds of thousands have their appetite so
  depraved" (J. H. McIlvaine)   43

4 "My non-compliance would almost always produce
  much confusion" (Frederick Douglass)   49

5 "Opium-like listlessness" (Herman Melville)   55

6 "Morbid attention" (Edgar Allan Poe)   59

7 "The shell of lethargy" (William James)   66

PART II. REFORM   69

8 "A white man could, if he had paid as much
  attention" (Lydia Maria Child)   77

9 "The cultivation of attention as a moral duty"
(Elizabeth Palmer Peabody)   80

10 "The heart must be cultivated" (William Watkins)   86

11 "You might see him looking steadily at something"
(Susan Paul)   90

12 "Their nobler faculties lie all undeveloped"
(William D. Kelley)   94

13 "Subdued and tender" (A. D. Eddy)   99

14 "If he wanted to kill time" (Austin Reed)   106

PART III. REVIVAL   111

15 "All attention to the last sermon" (James Dana)   119

16 "The power of fixed and continuous attention"
(Robert Baird)   125

17 "The relations of business and religion" (Henry
Clay Fish)   131

18 "My mind was powerfully wrought upon"
(William Apess)   134

19 "I began to direct my attention to this great object"
(Nat Turner)   139

20 "Hear me now, love your heart" (Toni Morrison)   143

21 "Read these leaves in the open air" (Walt
Whitman)   146

PART IV: DEVOTION   153

22   "Noble sentiments of devotion" (J. S. Buckminster
     and Ann Plato)   159

23   "Savoir attendre" (Adrien Rouquette)   163

24   "The greatest exercise of mind" (Anonymous/
     Abraham Jacobs)   167

25   "A true sauntering of the eye" (Henry David
     Thoreau)   174

26   "If we do not guard the mind" (Hannah More)   179

27   "The valves of her attention" (Emily Dickinson)   188

28   "Aroma finer than prayer" (Walt Whitman)   190

     Afterword   194

                    Acknowledgments   207
                         Notes   211
                         Index   231

THOREAU'S AXE

Introduction

The piece that secures an axe's metal head to its wooden handle is called the wedge. The handle, passing through the head, splits open at the top, and when the wedge is driven down into the seam, like a *V* sinking into a *Y*, it pushes the sides of the handle out against the metal cylinder, the eye, to fix the bond. If the wedge rots or wears thin, the handle will narrow, and the head will rattle, coming loose. If you are not paying attention to your work, the head will fly completely off—and this is what happened, one day toward the end of March 1845, to the borrowed axe that Henry David Thoreau was using to cut white pines for timber as he built his house by Walden Pond.[1]

Repairing the tool took skill and patience. Thoreau had to fashion a new wedge from fresh wood, then fit his pieces together again. Soaking the wood in water would expand it, slowly tightening the bond between the handle and the axe-head. Thoreau was waiting, killing time, when something unexpected caught his eye. A little snake went slithering through his worksite. Thoreau watched it slip into the water and settle on the bottom, where it stayed for a long time, perfectly still.

So early in spring, Thoreau thought, the snake must have been just waking up from hibernation. Here is how he described the episode in *Walden* (1854): "One day, when my axe had come off and I had cut a green hickory for a wedge, driving it with a stone, and had placed the whole to soak in a pond hole in order to swell the wood, I saw a striped snake run into the water, and he lay on the bottom, apparently without inconvenience, as long as I staid there, or more than a quarter of an hour; perhaps because he had not yet fairly come out of the torpid state."[2]

In the snake's unresponsiveness, its lingering torpor in a thawing season, Thoreau looked for meaning. "It appeared to me," he recalled, "that for a like reason men remain in their present low and primitive condition; but if they should feel the influence of the spring of springs arousing them, they would of necessity rise to a higher and more ethereal life."[3] The people of the nineteenth century, like winter snakes, lay low, withdrawn into themselves. They did not feel the influence of the enlivening spring. Their minds were somewhere else.

What was wrong with them, exactly? A few of Thoreau's ideas—the notions of the "torpid state" and the "primitive condition"—came from natural history. Other images—the serpent, the tree, the fallen waiting for their resurrection—he adapted from the Bible. Thoreau was putting pieces together, assembling usable components from his culture. He was combining scientific concepts and Christian symbols to diagnose a state of mind.[4]

In *Walden* and in several other works, Thoreau kept developing his thinking about this low condition. The trouble, as he came to understand it, had little to do with "primitive" ways. In Thoreau's eyes, modern civilization itself did harm to nature, human and nonhuman. People were not really stuck in the past; they were lost in the present, suffering from the effects of new economic and social forces. And while Thoreau was enough of a middle-class Protestant to believe in the virtues of thrift and clean living, what he meant by "the torpid state" was not old-fashioned laziness. Bodies at rest were inoffensive. The sickening thing was the mindless, exhausting, machine-like activity of modern work and entertainment. It was making people numb instead of calm.

"The world is a place of business," Thoreau observed sorrowfully in "Life without Principle" (1863), an essay about how much is lost when human life is reduced to an endless cycle of earning and spending dollars. He went on: "What an infinite bustle! I am awakened almost every night by the panting of the locomotive. It interrupts my dreams. There is no sabbath."[5] Even the fish in Walden's depths, Thoreau noticed, felt the "rumbling" of the passing cars.[6] Leaving nothing untouched, the modern economy seemed to be invading every private sanctuary—even the cabin, even the mind. Thoreau thought that there was something obscene about all this industry and commerce, howling in the dark.

A word for the misery was *distraction*. "Our inventions are wont to be pretty toys, which distract our attention from serious things," Thoreau wrote in what has become one of *Walden*'s most commonly quoted lines.[7] He was talking about how the "infinite bustle" of modern life damages our capacities for care and wonder. The economy observed no sabbath. In the workplace, it demanded constant labor under someone else's supervising eyes. In the marketplace, it displayed an endless spectacle of trivial things. The more life accelerated, the more attention was debased.

Thoreau was speaking from experience. When he examined his personal habits, he found himself messed up, like everybody else. He knew he had been careless with a borrowed axe, and the snake he saw in the water represented, among other things, his own shame. It is unpleasant, as a reader, to feel yourself called out and scolded by Thoreau. But it is no less awkward to witness the ordeal of his self-reproach. "I believe that the mind can be permanently profaned by the habit of attending to trivial things," he writes. The line is both a creed and a confession.

Thoreau devoted much of his life's work to undoing the damage. For generations of readers, he has represented an American Romantic in rebellion against the soul-killing compulsions of market capitalism and, even more, a visionary in matters of attention. In *Writing Nature* (1985), the critic Sharon Cameron described him "advocating constancy of attention." A more recent academic study praises Thoreau's work as "courageous in its willingness to attend to nature without a defined project, to pursue an investigation without yet knowing its end." Another scholar argues that "cultivating habits of attention" is the first aim of Thoreau's work, an ambition that might inspire social justice movements to this day. In a different sector, software engineers have launched a *Walden* video game whose users can move a virtual Thoreau around the woods, playing at living deliberately.[8]

Naturally, Thoreau's legacy has its critics. Among skeptics, his name often serves as shorthand for a flawed ideological fantasy at the heart of American culture: a white man's quest for personal freedom and moral purity in the unspoiled wilderness. Some scholars, notably the political theorist Hannah Arendt, argue that Thoreau's obsession with clearing his own conscience made him unfit for the collective, compromising work that real political change demands. Some claim that Thoreau promoted an ideal of self-reliance while refusing to acknowledge his dependence on other people's labor, or that he misrepresented the Walden Woods as pristine nature while ignoring the indigenous, enslaved, and marginalized people who inhabited the land before and after he did. Thoreau can be caricatured as a narcissist, obsessed with his own reflection in the pond. The axe that he used to represent the problem of his own distraction was also a weapon of imperial conquest and settlement.[9]

Many of these criticisms have less to do with the realities of Thoreau's life and work than with his popular legend as a solitary voice in the forest. In fact, Thoreau did not ignore slavery or the violence of empire; he went to jail protesting his government's participation in them. His idea in moving to Walden was not to extricate himself entirely from social ties; it was only to reorient his life so that the woods, rather than the town, centered his spiritual map. He never pretended to be entirely on his own. Around the ponds, Thoreau got to spend time with a motley community of outsiders and nonconformists, people living beyond the confines of Concord's white, middle-class, Protestant mainstream. He also found himself communing with plants and beasts.

There are some good reasons to read *Walden* with a measure of ambivalence. Thoreau could not entirely break his culture's habit of recasting large-scale social and political problems as personal failings, best corrected by stringent moral rehabilitation. In ways I will explore throughout this book, Thoreau's program of self-correction mirrored the discipline that was forcibly imposed in the American prisons and reformatories of his time. Whether you think these paradoxes make Thoreau's work intriguing or just irritating, however, they are not peculiar to his thought alone, and they have never really been resolved. When Thoreau described the proliferating distractions of an industrializing market economy—and when he called for a bracing self-discipline to reawaken the powers of attention—he was joining the company of many others, then and now.

"Attention," the Massachusetts-based activist and novelist Lydia Maria Child announced in the first issue of a new children's magazine in 1826, "is the grand key to all knowledge, to all perfection, in whatsoever appertains to the mind." By learning better habits of attention, Child advised, impressionable minds could be improved, and wayward souls brought back into the fold. Two decades before Thoreau borrowed a friend's axe and went off to Walden, the concept of distraction was already gaining currency as a way to explain modernity's bad effects, and attention promised a psychological and moral solution to large-scale social problems.[10]

The modern cityscape was "busy and splendid," a New England minister preached on Thanksgiving Day, but its "unnatural wants" and "fictitious pleasures" could "completely engross the attention," with corrosive effects. It was better to settle in the country, where Christians could devote their full attention to God. In 1841, the young Connecticut poet Ann Plato studied these words and incorporated them into her own essay about the virtues of agrarian life. By doing so, she demonstrated her faithfulness not only to God but also to a Christian nation. After publishing her book of poems and essays as a teenager, Plato became a teacher in a school for children of color, like the one where she received her own formal education, cultivating attention in the interest of racial progress.

"In our age of machines and money," the creole mystic Adrien Rouquette wrote in French from his hermitage in the Louisiana woods in 1852, two years before the appearance of *Walden*, "people know nothing, anymore, of godly things."[12] Rouquette adapted Roman Catholic devotional practices to an ascetic, missionary life among the Choctaw people near Lake Pontchartrain, outside New Orleans. Like Thoreau, whose book Rouquette came to admire, this self-styled primitive conducted an experiment on himself, trying to revive his depleted powers of attention. He saw himself as a voluntary exile, like one of the ancient desert fathers. The truth was that his diagnosis of modernity, along with his call for an attention revival, was becoming commonplace.

These writers and many others like them are the leading characters in *Thoreau's Axe*, and their writings about divided attention and moral discipline are my objects of study. The writers came from different regions and different social ranks, even different languages. Their politics ranged from reactionary to reformist and radical. Still, they shared some crucial things. They were all spiritual seekers, all interested in moral education and self-culture, all uneasy about the civilization that was taking shape around them. In the idea of distraction, they found a way to express the damage done by new economic systems and technologies. They responded by promoting disciplines of attention—regimens for cultivating perception, concentration, and presence of mind in a distracting world.

Today, in our age of new media and chronic attention deficit, these passages from the nineteenth century have a strange resonance. Are they just the artifacts of an old-fashioned, religious mentality, unable to adjust to modern times, or are they eerily familiar prophecies, anticipating our own worries about what screens and algorithms are doing to us now? What kind of problem is distraction, and how did we come to care so much about attention, as if we could repair the harm that the world has done to us by changing our ways of taking the world into ourselves?

Distraction often appears in the guise of a novelty, but some of the psychic and social calamities that seem new have really been unfolding for a long, long time. Likewise, some remedies that might feel secular—or, in the common phrasing, "spiritual but not religious"—partake of Christian moral regimens devised two hundred years ago or more. We may think that our distraction is unprecedented; so did many poets, preachers, and activists in the days when trains and cheap newsprint first moved across the continent. They believed that they were living in a new era, the age of machines and money. Distraction was their name for how it hurt.

Disciplines of attention were their therapies and rehabilitation programs. In the nineteenth century's attention revival, there were heavy-handed moralists who preached attention in the service of social control. They tried to reconcile the unruly, especially the powerless, to an existence of hard work and meager pleasure. There were plenty of middle-class escapists, too, who wished for little more than a spiritual vacation. They did what they could to soothe their frazzled nerves, then clocked back in to business as usual. And then there were a few wild mystics, pushing the limits, seeking spiritual freedom and ecstatic intimacies. Even the militants, however, did not dream of liberating themselves entirely from discipline, into a life with no direction or constraint. Instead, they tried to craft new disciplines, or counter-disciplines, for their movements and themselves.

This book is a genealogy of distraction and the disciplines of attention, going back to Thoreau's era. In the documents of nineteenth-century American literature, religion, and social reform, I find the sources of a predicament that still bedevils us today: even after we understand that distraction's real causes are in the large-scale economic systems and technologies that shape our world, we keep trying to solve the problem with personal, moral remedies. For instance, we adjust our consumption habits, or we make efforts to ensure that our leisure time is quality time, spent mindfully. By doing so, we repeat a pattern that took shape under the nineteenth century's versions of accelerating, industrializing market capitalism and spiritual revival.

I study the archives to understand this long, conflicted cultural history. At the same time, *Thoreau's Axe* is something of a salvage operation. I find, in the nineteenth century's ways of valuing and practicing attention, some resources for living through the present. For me, as a critic writing about others' writings, this means approaching my sources both as relics of a troubled past and as crafted objects of sustaining beauty. I read with a cautious eye, watching for the ways that writers exercise and disavow their power, even as my mind becomes absorbed in their poetry, taking shelter. There is some wariness in my way of reading, along with some attachment and desire; that's what closeness feels like, anyway. Maybe attention can be a way of engaging with the world instead of trying to transcend it, and discipline can be for self-composure, not for purity.

———

To the distracted, attention makes alluring promises. It opens a way to fuller, more satisfying experience, or it brings people into deeper contact with the ones they love. In the midst of hustling and noise, disciplines of attention offer peace of mind. At the same time, though, they call for certain sacrifices. Some kinds of pleasure and freedom will have to be surrendered on the way to attention's more enduring ones. Distraction is a kind of suffering, but suffering has also been inflicted in attention's name. This give-and-take, the interplay of rehabilitation and submission, was already happening along the shores of ponds in nineteenth-century Massachusetts.

Out in the woods, Thoreau set up his little house and devoted his time to the work of self-recovery. In "Life without Principle," he explained his therapeutic regimen for people who had let their minds become distracted: "If we have thus desecrated ourselves—and who has not?—the remedy will be by wariness and devotion to reconsecrate ourselves, and make once more a fane of the mind." With the archaic word *fane*—from Latin by way of Late Middle English, meaning a sacred place, a temple—Thoreau reached back through the ages, trying to recover some ancient, less degraded state. He continued: "We should treat our minds, that is, ourselves, as innocent and ingenuous children, whose guardians we are, and be careful what objects and what subjects we thrust on their attention." Treating his own mind like a child, Thoreau aspired to a second innocence. His program was a discipline of "wariness and devotion."[13]

Thoreau took an interest in the tradition of spiritual exercises, developed over many centuries by mystics and philosophers. Spiritual exercises are practices designed to detach people's minds from the passions and dramas of everyday social life so they can focus on higher, more enduring realities. Some of these practices, like solitary meditation, are perfectly tranquil. Others involve repressing the appetites and mortifying the flesh. In the opening pages of *Walden*, there are references to elaborate rituals of self-torment: ascetics "sitting exposed to four fires and looking in the face of the sun" or "dwelling, chained for life, at the foot of a tree."[14] Closer to home, for Thoreau, was New England's deep history of Christian devotional practices. Even the Puritans, remembered for their frigidness, had recorded weird, ecstatic ravishments by their God.

Thoreau was not the kind of hairshirted monk who would reject the pleasures of the senses or cut up his natural body. He meant to situate himself in the physical world and intensify his own experience. He wished to feel more wakeful, more alive. But he did try to adapt old-fashioned spiritual exercises to his nineteenth-century circumstances. When Thoreau went walking in the woods, he practiced what he called "the discipline of looking always at what is to be seen." When he studied the literary classics, he put himself through "a training such as the athletes underwent, the steady intention almost of the whole life to this object." He worked on reconditioning his distracted mind with disciplines of attention.[15]

At Walden, Thoreau felt he had discovered just the right place to get himself together. It was a quiet situation:

> The scenery of Walden is on a humble scale, and, though very beautiful, does not approach to grandeur, nor can it much concern one who has not long frequented it or lived by its shore; yet this pond is so remarkable for its depth and purity as to merit a particular description. It is a clear and deep green well, half a mile long and a mile and three quarters in circumference, and contains about sixty-one and a half acres; a perennial spring in the midst of pine and oak woods . . . [16]

Thoreau's technical training as a land surveyor helped him here, but he also needed to unlearn his habitual ways of seeing. Being humble itself, Walden required humility from its observer. For Thoreau, writing a careful description was a way to show the fruit of his self-discipline. He had turned himself into the kind of person who could appreciate simple, rather than spectacular scenery.[17]

Sometimes, though, the history of attention's disciplines is less free-spirited, less sweet. It is not only a history of people's efforts to save themselves from mind-corroding economic circumstances by reawakening their own powers. It is also a history of captivity and psychic manipulation. Take a look, for instance, at this other description of a rural New England scene, composed (like much of *Walden*) in the 1840s:

> The pond is of clear, pure water, about thirty feet in depth, and covering one hundred and seventy-eight acres of land. The ground rises, by a gentle acclivity, from the shore of the pond, to a height which overlooks this beautiful sheet of water, and an extent of country beyond, embracing, in part, the village of Westborough, and gives a very pleasing prospect. There are no manufacturing villages in the vicinity, and the farm-houses are

not more numerous than in most of the agricultural towns in the State, in proportion to the area. The situation, therefore, is sufficiently retired.

This passage celebrating pure water and gentle beauty, out in the country, far from modern noise, appears in an 1847 Massachusetts state legislature committee report, proposing the site for what would become America's first state-run juvenile reformatory.[18]

Drawing up the plans for its youth prison, the state chose a rustic, rural setting, distant from the temptations of urban consumption and the noise of factories. The planning committee noted, approvingly, that there was no industrial infrastructure in sight. The water was clear and clean, the views agreeable. It was almost as if the surveyors had stepped back in time. This, they determined, was the ideal setting for a new kind of incarceration.

Animating the committee's pastoral vision, there was a distinctly modern theory of delinquency and rehabilitation. The theory held that new manufacturing systems, along with the poisonous attractions of the marketplace, were corrupting vulnerable minds. Among the reformers who took an interest in such problems, the effect was called "hardening" (as in "hardened criminal"), or "blackening." Poorly supervised children, in particular, were said to suffer from bad influences, which coarsened their minds.[19]

Though juvenile delinquents were damaged, however, they were not incorrigible. Reformers saw their hardening as an effect of their experiences and circumstances, not some innate moral weakness or biological deficiency. What history had done to these victims of neglect could be undone by discipline. As the reformatory's founders put it, "It is proposed, by the discipline which awaits them here, to quicken the torpid action of conscience, by calling into play the moral sentiments which have been suffered to lie dormant."[20] Delinquents appeared, to their keepers, to be "torpid" animals, their moral sentiments in hibernation, like Thoreau's snake. To correct their ways, the state would begin by removing them to a purer atmosphere.

The property was secured; the facility was constructed near the pond. Just as Thoreau had exhorted his readers to treat our minds as "children, whose guardians we are," state-administered juvenile rehabilitation promised to repair delinquents' habits of attention. In custody, children would work all day and, in their free time, look out over the "beautiful sheet of water." Under strict supervision, they would learn industry and self-control. Correction was being redefined as therapy, punishment as pastoral care.

Unlike Thoreau's voluntary removal to Walden, however, serving time at the reformatory was compulsory, and it required submission to authorities. Although its propagandists talked about love and mercy, this was the kind of place that the sociologist Erving Goffman called a "total institution," the style of enforcement that the philosopher Michel Foucault analyzed with devastating elegance in *Surveiller et Punir* (1975).[21] Rather than a retreat for unhappy poets, the reformatory established a severe labor discipline and moral reeducation, under lock and key, mostly for the children of the poor. They were not "chained for life," but they were forcibly confined. Their assigned work was supposed to prepare them for the rigors of industrial market capitalism. Their moral training assimilated them into the culture of white, Protestant respectability.

They tended the reformatory's farm, or they made shoes and chairs in its workshops. Private contractors leased their labor from the state. If they failed to comply with the rules or to complete their work on time, guards and superintendents punished their insubordination. When their terms were over, the institution would unload them back into the same environment which, according to its own theory, first put them in harm's way. Rehabilitated, they were supposed to "go forth with the habits of industry, of purity, and self-respect," back to work.[22] The reformatory was a supplement to the market economy, then, not a monastic world apart.

Thoreau's self-culture and the reformatory's punishment, his self-discipline and its compulsory rehabilitation, resemble each other in disquieting ways. Rather than resisting modern economic forces, it appears, spiritual exercises can be used to reinforce them. Instead of striking against the true sources of distraction—the exploitations and manipulations of industrial capitalism—disciplines of attention were often used to keep the machinery running smoothly. This was the aim of the nineteenth century's most elaborate experiments in top-down social engineering, from evangelical missionary campaigns to industrial prisons.

Among the reformers who built the nineteenth century's correctional institutions, distraction was thought to cause two kinds of trouble: one at sites of production (the workplace), the other at scenes of consumption (the marketplace). First of all, there was inefficiency on the job. Distracted workers wasted time. The absent-minded sailor on the masthead in Herman Melville's *Moby-Dick* (1851), dissociating from his labor in "opium-like listlessness," had many thousands of real-life counterparts on farms, in workshops, and on factory floors. Withholding a part of themselves, these mental drifters slowed production down.

In *Capital* (1867), Karl Marx defines attention specifically as a force that keeps workers focused on the work in front of them. Over the time it takes to do a job, Marx notices, the mind inevitably wanders. This happens in every kind of labor, including the least exploitative; it happens even when you freely set your own task for yourself. After a while, you lose your concentration. You might start wishing you were doing something else, or just to take a break. Marx introduces the term *attention* to identify the power that holds you fast. Subordinating your fickle will to the purpose of your work, he writes, "means close attention."[23]

In Marx's theory of attention, it is not the laborer's tools that fall to pieces, like Thoreau's axe. It is the laborer himself. Inside the mind of every worker, there is a purpose, the will to complete a task, but then there also arise other desires and impulses, at odds with the original plan. Attention, like an axe-wedge, holds these two parts of the self together, in alignment. Although attention is often imagined as a person's way of relating to a thing, like reading a poem or cutting down a tree, Marx suggests that it is really a relation between two agents. Even when the worker is alone, there is something antagonistic about attention, maybe even something social.

The less the worker identifies his own freedom and pleasure with the purpose of the work, Marx writes, "the closer his attention is forced to be." As work becomes more alienating and exploitative, the "exertion of the working organs" must be forcibly cajoled.[24] It is as if an outside, hostile will, at odds with the worker's own, takes hold of him, using his attention to manipulate his body so that he can execute its plans. Attention means subordination.

Anyone who has done hard, unpleasant work can probably recognize the feeling of pushing themselves to get it over with. But in the middle decades of the nineteenth century, when Marx and Thoreau were writing about economies, the dynamics of productive labor under American capitalism were changing in profound ways, on a vast scale. Industrialization (of agriculture and manufacturing alike) and the market revolution wrought severe social and psychological dislocations. For many workers, the gap between the purpose of their labor and the freedom of their "physical and mental powers" was painfully intense.

The starkest example was chattel slavery. According to the American slave system's legal fictions, there was no significant conflict between the master's designs and the worker's will, since the worker was not supposed to have any free will at all. "The tragedy of the black slave's position was precisely this," W.E.B. Du Bois writes, surveying antebellum Southern legal codes: "his absolute subjection to the individual will of an owner."[25] On the ground, though, as Du Bois knew, the transaction was never so clean. This kind of owner-property relation was a human relation, fraught with conflict. "To coercion and punishment," the historian Eric Williams observes, the enslaved "responded with indolence, sabotage, and revolt." There was always resistance, ongoing drift.[26]

The violence of plantation labor discipline became notorious, as did the monstrous figure who embodied attention as a subordinating force—the overseer. In Marx's theory of productive

labor, two purposes within a single mind strained against one another, and attention mediated between the two. In the ideology of
the American slave system, each of these three parts was played by
a different actor. There was the master, with his will to raise a crop for
market. There was the enslaved worker, whose body had productive capacity but also strong impulses toward pleasure, rest, and
freedom. And then there was the overseer, who stood for attention
itself.

The overseer's business was to keep the enslaved on task, enforcing submission to the master's purposes. His methods included both harsh violence and hypervigilance. Slavery's arsenal
held many grotesque implements of torture, but it also included
subtler styles of psychic and emotional control. "There was no
deceiving him," Frederick Douglass writes of the infamous overseer Mr. Covey. "He had the faculty of making us feel that he was
ever present with us."[27] Surveillance seemed to get under the skin,
into the feelings, as unremitting wariness. In practice, overseers
negotiated with the agency of those whose personhood the law
denied. Even "the heart, the soul, and the mind," as Saidiya Hartman teaches us, can be "inroads of discipline."[28] Meanwhile, creating distractions became a prized tactical skill among subversives
and fugitives.

As for the nineteenth century's wage laborers, they were "nominally free," in possession of themselves, contracting to sell their
time and work consensually. All the same, though, there were ten-
sions between entrepreneurs' purposes and laborers' wills. In one
of Marx's source texts, *The Philosophy of Manufactures* (1835), the
Scottish business theorist Andrew Ure complained about the wandering minds of men recruited into factories from other, pre-
industrial sectors. "After struggling for a while to conquer their
listless and restive habits, they either renounce the employment
spontaneously, or are dismissed by the overlookers on account of
inattention."[29] Distraction was gumming up production on the factory floor. The art critic and theorist Jonathan Crary sees subversion in this kind of mental truancy: "Though its history will never

be formally written, the daydream is nonetheless a domain of resistance internal to any system of routinization or coercion."[30]

Ure determined that grown-up laborers, "past the age of puberty,"
were too far gone in their undisciplined habits. Industrialists found
themselves searching for more innocent, malleable subjects (namely
children) and more effective ways to motivate them. Ure fantasized
about "willing menials" happily giving their "attention and dexterity"
to the machine. If workers could be made to identify with the purpose of the labor, he imagined, they would acquiesce more readily.
They would practically supervise themselves.[31]

Sophisticated labor discipline sought more than the menials'
rote obedience to the boss's commands. It tried to change their
hearts. The right kind of training, as nineteenth-century managers
envisioned it, translated economic imperatives into the language
of the worker's private, moral conscience. And here, in the effort
to educate minds and souls, industrial labor discipline found its
common cause with a broader, Christian moral campaign to convert and civilize the nation's population.

Securing social order in an era of rapid economic disruptions
was not only about keeping workers at their ploughs and stations,
turning out more goods. It was also about regulating how they
spent their money and their free time, after work. The marketplace
was a source of growing wealth for businessmen and merchants, but
it was also a scene of social instability. Wayward, wandering types
appeared to be assembling at the temples of indulgence—taverns,
shops, and theaters—where their appetites got them into trouble.
The authorities saw distraction as a source of delinquency and
crime. Consumption, like production, needed supervision, and so
the disciplines of attention were brought to bear in institutionalized
moral training.

The theory of rehabilitation that shaped nineteenth-century
disciplines of attention was drawn, in part, from enlightened philosophies of the human mind. The reformers who developed it
were familiar with Jeremy Bentham's utilitarian proposals about surveillance as well as John Locke's ideas about mental development.

In his *Essay Concerning Human Understanding* (1689), Locke had explored how acts of attention involve both a passive receptivity to influences and an active selection of objects. Attention opened up the mind. It also exercised the will, focusing on certain things instead of others, filtering out the rest as background noise. Young people were available for rehabilitation because they remained malleable, receptive to new impressions from their superiors. The best way to shape their moral character, over time, was to enlist their own participation in the procedure.[32]

Although some of the philosophers who developed this account of the mind were dissenters and freethinkers, not orthodox Christians, their ideas were easily taken up by religious authorities and missionaries. "The mind will unavoidably take its character from the objects most frequently presented to it," one Unitarian minister preached in the early nineteenth century. "If these be low and trifling, so will be its pursuits and its desires." Here, as in Thoreau's remarks on self-discipline, attending to frivolous things was proscribed as a corrosive habit. To guard against the trifling that led to a vicious life, the minister recommended a regimen of prayer and devotional reading. He guided his young readers toward the "practice of piety," a set of techniques that would "excite constant attention to virtuous and active pursuits." By managing your objects of perception and desire, you could sanctify yourself.[33]

"The degree of attention we pay," another minister preached in 1850, "depends upon our own disposition to attend. This shows us that the matter, after all, is very largely one of *discipline*."[34] During the years when Thoreau built his cabin and the state of Massachusetts opened its reformatory, each along a waterfront, the longstanding alliance between Protestant ethics and the spirit of capitalism, famously analyzed by the social theorist Max Weber, was entering a new phase. Christian morality made its peace with large-scale plantation and factory work, a free market for consumer goods, and a flood of cheap print. Schools and penal institutions imposed disciplines of attention, tempered by love, so that industry and civilization could proceed.[35]

When the Massachusetts reformatory opened its doors and received its first delinquents, one reformer saw the future in these vivid terms: "Here ... where the sound of the orgies of the dram-shop never reach,—where no theatre opens its pit or gallery to entrap the unwary by its fascinations,—away from the oaths of ribaldry with which vice holds revel in the dens and stews of the crowded city,—washed clean of the filth with which vicious poverty defiles its children, the boy may learn the lesson of useful employment." Reform reached into "dens and stews," into a crowd of defiled, distracted children, and plucked out a single boy. Severed from the vicious social world that had shaped his character, he began to learn new lessons and to develop new habits of mind. When he was rehabilitated, he would be ready for employment.[36]

The literary theorist Eve Kosofsky Sedgwick introduces a beautiful phrase for the mental and moral lapses that nineteenth-century authorities meant to intervene against; she calls them "elopements of attention."[37] The wandering mind was a queer and worrisome thing, running off with its bad objects. Disciplinary institutions were designed to lock it down. To investigate attention's history, then, is not only to recover transcendentalist techniques of self-culture. It is also to encounter systems of exploitation, backed up by punitive mechanisms of social control. Along with free markets and free labor came the common school, the reformatory, and the prison. Thus, the industrial economy entered into an uneasy partnership with a civilizing mission, guided by white Christian nationalists who set the terms for social and political assimilation.

———

In revisiting the archives of nineteenth-century moral discipline, I come back to questions that have been at the heart of my own critical work for many years. I began the inquiry in my first book, *The Prison and the American Imagination*, and I have never really been able to let it go. Some questions seem unresolved; they still preoccupy my mind. Let me try to give some reasons why.

When I read the works of nineteenth-century reformers, revivalists, and transcendental mystics in the pages of old books and magazines, I know that I am looking at artifacts from a distant time. And yet I seem to recognize their ways of talking about distraction and the disciplines of attention. I can almost hear the grandfather who taught me how to tie a fishing knot and cast a lure; the public-school teachers who tried to keep me on task; the preacher turning our congregation to prayer in the evangelical churches down in Arkansas, where I was raised.

Most of these pastoral figures in my early life, I felt, spoke for a conservative social order. I was sometimes fidgety under their scolding, restless in their pews. I wanted distraction, and like most kids I found my share. As it turned out, though, most of my favorite kinds of expression and dissent, growing up, incorporated their own disciplines of attention.

In the Ozark Mountains back then, there were still some remnants of a hippie counterculture, people who had sauntered like Thoreau out of middle-class conformity, into the woods, living off the grid and getting mystical. In the college town where I went to public schools, there was a small but vital hardcore punk-rock scene, militant against consumer culture and white Christian bigotry. The assembly of beautiful freaks and misfits who came together at the local all-ages music venue was the closest thing I had to a congregation. I was in a band with a fifteen-year-old genius who skipped school just to practice playing his alto saxophone all day, until his lips would bleed. Maybe the police thought he was a delinquent, but to some of us he seemed more like a holy saint. All of this was about attention, too, somehow.

My friends in high school went straight edge, or went vegan, or shaved their heads. Dressed in combat boots and simple, thrift-store clothes, we weren't just shaking off the scolding that we disliked at Bible camp or dodging the managers who supervised us at our part-time jobs. We were also mimicking discipline, trying to adapt it to some other purpose. When we taught ourselves to play guitar, when we cooked for friends and strangers after rock shows in garages, when we pierced each other's faces with needles disinfected in the flame of butane cigarette lighters, late at night, it was sweet, but it was also regimented, in its way. We were doing work and practicing loyalty. The intimacies we nourished in private ended up sustaining us in public protest—against wars, against deportations, against police brutality, and against other kinds of state and vigilante cruelty.

I still hear all these voices now, I know, because I took them in, internalized them. They became part of the voice I use in silence when I am speaking only to myself. Trying to get my work done while the twenty-first-century attention economy chimes and flashes all around, I summon myself to concentration, to focus on my reading or my writing, in longhand, on a yellow legal pad. When I get distracted and blue, I tell myself that it is time to shut off my machines. I go out walking in the woods or by the sea, to recompose myself.

Even as I write critically about histories and fantasies of discipline, then, I cannot help practicing it. More and more, in middle age, I also find myself calling others to attention. In the classes I teach, some on a private university campus and some in state prisons, I try to cultivate my students' sustained concentration. I ask them to read closely, notice details, and think patiently about works of art. I use a similar voice when I instruct my son in drawing a picture of a hawk or setting up a hook with a jab in his tiny boxing gloves. "Watch this," he says all the time, calling my attention to himself.

Now and then, while I was writing this book, I drove out into the country to spend an afternoon at Miller's Pond, a spring-fed reservoir on a New England hilltop, where I like to swim and fish. Other days, I went to a particular bend in the Mill River, wading in the knee-deep water with my little boy. Once in a while we got lucky and caught sight of some wild bird of prey, an osprey or a red-tail hawk, or came across a snake, tightly curled among the rocks. I found that being by the water, in the company of those undomesticated creatures, cleared my mind.

On the way, I passed through Wallingford, Connecticut, a small city that was developed in the middle decades of the nineteenth century by utopian socialists from the Oneida Community. Oneida became notorious for experimenting with free love, but its economic ideas were similarly radical. Beside the river, Oneida laborers built industrial workshops to support their collective enterprise. One of their products, Oneida silverware, became well-known around the country. The commune's organizers believed that manufacturing could serve their social and spiritual improvement, as long as the work was fairly managed and the profits equitably shared.[38]

The community fell apart in the 1870s, but the company kept operating, and Wallingford grew and prospered as a manufacturing city for another century. It was only in my lifetime, after the 1970s, that most of the industry closed down or moved away. The infrastructure—old factories, warehouses, garages—stood empty for a while. Storms and vandals shattered the windows. The machines rusted out, and vines climbed over the walls, following the grooves between the bricks.

Nowadays, new enterprises occupy much of the commercial real estate. Where Wallingford laborers used to make things with machines, there are facilities for other disciplines. The industrial district houses a growing self-care industry for the multiracial working and middle classes. One former repair plant has been rebranded Forging Fitness, the gym where I work out. Upstairs, there is a martial arts studio. Nearby, you can find archery and axe throwing studios; you can get pierced and tattooed; you can practice yoga or Pilates. In these makeshift spaces, people come to find their regimens. The factories have been converted for new uses in a new economy.

Surveying this scarred and thinly touched-up landscape, it is tempting to take a disenchanted view, as the critic Christopher

Lasch did in his bitter indictment of postindustrial American society, *The Culture of Narcissism* (1979): "Having no hope of improving their lives in any of the ways that matter, people have convinced themselves that what matters is psychic self-improvement: getting in touch with their feelings, eating health food, taking lessons in ballet or belly-dancing, immersing themselves in the wisdom of the East, jogging, learning how to 'relate.'"[39] In the burned-out mill towns of our own century, such a critic might say, ex-factory workers and their children—pushed into the lower rungs of the health care industry, or trying their luck in the gig economy—have nothing left but a commodified self-care. Where there used to be an assembly line, now there are rows of weight racks and elliptical machines you have to pay to use. Business, having abandoned these people when it found cheaper labor somewhere else, comes back to sell them the opportunity to discipline themselves inside the very buildings it left empty.[40]

What are they seeking, really? What do we want? I like to think that the new disciplines of attention, like the ones that took shape two hundred years ago, register a widespread restlessness about economic conditions—a drive to realign our work with our own purposes. You can say that therapeutic self-care distracts people from the true, structural causes of human misery, but when you talk this way, you are doing your own moralizing about attention. The real question is whether disciplines of attention can be linked up with programs for economic and social—not just personal—transformation.[41]

The old utopian impulse might be revived, though the prospects for such a transformation remain uncertain. Since the nineteenth century, two prevailing forces have opposed it. One is market capitalism, which demands attention for its systems of production and consumption. The other is white Christian nationalism, which imposes moral discipline in the service of social repression. The first builds factories, shopping centers, and online marketplaces; the second drives evangelical missions, militarism, and a massive penal system.

The alliance between conservative religious discipline and the market economy has been a topic of critical study since the days of Marx and Weber. Still, seeing how they fit together can be tricky, not least because each of these formations sometimes makes itself look like a sanctuary from the other. An advertisement for a new brand of car or candy says that your consumer experience will feel like getting free from old-fashioned, repressive moral authority; meanwhile, right-wing evangelicalism represents itself as a campaign to save the nation's soul from base materialism. In reality, these two forged a strong bond in the early and middle decades of the nineteenth century, when slavery and indentured servitude gave way to free labor, the "market revolution" expanded consumer culture, and new publishing technologies produced the mass media. Trying to manage the social changes and dislocations that they understood as pervasive distraction, Protestants engineered a Great Awakening, and states built monumental penitentiaries.

Now, in a new millennium, the dilemma reappears. Our economy creates a thousand distractions, while our conservative religious and social movements absorb people's longing for spirituality and community, and our state governments lock away the unruly in mass numbers. The era of the digital attention economy has also been a boom time for evangelical megachurches and mass incarceration. At the margins are the armed libertarians and the right-wing vigilantes, with their quasi-military disciplines.

From the beginning, though, my work on *Thoreau's Axe* followed the intuition that a critical, historical reckoning with attention's disciplines cannot afford to treat them merely as methods of coercion, to be shaken off. Even degraded, commodified styles of self-culture appeal to a real, living hunger. They promise to satisfy the craving that arises, under normalized distraction, for some kind of transformation. The literary works and other writings that I study here point the way to mystical perceptions and redeemed intimacies. In the tradition of dialectical criticism, such promises are called "utopian."[42]

As a critical, historical study, this book is my effort to describe how so many American conflicts came to be imagined as problems of distraction or attention, as if they could be solved by retraining people's dormant capacities to see clearly and feel intensely. At the same time, though, I am interested in the possibilities that such an understanding opens up, not just its power to divert people from more authentic kinds of self-awareness or more effective kinds of action. Calling attention a mystification would not dispel its power, since mystification is another word for distraction.

Composing *Thoreau's Axe*, I wondered: What kind of thinking, what kind of critical writing, could grasp the histories of labor and power that shape the desire for a redeemed attentiveness while also recognizing—and pursuing—some version of this desire? Our methods of cultivating attention now are often escapist or therapeutic consolations, but other, fiercer ways have been imagined, and not all of them have been reactionary. Alone among the many disciplines of attention, reading can engage with attention's cultural history. Could I study the archive for both its coercive demands and its utopian cravings, both the violence that it disavows and the power whose pursuit it openly asserts? I decided to make an experiment.

I adapted an old religious genre, the book of devotion. Originally designed for Bible study, as an aid to prayer, devotional books incorporated brief excerpts from scripture or other religious works, supplementing the reprinted passages with the author's own meditations. Following the same model, I took some of my passages from religious works, but I also used the archives of literature and social reform.

I was looking for historical evidence that would help me reconstruct the cultural history of distraction and attention in the United States. I wanted to show the depth and the diversity of nineteenth-century writers' reckonings with these problems. More than artifacts, though, I wanted passages that would sustain slow, careful reading. I wanted to write with writers whose language had some music or some thunder and whose thinking harbored intellectual surprises. I chose passages that resisted paraphrase and seemed to become stranger, more paradoxical, and more beautiful the more I paid attention to them.

I began each of my reflections with a quotation, usually a selection where problems of distraction and attention are treated in some especially interesting way. Reading the passage closely and thinking about the historical conditions that informed it, I composed my reflection. Curiously, I found that I responded to the most didactic, pious works with feelings of suspicion and resistance, rather than acquiescence. By contrast, some of the wilder, more incendiary passages, whether they came from poets or militants, made me want to understand the discipline that guided them. If distraction means a division within the mind, pursuing two different purposes, then you could say that I tried to read my passages distractedly: one part of my reading accepted the work's demands, staying with its aspirations and its artistry, and another part dissociated, wandering to a further distance, thinking about history and power.

Just as some Christian devotional books offered one reflection for each day in a four-week cycle, I composed four sets of seven exercises. The four parts can be approached as deconstructed chapters, where the primary sources are examined in detail, with an eye for their complexities, rather than being smoothly incorporated into my own narrative. I know that there are some intellectual risks involved in laying out the book this way. My interpretations often end up in ambivalence, rather than a strong judgment about the passage at hand. But this, in my experience, is how attention really works—restlessly, reflexively, usually away from commands, especially when they come cloaked in disavowal, and often toward the charisma of other people's self-possession. Readers of *Thoreau's Axe* may choose to make their way through the reflections in their numbered sequence, from one to twenty-eight, tracking my argument about the cultural history of distraction and attention, or they may decide to skip around, making their own connections. If you read enough of them, you will see the patterns.

Part One, "From the Devil to Distraction," examines passages that deal with the changing meanings of distraction in modernizing times. The other three parts explore three ways the nineteenth century tried to regulate attention. "Reform" is about disciplinary institutions like experimental schools and penitentiaries; here I read passages about moral training, with reference to Foucault, Hartman, and other theorists of discipline. "Revival" goes to evangelical camp meetings and similar religious gatherings, studying passages about spiritual renewal while drawing from Marx, Weber, and other critics of Christianity under capitalism. "Devotion" examines nineteenth-century practices of self-culture, many of which were adapted from ancient spiritual exercises; here my readings focus especially on desire and disavowal, sometimes in a psychoanalytic mode.

The reformatory, the revival, and the scene of private devotion—as I make my way through this sequence of pastoral settings, I move from the one that is most obviously coercive to the one that seems most voluntary. Schools and correctional institutions impose compulsory disciplines, backed up by force. Evangelical churches use less formal kinds of paternalistic care and social pressure to ensure conformity. Devotional reading and prayer, when they are taken up by choice in private, might appear not to have any coercive force at all, though devotional literature usually models a kind of discipline for its readers, inviting them to try it for themselves, if they feel the calling.

Still, the story that unfolds across my four sections is not a neat progression from captivity to freedom. From the prison to the open-air sermon and the prayer closet, the politics of attention's disciplines are volatile. In schools and penitentiaries, reformers attempt to remedy the psychic harms inflicted by market capitalism, endowing wayward minds with the self-control required for freedom, yet disciplinary institutions have always been sites of counter-discipline as well, and they sometimes end up fostering, in spite of themselves, a spiritual militancy that turns against their own designs.[43] Revivals bring a Christian ethic of sober living to the working classes and the disenfranchised, but they can also become festivals of democratic intimacy, fiery and uncontained. Ascetic devotion mortifies improper desires, yet it occasionally prepares dissenters for resistance, even rebellion.

"I began to direct my attention to this great object," the rebel prophet Nat Turner is reported to have said of his insurrection plot against Virginia slaveholders in 1831.[44] Every kind of pastoral supervision exposes itself to evasion and inversion. This is the predicament of a modern economic system that incorporates spiritual exercises as its therapeutic, regulatory supplements. By setting devotional practices apart from its own systems and operations, the economy allows people to use them as ways of cultivating communities and identities in opposition to itself.

Many of my readings in the archive show how the literature of attention stages ethical encounters between two wills while, at the same time, disavowing any coercive willfulness. This paradox is easiest to identify in punitive situations, where authorities control delinquents by training them in self-control. It may be more difficult to see how the same dynamic plays out in practices of self-culture, as well. Achieving a greater receptivity to the outside world entails a deliberate choice, an exercise of will over oneself, often expressed in the imperative mode. One commands oneself to submit. Attending is surrendering, but willfully.[45]

My hope, in tracing these patterns of discipline and disavowal, is not just to expose some secret, unacknowledged complicity between power and attention. The worst effect of the developments I follow in this book is something other than hypocrisy or impurity. The diabolical thing is the breaking apart, the splintering of the world, so that each person or pairing seems isolated and condemned to its consoling therapy while the economy's machinery grinds on, grinding people down. The way beyond is not within, in purifying disciplines; it has to go, by way of work and love, into the world.

PART I

From the Devil to Distraction

When the devil left our world behind, if he ever did, he left us in distraction. The first edition of Noah Webster's *American Dictionary of the English Language* (1828) defined distraction as "confusion from a multiplicity of objects crowding on the mind and calling the attention in different ways." Distraction was a bad, divided feeling, a crowding on the mind, but it was also a wayward "calling," a sinister vocation. Like a serpent's whisper, distraction suggested the allure of sin. To give an example that nineteenth-century readers would be sure to recognize, the dictionary cited the King James Bible, 1 Corinthians 7:35, where the apostle Paul instructs his followers "to attend upon the Lord without distraction."

In Paul's letters, distraction means desire for the flickering, glittering attractions of this world. The distracted allow themselves to be carried away by thoughts of money, sex, and power. In other words, distraction is attention, even feverish attachment, but to all the wrong things. By contrast, attending to the Lord means straightening and constituting yourself through vigilant self-discipline. Paul imagines a painful tension between soul and body, spiritual devotion overmastering natural appetites. Holy attention is fidelity to the unseen. The apostle is always being drawn, through his flesh, into the crowding world, and he is always restraining himself, turning back to God.[1]

This ancient, dualistic way of thinking about distraction has never really disappeared. Writing about coming of age in upstate New York, the epicenter of nineteenth-century American revivalism, the African Methodist Evangelical deacon Julia A. J. Foote remembered wandering from the holy path. "The pomps and vanities of this world began to engross my attention," Foote confessed.[2] Lying to her mother, forgetting her faith, Foote snuck off to parties and the local playhouse, chasing pleasure. Her temperament was fickle, by her own account. She was drawn to crowds and given to distraction.

If listening in on these confessions now makes some of us feel nervous, this is partly because we have learned to associate old-time religion with repression. In Christian empires, jeremiads against worldly temptation have often justified political violence. Churches stifle unruly desire to reinforce their own power, and states impose restraints on populations whose appetites are deemed uncivilized. In assessments of devotion's purity, authorities draw social distinctions: religious identity, race, class, gender, and so on. Nathaniel Hawthorne's *The Scarlet Letter* (1850), with its rituals of public shaming and its scenes of private self-torture, has become a classic treatment of this cruel dynamic.

Wherever "the flesh" is targeted by punitive authorities, as skeptics know, certain bodies will be punished more severely than others. In Julia Foote's world, it was the indigenous and the enslaved who bore the heaviest burden.[3] Born into a society where religious hierarchies had been soldered to racial ones, Black Americans who published their own spiritual autobiographies were under pressure to demonstrate, against racists who doubted it, that they were capable of true, sober devotion. Conversion was a religious experience, but it also authorized the convert's claim to a measure of social and political dignity. For Foote, though, as for some other saints and martyrs whose stories circulated in popular narratives, the power conferred by spiritual exercises also went beyond the kinds of polite, respectable self-restraint that white Christian assimilationists wanted from them. Believers' contempt for "this world" gave them righteous fortitude against governments, slavecatchers, armies, and banks. Now and then, they let it rip.[4]

In the tradition of Christian confessional writing, a taste for sin was believed to be part of human nature. Temptation's first agent was the serpent in the Garden of Eden, and the same distraction flicked its tongue again whenever the devil whispered in some lost soul's ear. The carnal appetites were never satisfied; the world was always calling, always crowding on the mind. Only God could deliver grace, but only devotion could prepare the faithful to receive it. Attending to the Lord without distraction meant keeping yourself attuned, in readiness. Meanwhile, though, in everyday scenes of work and consumption, distraction was also going in the opposite direction.

Nineteenth-century life demanded and solicited attention—not to the heavens but to this world, here and now. To keep up with the times, to keep it together, a person had to stay focused at work, at home, and in the marketplace. And so, distraction signified not only a sinful attachment to this world but also the wrong kinds of absence from it. As the critical theorist Paul North says in *The Problem of Distraction*, detachment came to be regarded as a vice, "practiced by notorious figures, by sidetracked workers, bored students, and dissolute citizens, by the daydreamer, the sleeper who doesn't dream, the absentminded one."[5] North's list is like a litany; composing a sequence is one way to represent a crowd. The moods of disengagement range from sullenness to transcendental mysticism. Too much dissociation is a questionable habit, and people whose thoughts drift away from work and trade are likely to be mocked or even punished, rather than admired for their saintly ways.

As nineteenth-century writers, preachers, and social reformers reflected on distraction, they began to suspect that their economy was creating the disorder that interrupted its own smooth operation. Thoreau's lamentation that "the world is a place of business," for example, set the terms for his retreat, but Thoreau did not mean exactly what so many Christian monks and penitents since Paul meant by "the world." He was not talking about all natural desire or human commerce, everywhere, since man's first disobedience. Instead, Thoreau was pointing to some places in particular, during a special, relatively recent era, when social life had been reshaped by market forces and machines. Downtown Concord, Massachusetts in the 1840s was not Paradise or ancient Corinth.

If commerce in a New England town was bad for attention, life in the fast-growing capital cities and manufacturing towns was even worse. Industrial work strained the laborer's powers of concentration with its mind-numbing noise and repetitions. In the urban marketplaces, there was endless hawking and peddling, never-ending calls to want something, then something else, then something else again.

Edgar Allan Poe gave a vivid description in a tale about crowding, "The Man of the Crowd," when he compiled this list of city creatures: "Pie-men, porters, coal-heavers, sweeps; organ-grinders, monkey-exhibitors, and ballad-mongers, those who vended with those who sang; ragged artizans and exhausted laborers of every description, and all full of a noisy and inordinate vivacity which jarred discordantly upon the ear, and gave an aching sensation to the eye."[6] The urban economy, with its around-the-clock business, treated attention as it did most other resources—demanding it in ever-increasing quantities while also destroying its wellspring.

Civilization assaulted the senses—"jarred discordantly upon the ear, and gave an aching sensation to the eye"—and all this crowding, over time, did damage to the mind. Analyzing the psychic effects, Poe and many of his contemporaries set aside the language of diabolical temptation, perennial since the fall of man, and diagnosed distraction as a symptom of modernity. Rather than pointing the finger at the devil, they might blame the media, the slum, or new technologies. They saw distraction as unnatural, not a failure of human nature. It happened when the environment became mechanized and artificial, when the business of civilized life, as measured by the clock, was no longer in sync with the rhythms of the earth.

Distraction was diagnosed as a disease of the historical present; disciplines of attention, in turn, promised spiritual and natural remedies. This development itself invites historical reflection. Maybe it is not surprising that changing economic and social conditions inspired new, less openly scriptural ways of talking about distraction's causes. Where the devil had always been, now there was also coarse materialism, mechanization, mental disease, and the din of the crowd. It will take some careful reading, though, to see how mysticism and moralism infused themselves into even the most seemingly secular, modern programs to rehabilitate distracted minds.

The reflections that follow consider several kinds of distraction that troubled nineteenth-century preachers, writers, and social reformers. I begin in churches and other sites of Christian worship, then travel to workplaces, crime scenes, and the high seas— all of which became territories for the wandering mind and arenas for disciplining attention.

1

"Wandring or distraction"

When our thoughts should be wholly employ'd about some one thing, we either fix them on it, or suffer them to rove after a great many other Objects: If we keep our Thoughts close about the Matter we are engaged in, this may be properly said to be Attention; but if we give them their Liberty, and suffer them to range after things of another Nature, this is the Wandring of the Mind. So that for the purpose, in the Worship of God, the Wandring or Distraction of our Mind may be said to be two-fold: First, as it is the Act of our Will, and then without question it is a Sin: And, secondly, as it is the Effect of the Temper and Constitution of our Body; and then I no less doubt, but if striven against, it will be accounted by Almighty God as only a pitiable Infirmity.

—THOMAS CLAYTON, *SERIOUSNESS OF ATTENTION*
AT THE TIME OF DIVINE WORSHIP, EARNESTLY
RECOMMENDED (1712)

When is distraction a sin, and when is it something less than that, just a "pityable Infirmity" of fallen human nature? While we are listening to a sermon, strange thoughts begin to appear in our minds, unbidden. They seem to come to us from elsewhere. Their origins are in our natural bodies or in the devil's mischief, not our souls. When they arrive, though, we have to make a choice: either we strive against them, or we give them our attention. For fleeting temptations, brief wanderings of the mind, Christians who exercise the proper discipline will be forgiven. But if distraction takes our will, "then without question it is a Sin."[7]

At St. Michael's Church in Norwich, England, in November 1711, the reverend Thomas Clayton was telling his parishioners a story about religion's decline. Too many Christians, he said, had drifted away from reverence, into frivolous pursuits. Even while they sat in church, their thoughts were roving somewhere else. Even when they bowed their heads, their hearts were cold. They had a case of the wandering mind.[8]

Clayton was a Cambridge graduate who would hold his post for more than fifty years before his death in 1743. If the printed version of his sermon says anything about the quality of his performance, he had a couple of gifts that served him in the pulpit: a righteous terror of backsliding and a good ear for cadences. His task, as he explained it, was to correct "the Wandring or Distraction of our Mind," and in this way "restore the Honour justly due to God." The phrases express the minister's desire to bring his congregation back from the brink of spiritual ruin. With their iambic rhythms, they could almost be lines from poems.

On this occasion, Clayton was not preaching against the most obvious kinds of wickedness. He had little to say about sex, gluttony, or crime. He was after something subtler, all but invisible, something that happened only in a person's mind. You might come to church on time. You might go through all the motions. Meanwhile, though, you might be lost in dissociation. If you did not give the service your full attention, Clayton believed, then you were holding something precious back from God.

The preacher put it this way: "As Decency of Behaviour in the outward part of our religious Worship is required, so no less is Attention of Mind, in the inward part, expected from us" (9). Participation in the ceremony of worship is not enough. Even the "barbarous" nations, Clayton reminds his listeners, have their rites and sacrifices. From civilized Christians, God wants more than a pantomime. He commands "the humility of our Minds, and the Attention of our Hearts" (7). Without attention, ceremonial worship devolves into savagery, and English Christians appear to go primitive.

Clayton's distinction between matter and manner, conduct and conviction, rests on a deeper division between the natural body and the eternal soul. "For how lame a Sacrifice it will be, and unbecoming the Majesty of Heaven, for any one to present to God his Body, which alone is but a mere Carcass, and at the same time to offer up his Soul, his Heart and Affections, which are by far the better part, to the World?" (14). There is a whiff of death and the occult in Clayton's preaching. Those who worship in a state of diversion are sacrificing a "Carcass."

Attention, as Clayton defines it, is a technique for offering the better, inward part of oneself to God: "If we keep our Thoughts close about the Matter we are engaged in, this may properly be said to be Attention." Distraction, by contrast, happens "when we give [our thoughts] their Liberty." The drama of attention and distraction plays out within a context of obligation. Before we choose to attend or not to attend, we first have a sense of the task at hand, the specific purpose or "Matter we are engaged in." Attention is compliance, keeping our thoughts close. It might even be understood as a kind of captivity, as opposed to "liberty" and "wandering."

For Clayton, though, paying attention is not about being captured; it is a free act of the will. The worst thing we can do is to choose distraction: "As it is the Act of our Will, . . . then without question it is a sin." The sinner's mind, as Clayton describes it, *decides* to linger with its carnal, worldly thoughts; it might even take the devil's place, calling them forth from the beginning. Rather than passively suffering distraction, the sinner actively pursues it. Because attention is a matter of choice, it is rightfully subject to divine judgment; with freedom comes culpability.

Drawing his distinction between the kind of distraction that is an infirmity and the kind that is a sin, the minister collapses distraction back into attention. Sinful distraction means nothing more or less than withholding your attention from God and giving it, instead, to worldly things. If Clayton's sermon shows how the phenomenology of attention was already a problem for religious reflection in 1712, then, it also reveals how the minister's way of thinking about the problem was still shaped by ancient, dualistic oppositions between the heavens and the world, the spirit and the body. What mattered to Clayton was the object of attention, not its quality.

2

"Satan had hidden the very object from my mind"

I had struggled long and hard, but found not the desire of my heart. When I rose from my knees, there seemed a voice speaking to me, as I yet stood in a leaning posture—'Ask for sanctification.' When to my surprise, I recollected that I had not even thought of it in my whole prayer. It would seem Satan had hidden the very object from my mind, for which I had purposely kneeled to pray. But when this voice whispered in my heart, saying, 'Pray for sanctification,' I again bowed in the same place, at the same time, and said, 'Lord sanctify my soul for Christ's sake.' That very instant, as if lightning had darted through me, I sprang to my feet, and cried, 'The Lord has sanctified my soul!' There was none to hear this but the angels who stood around to witness my joy—and Satan, whose malice raged the more. That Satan was there, I knew; for no sooner had I cried out 'The Lord has sanctified my soul,' than there seemed another voice behind me, saying 'No, it is too great a work to be done.' But another spirit said 'Bow down for the witness—I received it—thou art sanctified!' The first I knew of myself after that, I was standing in the yard with my hands spread out, and looking with my face toward heaven.

I now ran into the house and told them what had happened to me, when, as it were, a new rush of the same ecstasy came upon me, and caused me to feel as if I were in an ocean of light and bliss.

—JARENA LEE, RELIGIOUS EXPERIENCE
AND JOURNAL (1849)

Hiding away in a secluded place, a Christian tries to pray, but she finds that her heart is cold, and her thoughts are all gone wayward, out of line. She wishes to speak to God, but something is distracting her. When she rises from her knees, about to abandon her efforts, a mighty voice commands her to renew them. Startled, she realizes that the devil has been playing tricks on her. "Satan had hidden the very object from my mind, for which I had purposely kneeled to pray." She came to this place with a certain purpose. Satan tries to drop a shroud between her mind and the object of her attention, but God intervenes.[9]

Jarena Lee knew some things about the devil. According to her spiritual autobiography, Satan had hounded her through her early life. Lee was born in Cape May, New Jersey, in 1783, to a free Black family, but from the age of seven she labored in servitude as a maid to another household, sixty miles away. The earliest memory she recorded was of lying to her mistress about work, and of the guilt she came to feel. God's spirit "moved in power through my conscience," Lee writes, and "great was the impression" (3). The drama of her life story begins with the feeling of being watched and judged by unseen eyes.

"My heart grew harder, after a while," Lee confesses, "yet the Spirit of the Lord never entirely forsook me." Her *Religious Experience*, probably the first autobiographical narrative written and published by an African American woman, follows her progress from sin to conversion, sanctification, and a call to preach the gospels. As she comes of age, she gets a religious education, finding herself ever more preoccupied with her own wickedness. She undertakes the spiritual disciplines available to a woman in her circumstances, but she struggles to get back to the intimacy of that first dialogue with God, where she felt known and open to his purifying influence.

All along the way, the devil seems to lie in wait. The crucial episodes in Lee's conversion narrative are almost all about how Satan made her swerve from the path of righteousness. But Lee's devil is a peculiar kind of bad company. He is not a seducer, whispering temptations; he is more like a monster, killing hope. Rather than kindling desire, he extinguishes it. Rather than whispering temptations, he spreads a cold despair. "It seemed as if someone was speaking to me, saying put your head under," she remembers of the time she nearly drowned herself. The voice is Satan's, calling her to "self-murder" (4).

Whenever a crisis comes in Lee's life, so does the devil. "I was strangely buffetted by that enemy of all righteousness," she writes (5). It happens again and again. Lee finds a spiritual mentor in the minister Richard Allen, bishop of the African Methodist Episcopal Church, but her struggles do not end there. She still has to contend with fiendish tricks, diversions from her purpose. One night, while she tries to pray, Satan appears in her room, in the form of a hideous dog, in a rage, "his tongue protruding from his mouth to a great length, and his eyes looked like two balls of fire" (6). Another day, Lee kneels with her mistress, but someone knocks at the door, distracting them from prayer. "This interruption," Lee decides, "was, doubtless, also the work of Satan" (7).

In the scene of Lee's sanctification, she triumphs over the diabolical agent of distraction, but the fight is hard. First, he tries to hide her chosen object from her mind, to make her forget the purpose of her prayer. It works for a spell, and she is almost ready to abandon her devotions, but then another voice brings her back around, recalling her to her own intentions. She obeys; she prays to be sanctified. And now, at long last, the holy lightning moves through her.

One final time, Lee's old, familiar enemy tries to interfere. "No, it is too great a work to be done," he says, casting doubt. But the devil's voice is answered by another, one who affirms that the work is truly done. Transported, Lee finds herself standing in the yard with her arms flung open, her face tilted to the sky. She testifies to her own sanctification, and her words are affirmed, again, with a rush of bliss. The devil has done his best to deaden Lee's senses, but her disciplined attention opens her up to a mystical delight.

The passage began with a belabored struggle, an absence of desire in the penitent's heart. It ends up floating in ecstasy.

In the years that followed, Lee would become the first woman authorized to preach the gospels in the African Methodist Episcopal Church. The spectacle of a woman preaching was a scandal, and controversy swirled around her. Her autobiography was, among other things, an effort to justify her claim to evangelical authority. She arrived by way of a story about devotion, overmastering Satan and his interruptions. Those who asked questions and raised doubts, who tried to sway her from her path, would find themselves playing the devil's part.

Describing her sanctification, Lee represents herself as a somewhat passive figure. Other voices speak their strange commands, and she responds, more or less obediently. When she moves at all, of her own will, it is to bow and kneel. When she speaks in her own voice, it is mainly to testify about the work of other forces. "I now ran into the house and told them what had happened to me." All the while, though, Lee's willful surrender is also an access of power. Commanded to bow down, she is lifted up. She reaches toward the sky. By way of submission, she has tapped into a new kind of authority.

3

"Hundreds of thousands have their appetite so depraved"

Shrinking from every effort of VOLUNTARY ATTENTION, they can find no interest in any subject of depth or difficulty; they are disgusted with the first page of an author who refuses to minister to their imbecility; and they fly to that pernicious literature which, conscious of its own emptiness—that it can offer nothing worthy of a reasonable mind—yet seeks to entrap the attention by the illegitimate and base means of stimulating the appetites and passions. Thus their taste for reading becomes a diseased and depraved appetite, which rejects all wholesome nutriment, and devours with a loathsome relish only a certain offal and garbage of literature. Fictitious tales of the supernatural, of wonderful robberies and impossible escapes from prison, of sentimental swindlers, of generous thieves, of heroic gamblers, of refined and cultivated murderers, of romantic and tender-hearted pirates—the thieves' literature; novels of crime, whose sole charm is their power to stimulate the vilest passions; infidel writings of the Paine school, whose strength is in the recklessness of their blasphemy; sensuality under the flimsy garb of sentiment; and finally, undisguised and bestial obscenity—all this is now vomited forth from the public press as a flood; while thousands, and hundreds of thousands have their appetite so depraved that they receive the foul and fetid stream into their upturned and open mouths.

—J. H. MCILVAINE, A DISCOURSE UPON THE POWER OF
VOLUNTARY ATTENTION (1849)

43

Nobody in the nineteenth century preached the gospel of disciplined attention with more fire than the reverend J. H. McIlvaine of Rochester, New York. McIlvaine was a Presbyterian minister, the author of an eccentric book about how to read the Bible, and a righteous voice in upstate New York's crowded revival scene. In 1849, when the Rochester Atheneum and Mechanics' Association opened its new library, devoted to working-class self-culture, the club invited McIlvaine to deliver its inaugural lecture. It was a chance to celebrate the diffusion of knowledge and to offer some guidance for laborers who wished to broaden their learning. McIlvaine gave his listeners a scorching jeremiad called "A Discourse upon the Power of Voluntary Attention."[10]

If you were wondering how much evil might come from letting your mind wander, how much damage might be done by a little diversion, McIlvaine was prepared to test the limits. A library was a fine institution, but reading alone, he insisted, would never suffice to lift up the untutored mind. To practice true self-culture, you had to choose the right books, and you had to read them with the right kind of attention. Reading must not be an affair of the appetites; it has to be an assertion of will. The discipline of attention means everything to McIlvaine. The difference between slavery and mastery is hanging in the balance.

McIlvaine's "Discourse" approaches the problem of attention in a peculiar way, by laying out a taxonomy of literary genres. Some kinds of books require the exercise of voluntary attention. The rest are just so much distracting trash. Among the good works, worthy of a young man's study, McIlvaine includes the highest of them all, the holy Bible. Building a ladder that can lead up to revelation, he puts other worthy texts in their proper place—first, those by men of science like Bacon and Newton; above them, the poetry of Homer, Shakespeare, and Milton; and at last, the scriptures, especially Paul's letters and the gospels. A good education makes its way heavenward along this sequence. From the truths of nature, it ascends to those of art. From poetry, it climbs up to divinity.

And then, on a lower shelf, there are the varieties of "pernicious literature," those publications that "entrap the attention by the illegitimate and base means of stimulating the appetites and passions." The mass press in the 1840s, as McIlvaine imagines it, is flooding the marketplace with blasphemous, sensual, obscene works. This stuff includes fantastic stories of crime and escape, "infidel" assaults on religion and the churches, and pornography. Devilish and seductive, sweetening its moral poison with easy pleasures, this literature disarms its readers. As it takes hold of them, they lose their self-possession. McIlvaine describes them with "upturned and open mouths," as if on their knees, regressing to passive consumption.

In McIlvaine's view, then, you reveal yourself, and you might transform yourself, in choosing what to read. Taste is character. "Some of these tastes are higher and nobler than others, relatively to an absolute standard, and belong to humanity at a more advanced stage of its progress towards perfection" (28). Every aesthetic judgment is an ethical test, and no moment of appreciation or delight escapes moral judgment.

As McIlvaine develops his genre hierarchies, it becomes clear that education means civilization for him. In other words, it means refining individual minds in order to improve the population. The condition of a single wayward person might be a minor concern. What really gives McIlvaine nightmares is mass distraction, the sickening of the "thousands, and hundreds of thousands" who drink from the sewer-pipe of the "public press." He wants to see the mechanics' library contribute to a quasi-colonial mission, assembling and civilizing impressionable minds on a continental scale.

There is a strong current of racism (though less nationalism) in McIlvaine's moralized aesthetics. Again and again, when he praises one work of art and condemns another one, he is lifting up the Western tradition and condemning some other culture. He is especially troubled by the imagery of Africa. "Even in physical beauty, it is not a matter of indifference whether your taste prefers that of the Venus di Medici, or that of the Hottentot Venus; nor whether you regard as the expression of manly perfection, the form and features of the Pythian Apollo, or those of the South African Bushman" (27). An undisciplined appetite craves African bodies; Mediterranean goddesses and gods are objects for a finer style of contemplation.

McIlvaine's central metaphors are lordship and bondage. "Man," he reminds his listeners, "was made to be the lord of his affections, passions and appetites, and not their slave" (9). Committed as McIlvaine is to his hard distinctions between body and soul, sensuality and self-control, he cannot resist racializing voluntary attention, making it a feature of Anglo-American character in an imperial march across the continent. Pointing toward the recently acquired territory of California, he uses the gold mines as a figure for the library bookshelf: "The indolent Mexican hunter, and the rude Indian, had wandered for generations over that country of which the very dust was gold, and whose stones were jewels, and knew it not. But the man of another race came, with an eye that could see, and an arm inured to toil, and to him the earth revealed those inexhaustible riches" (15). Voluntary attention comes more naturally to some populations than to others.

Thus, education plays its part in a civilizing mission, absorbing and purifying a multiethnic working class. But it does so by restraining the appetites and instrumentalizing the will in self-regulation. It is not only a matter of informing the mind; it also entails cooling and hardening the body, straightening erotic life. Consider McIlvaine's examples of undisciplined appetite. He imagines a wretched, lost soul who is "tickled with the Sailor's hornpipe"; who "revels in the groans and tears and blood of his brethren"; who "is charmed by the music of a Scotch jig"; who likes "to groan with Paul de Kock" (27). These are images of passivity and penetration, of spillage, of bodies opened and defiled. Against them, McIlvaine preaches a discipline of girded self-possession.

Like other high-handed moralists, though, McIlvaine discloses his own deep attachment to the sins he loves to condemn. His prose winds its way, tendril-like, around its bad objects; here and there along its lengths, strange blossoms open up. The author lingers with them, drawn in and transfixed. He becomes, in spite of himself, a poet of distraction's pleasures.

Listeners in Rochester in the 1840s might recognize McIlvaine's figure of the bad reader from the Temperance tracts. "He can only skim the surface of what he reads, hastening on from page to page, and often from volume to volume, while his mind becomes more lean and starved. By such aimless and desultory reading the intellectual powers . . . are dissipated and prostrated, as the energies of the body by licentiousness or gluttony or drunkenness" (6). The distracted reader's mind is in thrall to the cravings of his body, but he finds no nourishment, no lasting satisfaction in feeding them. The more he consumes, the more he withers away. The servant to his own appetites, he is sure to destroy himself before too long. McIlvaine would line his tomb with the "offal and garbage of literature" and bury him for good (7).

McIlvaine's lecture is steeped in the old-fashioned language of vices and passions, of corruption and spiritual darkness. But he is clear and explicit about the sources of these evils, which fester in atheist polemics and pornography alike. The problem is secular modernity and, in particular, the sensational press that in the antebellum period was rapidly becoming the first mass medium. "All this is now vomited forth from the public press as a flood." *Now*: a time of sickening novelties. The distracted reader is not the bearer of natural depravity. He is a creature of history, the child of a corrupt civilization.

Here is the secret to McIlvaine's peculiar notion of self-liberation. The preacher traces the sources of distraction to the powerful economic and technical machinery that controls the masses, not by oppressing them but by stimulating their appetites and satisfying them, briefly, so that they need to keep coming back for more. If your very cravings are the effects of power, if modernity has taken hold of you beneath the skin, making you its consumer, then the exercise of self-restraint can promise freedom.

Bringing a discipline of attention to bear on the problem of civilization, then, even an open racist like McIlvaine works from the premise that self-mastery is a practice, not just a birthright: even for the free, white laborers of Rochester, it has to be "awakened" by "effort" and "strengthened" by "struggle" (11–12). The cultivation of attentiveness will lift its practitioners up from mortal, creaturely life and give them a chance at salvation. "A struggle commences between nature and the will for the possession and control of the intellectual powers," McIlvaine observes, "the first movement of which, in such a man, is ever a prophecy of the victory of the will" (11). The reformer sees his modernizing society as a place of multiplying and pernicious distractions, and he proposes that a kind of salvation might be acquired by disciplined attentiveness to the right kinds of books.

4

"My non-compliance would almost always produce much confusion"

Mr. Covey's forte consisted in his power to deceive. His life was devoted to planning and perpetrating the grossest deceptions. Every thing he possessed in the shape of learning or religion, he made conform to his disposition to deceive. He seemed to think himself equal to deceiving the Almighty. He would make a short prayer in the morning, and a long prayer at night; and, strange as it may seem, few men would at times appear more devotional than he. The exercises of his family devotions were always commenced with singing; and, as he was a very poor singer himself, the duty of raising the hymn generally came upon me. He would read his hymn, and nod at me to commence. I would at times do so; at others, I would not. My non-compliance would almost always produce much confusion. To show himself independent of me, he would start and stagger through with his hymn in the most discordant manner. In this state of mind, he prayed with more than ordinary spirit. Poor man! such was his disposition, and success at deceiving, I do verily believe that he sometimes deceived himself into the solemn belief, that he was a sincere worshipper of the most high God; and this, too, at a time when he may be said to have been guilty of compelling his woman slave to commit the sin of adultery.

—FREDERICK DOUGLASS, *NARRATIVE OF THE LIFE OF
FREDERICK DOUGLASS, AN AMERICAN SLAVE* (1845)

Recalling his time at the infamous Mr. Covey's farm, Frederick Douglass writes, "I was somewhat unmanageable when I first went there, but a few months of this discipline tamed me." Covey is a "slave-breaker," known for his power to overmaster unruly spirits, and he runs his property as a makeshift penal institution. When enslaved men and women cause trouble on the plantations of richer, more refined slaveholders, they are sent off to Covey to be "tamed." Thus, his reputation for brutality allows him to procure labor at a discount, and to reap the profits. He is raising crops for market, but he is also in the business of correction.[11]

Although Covey's origins in poverty have made him into an unusually hard, violent man, his real gifts are in the arts of deception. He is a master of surveillance, seeing without being seen. Covey does not watch over his fields from above like an angel or a pastor. He crawls on his belly, on the ground. He understands how to hide and lie in wait, tricking his workers into thinking they are unobserved. He likes to tempt them into breaking his rules, just so he can ambush them and make them pay. "He was under every tree," Douglass writes of Covey's serpentine vigilance. These tactics earn the overseer a nickname among the women and men who live in terror of his cruelty; they call him "the snake."

Douglass's account of Covey's farm reads, in part, like a nightmarish revision of the Book of Genesis, set in the plantation South. The woman Douglass mentions, compelled into adultery, is Covey's unconsenting Eve, his first investment in human property. "He bought her, he said, for a *breeder*." She gives birth to twins. Covey, an agent of sin who claims a virtually unlimited power to punish his own victims, plays both a serpent and a petty, vengeful god. He also plays the part of a devout Christian believer. As Douglass notes, Covey always says his daily prayers, and he conducts religious services for his household, including the enslaved. He thinks of himself as a "sincere worshipper of the most high God." In this way, Douglass concludes, Covey falls for his own deceptions.[12]

As Douglass recollects the religious services performed on Covey's farm, he writes with bitter irony. When the overseer brings Douglass into "the exercises of his family devotions," he finds himself conscripted into absurd hypocrisy. Douglass's special job is "raising the hymn," or leading the group in song. He balks at the task, sometimes committing little acts of "non-compliance." Receiving Covey's cue to sing, "I would at times do so," Douglass remembers, but "at others, I would not." Withholding his voice from the ceremony, he is able to create "much confusion"—a disturbance in the exercise.

The overseer, accustomed to being obeyed, now finds himself under pressure "to show himself independent of me." Covey begins to "start and stagger." His song becomes "discordant." When Douglass writes that Covey "prayed with more than ordinary spirit," he is mocking his overseer's flailing, failed performance. Thus, the relations of autonomy and dependence, mastery and servitude, are momentarily jeopardized. By creating a distraction, Douglass has exposed the gap between the purpose of the ritual and Covey's personal will. The hymn is no longer a demonstration of the believer's submission to God; it has become a "show" of aggression, one man against another.

Later in the same chapter, Douglass tells the story of a high-stakes physical struggle against Covey. He becomes so miserable under the slave-breaker's discipline that he is no longer afraid to die. He feels that nothing, not even death, could be worse than his present suffering and humiliation, and so he decides to fight. When he throws down the overseer, he experiences the victory as a spiritual resurrection—the return of his true, unmanageable and unbroken nature.

Here in the hymn scene, though, Douglass is describing a different style of insubordination. Compared to the climactic fight, his refusal to sing is less heroic and a little bit more punk. At this stage, he has hardly any thought of reclaiming his dignity. He satisfies himself with sabotaging the theater of sanctimony, embarrassing the overseer who cannot sing without his voice. Rather than doing battle, he shirks his "duty." Thus, Douglass sets a rare kind of scene, one where his religious noncompliance—causing a disruption in church—can be understood by his readers as justifiable, both spiritually and politically. In a diabolical situation, the ordinary moral order goes upside down. What looks like devotion is really sin, and distraction tricks the snake.

Douglass has demonstrated the strategic use of distraction under circumstances of dehumanizing discipline and religious hypocrisy. But this darkly comic anecdote about distraction depends for its rhetorical success on Douglass's subtle, sophisticated coordination of attention. After all, if Covey is going to be embarrassed, an audience will be required; someone has to see him at his worst. If Covey is going to be judged—if, as Douglass writes, "he may be said to have been guilty"—then some kind of court will have to pass the verdict. Who is watching the overseer?

The beginnings of an answer can be found in Douglass's grammar, especially in his use of the modal verb *would*, as in the phrases "sometimes I would do so," and "he would start and stagger." In English, this verb tense or mood has at least two functions. It can be used to indicate the "habitual past" tense—that is, actions that have been regularly repeated over a long time. But the same phrasing can also indicate the "conditional" mood, imagining something that might happen in the future, if certain conditions are met. The habitual past is grinding, routinized history; the conditional is the mood of uncertain, future-oriented possibility. Douglass takes advantage of this ambiguity.

When he writes about Covey's farm, Douglass is telling his own story about the villain he encountered and eventually defeated. But a careful reader of Douglass's grammar will notice how he is also choreographing a larger drama of habitual perception and conditional knowledge. In other words, Douglass is not writing just from his own point of view. The autobiographer is not the only agent of attention here; he becomes the transmitter of what others *would* see and know.

If you take Douglass to be using the habitual past, recording the routinized events that kept happening at the farm, then you will understand that he is speaking not just for himself but for the whole community of enslaved people under Covey's supervision. While the overseer has been watching them, they have been watching him, too. They have been observing his ways and learning his favorite tricks, and they share this knowledge with each other. He is a master of deception, but in the end, they are not deceived.

Douglass shows his own embeddedness in this countersurveillance network when he writes in the first-person plural. "He appeared to us as being ever at hand." *To us*—that is, to collective eyes. This is an audience that Douglass can perform for, one that can see and hear Covey's embarrassing awkwardness as he tries to raise the hymn. "We used to call him, among ourselves, 'the snake.'" *Among ourselves*—when that monster was not listening, or when he did not understand what he was hearing. Either there were lapses in the overseer's vigilance, or else Douglass and his friends were speaking in some secret language.

Douglass does not keep the secret, though. He shares it on the page, inviting the public into the scene. While Douglass is tracking surveillance and countersurveillance, while he is disclosing the facts that the enslaved have gathered, he is also managing the public's attention. He does so most obviously by confronting nineteenth-century readers with violent, disturbing scenes. In the pages of his narrative, he documents the brutal realities that many white Americans would have preferred to ignore. In a time of distraction, Douglass is calling the public's attention to some urgent truths.

Here, in the court of public opinion, Douglass's writing has not only its documentary force as a record of the habitual past but also its conditional, aspirational resonance as an opening onto future insight. The whole passage about Covey's disciplines invites you to see through the snake's deceptions, perceiving the realities beneath the show of false appearances. If you paid attention, Douglass's rhetoric suggests, then you would perceive what you have been distracting yourself from. To those who are willing to take it up, reading the *Narrative* thus offers its own moral discipline.

In fact, in one crucial line about attention, Douglass goes so far as to isolate an imaginary observer out from the enslaved community. He addresses *you* directly: "You would see him coiled up in the wood-fence, watching every motion of the slaves." In this tableau, three subjects of attention occupy their separate positions. There is the overseer, coiled like a snake, who watches the enslaved; there are the enslaved, who have their own observations and knowledge about the overseer's habits; and then there is you, the reader, whoever you are, the one who *would see*, if only.

5

"Opium-like listlessness"

Lulled into such an opium-like listlessness of vacant, unconscious reverie is this absent-minded youth by the blending cadence of waves with thoughts, that at last he loses his identity; takes the mystic ocean at his feet for the visible image of that deep, blue, bottomless soul, pervading mankind and nature; and every strange, half-seen, gliding, beautiful thing that eludes him; every dimly discovered, uprising fin of some undiscernible form, seems to him the embodiment of those elusive thoughts that only people the soul by continually flitting through it.

—HERMAN MELVILLE, MOBY-DICK (1851)

Ishmael climbs to the masthead, taking his turn at the watch. His job is to scan the waves for signs of whales. If he glimpses a fin or a spout, he is supposed to give the signal to the men below, down on the decks, so they can launch a hunt. Ishmael's shipmates go about the business of sailing and housekeeping; he stands guard, enjoined to vigilance. While they act, he keeps an eye out.[13]

Working the masthead is a discipline of attention, and Ishmael does it poorly. "Let me make a clean breast of it here, and frankly admit that I kept but sorry guard" (135). Over the course of three years at sea, he fails to call out a single whale. What is his problem?

Ishmael, for his part, attributes his poor record to his dreamy absentmindedness. He finds himself constitutionally unsuited to the watch. Meditating on his tendency to drift, recalling how he became estranged from himself and melded with the world, he slips into a languid, impersonal prose. "Half-seen, gliding, beautiful": his writing, like his mind, is listless. There is no boundary anymore between the self and the sea. The masthead watchman is supposed to focus, but instead he drifts away.

Given to the kind of distraction that has come to be known as *dissociation*, a detachment of the self from its location in social space and time, Ishmael surmises that he belongs among "romantic, melancholy, and absent-minded young men, disgusted with the carking cares of earth" (135). Such men are drawn to the ocean, but when they arrive, they find themselves ill-suited to a seaman's labor. While he ought to be watching for whales, the daydreamer on the masthead gives his thoughts over to "the problem of the universe" (135). He costs the crew some chances to make kills, and he puts himself in danger of tumbling into the sea. He seems more likely to die than to play his appointed role in the whaleship's murderous business.

The chapter entitled "The Mast-Head" is, in part, a gently comic treatment of the Romantic temperament. The chapter makes a fool of Ishmael by exposing the dangerous incompetence that comes with transcendence. It laughs at his oceanic reveries (as, in retrospect, he laughs at them himself) because they alienate him from the crew and put his own life at risk.[14] Melville draws from the practical common sense of his business-minded age, which often mocked Transcendentalists and other visionaries for being out of touch.

Ralph Waldo Emerson was one of those who felt the sting. In "The Transcendentalist" (1842), he had defended the lonely idealists who "withdraw themselves from the common labors and competitions of the market," preferring what he called "a certain solitary and critical way of living." Such misfits, Emerson knew, were scorned for entertaining weird ideas about nature and the soul—and, even worse, for "striking work."[15] They were called lazy, useless, and odd.

Emerson loved and defended them as keepers of a timeless flame: "When every voice is raised for a new road or another statue or subscription of stock; for an improvement in dress, or in dentistry; for a new house or a larger business; for a political party, or the division of an estate—will you not tolerate one or two solitary voices in the land, speaking for thoughts and principles not marketable?"[16] Popular attention to worldly things had become the governing norm; in a thoroughly materialist culture, it was the idealist, the one who cared for "principles not marketable," who had to beg for toleration.

Melville's chapter "The Mast-Head," then, is working out the ethics of a certain relation between observers and objects. Summoning the romantics down from the heavens or up from the depths of the sea, it calls for a more practical, grounded attention to the world. But if this style of watchfulness is a virtue, then it is a distinctly modern, secular one. When Melville's narrator argues for attending to the world and for an attachment to mortal life, he is not just developing a critique of Transcendentalism; he is marking a profound reversal in the much longer history of attention and its disciplines.

As it turns out, the intertwining histories of vigilance and virtue are among Melville's topics in "The Mast-Head" and elsewhere in *Moby-Dick*. Ishmael reconstructs an ancient and far-reaching tradition of masthead-standing. There was, for instance, the Tower of Babel. There were the Pyramids of Egypt. And then there was "Saint Stylites, the famous Christian hermit of old times, who built him a lofty stone pillar in the desert and spent the whole latter portion of his life on its summit" (132). Curiously, the first "standers-of-mast-heads," according to Ishmael, were mystics and anchorites, rather than watchmen. They were not looking for whales. They were trying to get closer to their gods.

In "The Mast-Head," Melville may invoke the temptations of Romantic melancholy, but he also gestures toward Christian asceticism, prayer, and devotion. He does so by revising some canonical religious and literary works. Drink too much, according to Proverbs 23:34, and "thou shalt be as he that lieth down in the midst of the sea, or as he that lieth upon the top of the mast." Lust after the "momentary grace of mortal men / which we more hunt for than the grace of God" according to Hastings in Shakespeare's *Richard III*, and you live "like a drunken sailor on a mast, / Ready with every nod to tumble down / Into the fatal bowels of the deep."[17] In these earlier texts, the drunken sailor turns away from divine concerns to pursue worldly ones, thus endangering his eternal soul. In Melville, the situation is reversed: a quasi-religious experience distracts the worker from his worldly task.

In "The Mast-Head," attention has been harnessed to labor, the mind's capacities for vigilance weaponized in the hunt for oil. In this new world, daydreaming, drugs, and the wilder forms of mysticism might become styles of escapism from secular time, ways of leaving behind a self that has become an instrument in someone else's enterprise.

6

"Morbid attention"

Yet let me not be misapprehended. The undue, earnest, and morbid attention thus excited by objects in their own nature frivolous, must not be confounded in character with that ruminating propensity common to all mankind, and more especially indulged in by persons of ardent imagination. By no means. It was not even, as might be at first supposed, an extreme condition, or exaggeration of such propensity, but primarily and essentially distinct and different. In the one instance the dreamer, or enthusiast, being interested by an object usually not *frivolous, imperceptibly loses sight of this object in a wilderness of deductions and suggestions issuing therefrom, until, at the conclusion of a day-dream often replete with luxury, he finds the* incitamentum, *or first cause of his musings, entirely vanished and forgotten. In my case, the primary object was* invariably frivolous, *although assuming, through the medium of my distempered vision, a refracted and unreal importance. Few deductions, if any, were made; and those few pertinaciously returning in upon the original object as a centre. The meditations were* never *pleasurable; and, at the termination of the revery, the first cause, so far from being out of sight, had attained that supernaturally exaggerated interest which was the prevailing feature of the disease. In a word, the powers of mind more particularly exercised were, with me, as I have said before, the* attentive.

—EDGAR ALLAN POE, "BERENICE" (1835)

In the gothic tale "Berenice," Edgar Allan Poe diagnoses a peculiar kind of psychic malady. The disease expresses itself "in a morbid irritability of those properties of the mind in metaphysical science termed the *attentive*." The problem, for Poe's narrator, is not an inability to concentrate. It is a tendency to become too absorbed, for too long, by the wrong things. "Monomania," he calls it: pathological fixation to a single object or purpose.[18]

This neurosis manifests in an attention surplus, not a deficit. A shadow on the wall captures the man's thoughts for hours. The smell of a certain flower becomes his obsession. He finds himself repeating "some common word" to himself until the sound loses its meaning. He cannot direct or regulate his attachments; he loses himself in the contemplation of "frivolous" things. The objects of his meditations are trivial, but the consequences are awful. "Berenice" is a story about how a malady in the faculty of attention leads to a murderous "dental surgery" (217).

The tale first appeared in the *Southern Literary Messenger* in 1835. Poe would revise it, repressing one scene, before he republished it in volume 2 of his *Tales of the Grotesque and Arabesque* (1840). The first version of "Berenice" seems to have caused a minor scandal. In a letter to the *Messenger*'s editor, Poe acknowledged that the tale "approaches the very verge of bad taste."[19] This was a qualified defense of the work, suggesting that it *approaches* but does not cross the line into vulgarity. But Poe was also punning. The nastiest parts of his tale have to do with the title character's teeth, the exposed tips of bone at the threshold of the mouth—the verge, you might say, of the organs of taste.

The narrator, Egaeus, presents himself as the heir of a distinguished family, known as a "race of visionaries" for their achievements in painting and literature, and famous for their "very peculiar" library. The library is the setting for the tale, and for most of Egaeus's experience. "Here died my mother. Herein I was born" (209). It was not his mother's body, he suggests, but the library itself that delivered him to life; he recalls his own birth as an awakening "into the wild dominions of monastic thought and erudition" (210).

He enters not, like other children, into the material world. From the beginning, he departs into ethereal "revery."

Egaeus is raised in the company of his cousin, the beautiful Berenice. The two are complementary souls. Egaeus is a gloomy, brooding type, "addicted, body and soul, to the most painful meditations." His cousin is his "light-hearted" counterpart, his opposite but also his intimate companion, "roaming through life, with no thought of the shadows in her path" (210).

In a tale by Poe, such a creature of the light can only be doomed, and everything changes when an illness takes hold of Berenice— "pervading her mind, her habits, and her character, and, in a manner the most subtle and terrible, disturbing even the identity of her person" (211). *Identity*, as Colin Dayan notes, is a keyword in Poe's tale, and one of his more sinister games is playing with the conceit that there is something dental, some dentistry, in the matter of personhood.[20] As the disease afflicting Berenice advances, she falls into lifeless trances. Her skin goes pale, and there is a hollowness in her face. Ghostly and emaciated, wasting away, she has survived her illness, but it has left her close to death.

For reasons that Egaeus cannot quite explain, the changes in Berenice's condition bring about a change in his feelings for her. Before she got sick, he says, she had been an "abstraction" to him. In their youth, he had apprehended her "not as an object of love, but as the theme of . . . speculation." She had appealed to his faculties of reason and imagination, not to his passions. But now, as her body shows the signs of illness, approaching death, he comes to see her otherwise, "as the living and breathing Berenice" (214).

It happens—Berenice becomes a creature of flesh and blood for Egaeus—because her disease provokes his own. Her epilepsy finds a sympathetic response in his monomania. When she begins to slip into trances, he is seized by his fits of morbid hypervigilance. "My disorder reveled," he says, "in the . . . changes wrought in the *physical* frame of Berenice—in the singular and most appalling distortion of her personal identity" (213). Egaeus perceives the withering of Berenice's body as a kind of incarnation, an enfleshment.

Paradoxically, her body's decay seems to bring it to life for him. Disease—her own, or maybe his—converts Berenice from an abstraction into "a being of the earth, earthy." It kindles his desire. He asks her to marry him.

But the marriage of Egaeus and Berenice never takes place. Instead, they play out another consummation, fantastically grotesque. Some days into their engagement, she visits him in the library, and his attention fixes itself on her face: "The eyes were lifeless. . . . I shrank involuntarily from their glassy stare to the contemplation of the thin and sunken lips. They parted; and in a smile of peculiar meaning, *the teeth* of the changed Berenice disclosed themselves slowly to my view" (215). Egaeus's grammar, like his unsettled mind, dissects his intended. He dismembers her face, isolating its organs, then attributing a kind of agency to each of them. The lips *part*, as if of their own volition. The teeth *disclose themselves*.

"Berenice" is one of Poe's gothic confessions, similar in some ways to his more famous ones, "The Tell-Tale Heart" and "The Imp of the Perverse," but with a significant difference: the confessant in "Berenice" can provide neither the motive for nor the memory of his crime. As for Berenice herself, she seems hardly to play a role at all. Her sensory organs take on lives of their own, and Egaeus submits to the agency of the objects that capture his attention. He finds himself divested of power, shrinking "involuntarily" into contemplation. The beholder is held in thrall.

"Would to God that I had never beheld them, or that, having done so, I had died!" (215) This weird encounter, an unveiling scene rendered both gothic and comic, is wide open to psychoanalytic reading. In a classic study, Joel Porte describes "Berenice" as "a romance of sex and death" in which the narrator's idealism, his devotion to the purity of disembodied contemplation, is exposed as a strategy of displacement.[21] From the beginning, according to Porte, Egaeus has been repressing an erotic desire for his cousin. Unable to articulate this desire, much less to act on it, he allows himself to claim Berenice only after her disease has "desexualized" her.[22] He can acknowledge his desire for her, in other words, only after she has become undesirable.

The trick works for a while, but when she flashes her "smile of peculiar meaning" and reveals her teeth, the truth emerges. The man of reason can no longer disavow his appetite (or hers) by displacing it through abstraction. "Egaeus' passion for the mind has come to haunt him in the mouth of his cousin."[23] Into the library, into the space of contemplation, the specter of sex encroaches.

What happens after this crisis is hard to summarize. Egaeus himself gives only a broken, bewildered account of the events. The split between his conscious reflections and his unconscious motivations becomes so extreme that he seems not to know what he is doing, what he has done. His narration represents not his actions but the mental drama of his attention, his solitary reflections on the mouth of Berenice. By his account, he commits hardly any act at all; he simply remains in the library alone, thinking about his cousin's teeth. "And still I sat motionless in that solitary room— and still I sat buried in meditation—and still the *phantasma* of the teeth maintained its terrible ascendancy" (216). This goes on, he says, hour after hour, as the night gives way to morning, as the day gives way to another night.

And then, as the second night gives way to a second morning, a scream rings out in the mansion. A servant appears and tells Egaeus that Berenice has died. "The grave was ready for its tenant, and all the preparations for the burial were completed" (217). All this has happened without Egaeus's conscious participation; apparently he has not been paying attention.

In the 1835 version of the tale, Egaeus responds to the news by making a visit to his cousin's body. She has been laid in her coffin, and the coffin has been placed on her bed, and the bed's curtains have been drawn around it. Feeling summoned to Berenice's side, Egaeus parts the curtains and enters, enclosing himself within her tiny chamber. For a moment, he thinks he sees her finger move, and he wonders whether it is a sign of life, but he does not trust his senses.

His eyes are soon drawn to her face. "There had been a band around the jaws, but, I know not how, it was broken asunder. The livid lips were wreathed into a species of smile, and, through the

enveloping gloom, once again there glared upon me in too pal-
pable reality, the white and glistening, and ghastly teeth of Berenice"
(217). Horrified, he runs away, back to his sanctuary in the library.

This is the episode that Poe removed when he republished the
story in his own 1840 collection. Why did he extract it? The readi-
est explanation is a concession to popular "taste." Scholars have
understood the revision as Poe's response to the scandal that his
original version provoked, an effort to make it a little less shocking,
a little more palatable for readers of his *Tales of the Grotesque and
Arabesque*. While it may be true that some readers' revulsion led Poe
to read his tale with a more delicate eye, however, the second version is no less disturbing and no less explicit than the original one.
Cutting the scene of Egaeus's visit to his cousin's bedroom does
not make "Berenice" more tasteful.

Instead, it has another effect: it renders more extreme, indeed
it makes almost irreconcilable, the bifurcation between the narrator's actions and his conscious experience. Cutting the deathbed
scene, Poe intensified the tale's focus on the problems of attention and distraction; he transformed "Berenice" into a story about
dissociation.

In the revised version, readers never see Egaeus leave the library. After an indefinite period of time, indicated by a section
break, he is startled into consciousness, as if waking from a dream.
Whether he has returned to the library, or whether he has been
there all along, the tale does not indicate. As far as Egaeus can recall, he has not moved. But he does have the faintest, haunting
sense that something else, maybe something horrible, has happened in the meantime. "I had done a deed—what was it?" (218).

A little box sits on the table beside him. It gives him a bad feeling.
He turns his eyes away, and they fall on the pages of an open book.
He reads just a little. "The words were the singular but simple ones
of the poet Ebn Zaiat:—'*Dicebant mihi sodales si sepulchrum ami-
cae visitarem, curas meas aliquantulum fore levatas*'" (218). Readers
will recognize the line—apparently Poe's own invention, meaning,
roughly, "My companions said that if I visited the grave of my

friend, I might find a little relief from my worries"—since we have already encountered it as the tale's epigraph. Here, in its second appearance, it becomes a clue to what Egaeus has done, the deed he has performed in a state of such profound dissociation that he could not really confess to it, even if he wished to.

The mystery is soon dispelled. Another servant (Egaeus calls him a "menial") arrives in the library, looking "wild with terror." He reveals that the grave of Berenice has been opened in the night, that her body has been terribly disfigured—and that she is still alive, "enshrouded, yet still breathing," somehow (218).

The tale ends with a kind of catalogue, taking inventory of the evidence of Egaeus's crime. The presence of the servant brings Egaeus back to himself, awakening his attention so that he can read the traces of his own actions. He sees that his clothes are smeared with dirt and blood, that his hand bears the marks of another's fingernails. Against the wall, he notices a shovel. He discovers a box on the table in front of him, and as he opens it "there rolled out some instruments of dental surgery, intermingled with thirty-two small, white, and ivory-looking substances that were scattered to and fro about the floor" (219).

Poe's sensational tale has little to say about religion. It is a piece of magazine fiction, designed to entertain the public, rather than to preach a moral lesson. When it explores the deep forces motivating human action, when it reflects on desire and guilt, it takes its terms from psychology; it is more interested in mental sickness than in sin. The mind's dissociation from the body's performances had been a source of concern among ministers for a long time. Now it was a way of diagnosing criminal pathology, as well.

7

"The shell of lethargy"

Most people probably fall several times a day into a fit of something like this: The eyes are fixed on vacancy, the sounds of the world melt into confused unity, the attention is dispersed so that the whole body is felt, as it were, at once, and the foreground of consciousness is filled, if by anything, by a sort of solemn sense of surrender to the empty passing of time. In the dim background of our mind we know meanwhile what we ought to be doing: getting up, dressing ourselves, answering the person who has spoken to us, trying to make the next step in our reasoning. But somehow we cannot start; the pensée de derrière la tête fails to pierce the shell of lethargy that wraps our state about. Every moment we expect the spell to break, for we know no reason why it should continue. But it does continue, pulse after pulse, and we float with it, until—also without reason that we can discover—an energy is given, something—we know not what—enables us to gather ourselves together, we wink our eyes, we shake our heads, the background-ideas become effective, and the wheels of life go round again.

—WILLIAM JAMES, "ATTENTION" (1890)

It happens, probably, to most people, several times a day. We fall. Our consciousness is filled by a solemn sense of surrender. We know what we ought to be doing, and something keeps us from starting. Something, but what? Call it a fit; call it a spell. Call it "the shell of lethargy that wraps our state about." It disperses our attention, and we float with it until another "something—we know not what—enables us to gather ourselves together," and we break the spell, we pierce the shell, emerging into life again.²⁴

In his monumental *Principles of Psychology* (1890), William James devotes a crucial chapter to the problem of attention. From the beginning, the topic causes some peculiar troubles for his writing. Even before he offers a definition of attention, he pauses to acknowledge that the concept is so basic, so well-known, that whatever he says can only be redundant. This is his opening gesture: "Everyone knows what attention is" (381). He will be rehearsing common ideas, not introducing new ones. Worse, if everyone already knows what attention is, then all readers will have their own sentiments and prejudices about it, and it is a difficult task for the writer to give an account that matches theirs. Every word he sets down on the page might seem to be measuring the distance between his thinking and the reader's own.

At the same time, "everyone knows" is an invitation into the community of the knowing, a rhetorical move that asks readers to recognize what follows as an expression of their shared understanding. James goes ahead with his definition of attention: "It is the taking possession by the mind, in clear and vivid form, of one out of what seem several simultaneously possible objects or trains of thought" (381). *The taking possession*: not simply possessing, but actively reaching and grasping. Attention is animated by desire, acquisitiveness, even aggression. *By the mind*: this is the agent of attention. The mind is the subject that takes possession. But if the mind is the source of attention, it may also be attention's effect. As James goes on, he will disclose his view of the mind as a kind of substance that becomes a subject, becomes an active agent, only when it rouses itself to attend.

In clear and vivid form: When the mind takes possession, what does it obtain? James's syntax defers arrival, waits to name its object. First, it describes the object's "form," the qualities that attention gives to the thing it takes possession of. The qualities are clarity and vividness. *Of one out of what seem several simultaneously possible objects or trains of thought*: This form is not the thing but the appearance of the thing, its radiant singularity, the effect of its extraction from a multiplicity, an operation performed by the attending mind. Attention isolates (or reifies) one object or train of thought. It is an act of selection that confers a distinct form. Is attention taking or giving? Receiving or making? James's writing begins to cross the lines.

The field of objects is vast. The possible trains of thought may be many. James doesn't linger on either the objects or possible trains of thought, and he draws only the sketchiest line between the objective and the subjective domains. He is trying, instead, to render what it feels like to come into, or to be within, the attentive state. "Focalization, concentration, of consciousness are of its essence." We know it because we also know its opposite—a "confused, dazed, scatter-brained state" (381–382). This is the distinction that matters to James: not the difference between one kind of object and another, but the one between attention and distraction. It is almost as if attention is itself the cause, the agent that composes both a subject and an object out of an otherwise inchoate "confused unity."

There may be some drowsy pleasure to lingering in a "fit of something," but in James's story we dazed creatures are nagged by the knowledge that we really should be rousing ourselves. "We know meanwhile what we ought to be doing." Again, it doesn't really matter what, in particular, calls for our attention. It might be the voice of a neighbor. It might just be rising from our beds. It is none of these objects that really rouses us, and we hardly have the power to rouse ourselves. Instead, something mysterious happens: not only the distinct object but also the subject is called forth from dissipation into focus and singularity; attention is the relation that constitutes them both. Rendering this change, James seems almost to stutter, to slip into vagary, never finding the right words—"without reason that we can discover—an energy is given, something—we know not what—enables us." It is like a resurrection narrative. A little influx of grace, and the shell of lethargy is cracked. We come back to life.

PART II

Reform

In the far-reaching program for the diagnosis and treatment of distraction, education plays a special part. In our time, after the triumph of newer media, under the empire of spectacle, the mode of careful, sustained attention associated with studying culture and history is more and more endangered, and students are drifting away from the humanities.[1] And yet some educators, including many critics of the arts, have described this trouble as an opportunity. It seems to offer a new justification for our academic disciplines. Rather than defending any particular canon of masterpieces, some scholars have begun to talk about the ethical and even spiritual benefits of attention itself. What counts, in these defenses of the critical humanities, is less attention's object than its quality or mode.

Looking closely at a painting, according to the art historian Jennifer Roberts, creates "opportunities for students to engage in deceleration, patience, and immersive attention," and "these are the kind of practices that now most need to be actively engineered by faculty, because they are no longer available 'in nature,' as it were."[2] Professors of literature say the same kinds of things: "Contemporary readers sometimes find the close attention required by eighteenth-century poems to be alien and difficult," the critic Margaret Koehler observes, but "readers can also reap substantial benefits" from learning "to exercise neglected attention skills."[3] In these accounts, university classrooms and libraries become therapeutic sanctuaries for distracted minds. Slow observation and close reading take their place among the disciplines of attention.

In other words, some critics have begun to promote the study of the arts as a therapy for distraction. "This destruction of attention is disindividuation," the philosopher Bernard Stiegler writes, thinking of the damage done by television, "and this in turn is precisely a *deformation*: a destruction of the individual that education has constructed."[4] The genealogy of these claims is a long one, and the implications are complex. If distraction is a deformation, what kind of reconstruction can an education system offer, in response? Can the individual be reformed?

In the early decades of the nineteenth century, too, many educators tried out therapeutic programs for distracted minds. Their cause was called *reform*. Reformers were teachers, chaplains, and other figures of pastoral authority who aspired to create a happier, more peaceful society by rehabilitating the moral character of the population. They were alarmed by the social disorder and antagonism that accompanied the transition to an industrial market economy, but they sought to raise awareness and change hearts, not the class structure. Rather than regulating industries or redistributing wealth, they offered regimens of personal improvement to the middle and laboring classes. Reformers belonged to many different churches, and they emphasized a shared, nondenominational vision of good character and conduct that transcended theological differences. Their watchwords included temperance, chastity, and love.

In schools, reformers opposed harsh corporal punishments, favoring a more tender, nurturing style. They insisted that intellectual education should be supplemented by lessons in moral self-conduct. In criminal justice, they promoted rehabilitation, rather than cruel retribution. They saw delinquents and convicts as candidates for conversion. Reformers often idealized the private, bourgeois household, featuring a sober husband, an angelic wife, and innocent children. In fact, they were crafting a fantasy of American civilization, setting the terms for social and political assimilation into the white, Christian nation.

By the 1840s, reform's monuments had risen up all over the landscape: the first large-scale charitable schools for the poor, for the indigenous, and for children of color; the first juvenile reformatories; the original penitentiary systems. All of these institutions were engaged in moral training of one kind or another. They were designed to educate wayward, impressionable people into better habits of labor and temperance. In reformed classrooms, workshops, and cells, teachers and keepers imposed compulsory disciplines of attention. As for the victims of distraction, reformers liked to imagine, their correction would feel like receiving care, and their submission to authority would be an act of love and freedom.

In 1834, for example, the educator Warren Burton addressed the members of the American Institute of Instruction, New England's most prestigious teacher's organization, with a lecture entitled "The Best Mode of Fixing the Attention of the Young." Like many other American reformers, Burton saw cultivating and directing young people's attention as the first step toward improving their moral character. The mission called for a soft touch: "The educator is no longer to be a whip-holding task-master—a daily prison-keeper, hateful to the eyes of his charge."[5] In the old days, as Burton recollected them, teachers had imposed stinging punishments with whips and rods. They had been feared by their students, but they had been also been resented. Beatings chafed and sometimes backfired; threats of violence prompted subterfuge or outright defiance.

Now, however, educators were going to lay their weapons down. "The new philosophy of education that is prevailing, will change the whole aspect of the vocation. The teacher's toil will become a pleasure." The best mode of fixing the attention of the young was with parental care, not battery. "The golden era of education has dawned," Burton announced, and "blessed auspices are brightening around." The age of the philosophy of love was in its dawn.

Burton was only one of reform's thousands of prophets and promoters. His lecture charted the rise of a popular, widely influential style of moral training, known to scholars of the period as

"disciplinary intimacy."[6] A custodian's task, according to this philosophy, was not to demand obedience with threats of naked force.
Instead, it was to cultivate a sweet affection between the guardian
and the dependent. Students who loved their teachers would not
follow commands begrudgingly, out of fear; they would acquiesce
more readily and cheerfully, demonstrating faithfulness. Over
time, as their habits improved, they would no longer need any
supervision at all. They would watch over themselves, even when
they were alone.

An 1825 pamphlet on early childhood education, printed in
England and reprinted in Massachusetts, clarified how disciplines
of attention prepared young minds for self-control. The anonymous author laid out a series of practical assignments. The tasks
combined observation with description: look closely at an object
for a while, then compose a careful, detailed account of what you
perceived. The accuracy of your rendering demonstrates the fidelity of your attention. The pamphlet affirmed that "exercises of this
kind are intended principally to AWAKEN the mind of the child,
and to lead him to more prolonged *attention*." According to the
pamphlet, however, this awakening was nothing more or less than
an initiation into disciplinary self-surveillance. Attention gave
children "strength of mind," but this strength was to be turned against
their own bad impulses, as a way to "regulate their conduct."[7]
While you were looking at an object, you were learning how to
monitor yourself.

Without the threat of punishment, some might ask, what would
keep distractable children on task? The trick, reformers thought,
was to place a mechanism of self-regulation in their minds. Burton
called this mechanism *conscience* or *the inward voice*. Each student's
conscience, he proposed, should be "educated to sit in judgment
on the thousand little actions and words, dispositions and motives, which really make up and indicate the character."[8] Reform's
most influential novelist, Harriet Beecher Stowe, learned this from
her sister, the schoolmistress Catharine Beecher: "Education was
not merely the communication of knowledge, but the formation

of character."[9] Teaching children was an intellectual exercise, but it also had to be a moral one.

In *Uncle Tom's Cabin* (1852), Stowe dramatized the lesson with a famous story about juvenile rehabilitation. Topsy is an enslaved girl whose brutal treatment at the hands of her masters has made her, in Stowe's language, "wicked" and "goblin-like." Topsy has a quick mind, but she tends to become distracted and get up to mischief. Her teacher, Miss Ophelia, sets out to convert this seemingly intractable "heathen." To accomplish the "missionary work," as Stowe calls it, Miss Ophelia has to set aside some old "ideas of education," the rigid methods "that prevailed in New England a century ago." To reform the delinquent, she first has to update her own techniques.[10]

Inspired by the death of her niece, the lamb-like little Eva, Miss Ophelia converts to the reformist program. She puts her whip away and shows a kinder, gentler attitude toward Topsy. Instead of threats, she makes promises of care. "I can love you," she affirms. The effect is almost magical, miraculous, as "from that hour," Stowe writes, the guardian "acquired an influence over the mind of the destitute child that she never lost."[11] By giving love, the teacher gains enduring power. Brutal punishments have weak effects. The soft teaching style of a surrogate mother secures a stronger hold.

As slave emancipation proceeded—gradually, unevenly—in most Northern states, white reformers before and after Stowe treated Black Americans as a kind of limit case. They asked whether disciplines of attention might be used to prepare the formerly enslaved for social and political membership into the national community. It was a controversial question. In *The Black Child-Savers*, a historical study of race, delinquency, and rehabilitation, Geoff K. Ward notes that many of the first American juvenile reformatories, built between the 1820s and the Civil War, refused to take in African American children. White supremacists, according to Ward, treated Black delinquents as "a strange species of rigid or inflexible human clay, a categorically incorrigible group, more suited to neglect and exploitation than to attempts at normalization and civic integration."[12]

With their infinite bad faith, American racists could also say the opposite—not that Black delinquents were too dull for the rigors of freedom but that they were too impressionable and excitable; not that they were too cold for the bonds of community but that their feelings ran too warm. As Curtis J. Evans shows in *The Burden of Black Religion,* many white reformers viewed the enslaved and formerly enslaved population through the lens of their own "romantic racialism."[13] They saw people of African descent as naturally gifted in spirituality and emotional attachment, yet inferior to whites in their capacities for moral self-discipline and intellectual reasoning. Reformers like Stowe might be strong critics of slavery, Evans shows, but they also shied away from racial integration. Thus, Stowe imagined that children like Topsy, of the "outcast race," should be trained in American homes and classrooms, then dispatched to Liberia, where they would serve as Christian teachers and colonists. Segregated institutions like New York's African Free School were founded to serve just this purpose: they proposed to do the missionary work of educating Black children who, in turn, would make the reverse Middle Passage to Africa as missionaries themselves.[14]

Elsewhere, though, many African American reformers and a few white ones did make the case for integration. When they did so, problems of distraction and attention were crucial to the stories that they told about their enterprise. In her *Memoir of James Jackson, the Attentive and Obedient Scholar* (1835), for instance, the schoolteacher Susan Paul insisted "that the moral and intellectual powers of colored children are inferior to the power of others, only as their advantages are inferior." Paul was arguing that the root causes of delinquency were in social structures, not human nature. Black children needed and deserved the advantage of a loving education. Treated with tenderness, the young James Jackson became a model of the two mutually sustaining virtues named in his biography's subtitle: attention and obedience.

He also became estranged from others of his race. Paul includes a poignant line about Jackson's loneliness: "He has often been known to remain a long time by himself, until he could cease cry-ing."[15] Reformers understood their movement as a philanthropic, humanitarian, Christian mission. They imagined extending the gifts of practical knowledge and religion to the lower classes. For her part, Susan Paul called on reformers to include children of color in their vision of an integrated future. At the same time, though, her story registered some of the harm that reform inflicted in the name of love. Her image for it was a solitary child, swallowing his own tears.

Wherever respectable society kept its gates, disciplines of atten-tion were likely to be imposed. In schools for minor children, in reformatories for convicts and delinquents, and in Christian out-reach programs for the unconverted, attention was supposed to open the way to social assimilation. Most of these institutions prom-ised to educate people for life at large in American society, under the prevailing norms of white supremacy and Protestant morality. Para-doxically, though, their disciplinary systems also imposed a stark moral solitude. Joining the civilized community required, first of all, seeing yourself in isolation, as a unit, regulating what kinds of influences you allowed into your mind. Every reformatory was an orphanage, in a sense. Before you could belong, you had to be alone.

Even as reformers were organizing a mass movement and open-ing large-scale institutions, then, they were recasting group an-tagonisms as problems of personal self-control. Their mission was not the redistribution of wealth or power to the lower classes; it was the rehabilitation of this delinquent mind, the conversion of that wayward soul, one at a time. In this way, as Saidiya Hartman writes, "the recognition of humanity and individuality acted to tether, bind, and oppress," not to liberate, and "the fashioning of the self-possessed individual" could be a strategy of subjection.[16] This was the deepest division that reformers inflicted so that they could set about repairing it: they extracted the delinquent mind from its social world.

Historically, it could be said of a nation cleaved into factions or a city torn apart by riots that it had descended *into distraction*. The term has always referred to a split within oneself, as in ancient

Stoic and Christian ideas about the wandering mind. For a long time, though, distraction also described divisions within communities. Webster preserved this definition in his 1828 *Dictionary*: "3. Confusion of affairs; tumult; disorder; as political distractions." Even in the nineteenth century, wars of religion, class struggles, and conflicts between regions were still sometimes described in terms of distraction. Over time, though, the political meaning receded, and a psychological and ethical one prevailed. Distraction became a private affair. Reform is one of the reasons why.

Reformers knew that they lived in a world of rigid hierarchies. They had their concerns about this world's frictions and inequities. They tended to see the misery afflicting the lower classes as an effect of historical conditions, not natural inferiority. They were quick to diagnose delinquency as a symptom of degrading social environments—"vicious poverty," or the "crowded city." In the end, though, the object of their condescending sympathy was always the individual victim, available to rehabilitation at close range. Reformers did see distraction as an effect of economic and social forces, but they also recast it as a personal, moral problem. One of their signature inventions was adapted from monastic architecture: the solitary confinement cell, a space for moral isolation within an institutional setting.

The exercises in this section are case studies in reform's disciplines of attention. I take up passages from several scenes of moral training and rehabilitation—schools, reformatories, and prisons— in the northeastern United States, from the 1820s into the 1850s. Together, these various sources show the significance and the centrality of attention to the reformist endeavor.

As reformers imagine the awakening of minds and the conversion of souls, they disavow their own power. They project the disciplinary agency of supervisory authorities like teachers and prison chaplains onto students and captives, who come to appear as autonomous, watchfully self-governing. Reformist writers execute this displacement through the figure of the mind in isolation, receiving benign impressions and guarding itself against distraction.

8

"A white man could, if he had paid as much attention"

James.—But then, some people are quicker at some things than others. A white man could never trace an animal through the woods as an Indian can.

    Aunt.—I ask your pardon. A white man could, if he had paid as much attention to the subject. The eyes of Indians are not gifted with any peculiar magnifying powers, more than ours. They merely attend to very trifling circumstances, and make up a judgment from them.

—LYDIA MARIA CHILD, "CONVERSATION
ON ATTENTION" (1826)

In "Conversation on Attention," published in the inaugural issue of a children's magazine called *The Juvenile Miscellany*, the reformer Lydia Maria Child called young readers to attention. Here the author, identifying herself as Aunt Lydia, guides her nephew, James, through a series of exercises designed to teach him patience and focus. He attributes the skills of "Indian" hunters to some natural gift of their race; she informs him that hunting is a discipline of attention, much like reading.[17]

    Although it includes a brief fantasy about tracking prey, "Conversation on Attention" is mostly about literary interpretation. It models, for parents and teachers, a lesson in reading. James is the sort of boy who likes sensational adventure stories, the kind of

stuff printed in cheap editions for mass entertainment, but he struggles to make sense of poetry. Aunt Lydia sets out to train him as a
critic. His confusion, she assures him, is not the effect of a weak
intelligence; it is just "because you have never paid any *attention*
to the cultivation of your imagination" (75).

How is reading a poem like pursuing an elusive animal through
the woods? Child proposes that both tasks call for "close active
attention" (76). The reader sees a literary symbol and, attending,
recognizes what it signifies, the meaning encoded by the author's
phrase or image. The hunter sees a footprint or a break in the forest
undergrowth and, attending, gleans some useful information
about the beast that left the mark. Child's point is that both reading and tracking are acts of interpretation. In the library or in the
woods, attention guides the senses, opening the mind up to impressions and preparing it to make judgments.

"Remember then," she concludes, "that *attention* is the golden
key to the immense mines of wisdom, which nature is ever ready to
open to the eyes of taste" (86). "Conversation on Attention" is a
pious, didactic work, but it is oriented toward this world, rather
than the heavens. Disciplines of attention do not carry the student
away from his physical environment. Instead, they intensify his
sensations and put him in touch with the things around him, close
at hand.

When the conversation turns to race, Aunt Lydia applies the
same lesson to the "Indian" and the "white man." James seems to
believe that "some people," by which he means some populations,
have a "quicker" attention than others. His example is the Native
tracker who, moving through the landscape, notices the subtle
signs of life that fall beneath a white man's notice. James enter-
tains a primitivist fantasy, probably shaped by the popular adventure novels that he loves to read. He pictures the Indian as a type
of person whose senses are keener than his own, better attuned
to "the woods."

"I ask your pardon," Aunt Lydia begins, addressing her student
not with harshness but with an almost submissive kindness, as if

he were her master or her judge. Then she turns to correcting his errors. She rejects the idea that there is any natural difference between indigenous and settler populations. In terms of physical gifts, in their capacities to see and hear, they are born equals. If one of them is more perceptive in the woods, according to Aunt Lydia's notion of racial development, then that distinction is an effect of their different social conditions and practices of self-cultivation.

"Conversation on Attention" promotes education reform to expand and refine American civilization, but with its brief foray into primitivist fantasy it also acknowledges that civilization itself is deadening some people's minds. The "white man" has lost touch with the natural world. His sight has withered, or his vigilance has slackened. When he goes into the woods, he goes distracted. By contrast, the "Indian" represents a better reader of the landscape. His attention is well disciplined in the wild. It is his culture, not his nature, that makes him quicker in the hunt. Child's program for a sophisticated, modern system of instruction, rehabilitating children from distraction, would reorient them toward the subtler truths not only of poetry but also of the American wilderness. The right kind of culture would recuperate the reader's natural capacities.

9

"The cultivation of attention as a moral duty"

In the first place, the cultivation of attention as a moral duty, with the constant exposition of all which interferes with it in instinctive habits, is of the first importance to the intellectual life. The mode in which this state of mind is cultivated, is not merely that of stating it as a duty, but stating it as a duty, after having used all the resources of his own and others' genius to attract and reward their attention. When a child has been led to enjoy his intellectual life, in any way, and then is made to observe whence his enjoyment has arisen,—he can feel and understand the argument of duty which may be urged in favor of attention. Those who commonly instruct children would be astonished, to witness the degree of attention which Mr. Alcott succeeds in obtaining from his scholars constantly. Indeed, the majority of adults might envy them. It is, generally speaking, complete, profound, and as continuous as any would wish the attention of children to be."

—ELIZABETH PALMER PEABODY, "METHOD
OF SPIRITUAL CULTURE" (1836)

A teacher makes a risky gambit. In disciplining his students, he tries to bring them around to a sense of their own power. By apprehending how their own acts of attention hold them fast, they will learn to see, and then to guide, the strong capacities of the will that directs this attention. Paradoxically, it is by remembering and analyzing their pleasurable entrapment that they come to discover their freedom and their strength.[18]

The scene is a classroom in the Temple School, and the teacher is Bronson Alcott. The author of the observations is Elizabeth Palmer Peabody, one of the most cosmopolitan intellectuals in the New England Transcendentalist circle. From her home in Boston, she ran Elizabeth Palmer Peabody's West Street Bookshop, specializing in international literature, natural history, and world religions. She helped to maintain the coterie literary journal *The Dial*, and she was active in movements for the abolition of slavery and for the legal rights of the Paiute Indians.[19]

Peabody belonged to liberal Unitarian circles, and as a writer and editor she explored traditions of spiritual exercises ranging far beyond Northern European Protestantism. In 1843 she brought out the first American edition of Augustine's *Confessions*. She helped to import South Asian philosophy to New England. In her bookshop, the curious customer might find a copy of Pringle's *Residence in South Africa* or Herder's *Hebrew Poetry*.

Peabody's life's work was teaching, or what she called "spiritual culture." Taking an interest in European theories and methods, she founded the first English-language kindergarten in the United States, and to the end of her life she would advocate for greater public investment in early childhood education. In the 1880s she sponsored Sarah Winnemucca's innovative school for Paiute children. But Peabody had made a name for herself in education reform debates a half century earlier, when she went to work with the controversial Alcott, publishing an account of the experience as *Record of a School* (1835).

Revised from Peabody's journals, the *Record* gives an intimate and sympathetic, though sometimes critical, portrait of daily life at the experimental primary school. In Peabody's account, Alcott teaches such ordinary topics as reading and natural history, but he subordinates every academic goal to his students' moral self-cultivation. On the opening page, Peabody notes that Alcott chooses and decorates his classroom with a feeling for how the physical environment impresses itself upon a child's character. "The objects which meet the senses every day for years, must necessarily mould the mind."[20] By way of attention, the curated atmosphere shapes each boy's impressionable character.

From the beginning, then, the problem of attention preoccupies Alcott. "It is very important in teaching young children to direct their attention very carefully to things in detail," Peabody insists.[21] Everything at the Temple School is organized to cultivate habits of steady, fixed attention—and to instruct the students in controlling their own attention as a style of moral discipline. By reflecting on the experience of being captivated, mentally "chained," they acquire a measure of freedom.

Alcott's approach to teaching one important lesson, Peabody writes, "was by reading to them, and by fastening their attention; and then bringing them to attend to the fact of having been thus chained to their chairs by thoughts and feelings in their own minds."[22] Here, a drama plays out in two acts. In the first, Alcott's reading attracts and fastens the boys' attention. And then, in the second, he turns their attention back on itself, asking them to remember what it felt like, just a few moments earlier, to devote such close attention to the reading.

Something of an avant-gardist in the arts of attention, the Alcott of Peabody's *Record* is exquisitely sensitive to the subtle, reversible dynamics of domination and submission. Like others working in the field of moral instruction, he seeks to build up the child's will, not to set it loose in the world but instead to instrumentalize it in restraining the child's own thoughts and actions. He cultivates personal agency for the purposes of self-supervision. Doing so was common practice among the more liberal educators of the early nineteenth century. At Alcott's school, though, the dynamics played out in extreme, sometimes bizarre forms.

Most notoriously, Alcott experiments with swapping the roles in corporal punishment: rather than beating his students for disobedience, he offers up his own knuckles to be rapped by the boys. If the class is unruly, according to Alcott's philosophy, it is the teacher's own fault. He has failed in teaching them how to monitor their own behavior, he explains, and he asks them to punish him for the lapse.

When Alcott introduces the idea, the students are stunned, but he insists: "He was determined that they should not escape the pain and shame of themselves administering the stroke upon him." Hesitant, the boys take up the rod and give him a few light blows. Alcott is not satisfied. Do they believe, he asks, that such gentle treatment is what they deserve? "And so," Peabody writes, "they were obliged to give it hard:—but it was not without tears, which they had never shed when punished themselves." Inflicting punishment, rather than receiving it, brings on their anguish. "This is the most complete punishment that a master ever invented,—was the observation of one of the boys." By submitting himself to receive the stroke, the teacher overmasters his most unruly boys. "Mr. Alcott has secured obedience now."[23]

As Peabody's account began to circulate, in New England and beyond, Alcott's peculiar methods brought some scandal on his school. Some people said that he was inculcating haughty egotism, rather than humility; that he was meddling with the proper relations of authority between the teacher and the student; that his doctrines were unchristian and his discipline corrupt.

Peabody responded to the criticism and, in a measured way, defended Alcott against it in the new introduction that she wrote for the second edition of her *Record*. The essay, "Method of Spiritual Culture," deals especially with the problem of discipline. "Mr. Alcott rests his chief dependence for the moral culture of his pupils, upon the moral discipline to which he subjects them," Peabody writes (xiii). His techniques are unusual and, she admits, not the ones she would use in her own school for girls. Strange as it might appear, though, Alcott's method works its magic.

The evidence is the students' focused and sustained concentration in the classroom. "Those who commonly instruct children would be astonished, to witness the degree of attention which Mr. Alcott succeeds in obtaining from his scholars constantly."

If the test of a disciplinary system is its capacity to secure attention, then Alcott's method is working beautifully.

The essential first task of intellectual life, Peabody observes, is "the cultivation of attention as a moral duty." Without obtaining attention—and without exposing, in order to overmaster them, the "instinctive habits" that tend to distraction—education can hardly begin. And so, the question of discipline is first of all the question of how to make students feel that attending to their lessons is their moral duty.

How can the sense of obligation be instilled? Another kind of teacher might just assert the command, "merely," as Peabody puts it, "stating it as a duty." *Pay attention.* But the obligation, so out of line with a child's natural tendencies for wandering and play, will not take hold simply because it has been spoken. Telling students that they have to pay attention feels at first like a strong assertion of authority, but its effects are weak. Unless the teacher can solicit their assent, he will have to use clumsy, ineffective methods of correction (losing his temper, raising his fist) that reveal the feebleness of his command.

Alcott therefore does not begin with statements of duty. Instead, he prepares the way. He will come around to his students' obligation in the end, but only "after having used all the resources of his own and others' genius to attract and reward their attention." On this account, teaching becomes a style of solicitation, even of seduction. The teacher has to spend his resources in courting the students' interest; he performs the work of attraction and hopes to stimulate enjoyment. He plays the jester or the suitor to their pleasures. He learns, or he anticipates, what will fasten their attention to him.

After the student has experienced delight, the teacher pushes him to reflect on its sources: "The child will be made to observe whence his enjoyment has arisen." And from this consideration of his own capacity to experience an enthralling pleasure through acts of attention, he will come to understand his moral duty. If he is capable of fixing his senses and his thoughts so devotedly, then he is obliged to do so. The student has become interested in his own obedience.

On the surface of the passage, there is very little sensational drama. The reader finds no wild transgressions here, no scolding or flogging. The teacher does not mortify unruly boys or expose his own hand to be struck. As the passage develops its theory of attention, however, it moves through a subtler choreography, performing conceptually some of the same moves that Alcott makes in his classroom. There is the doubling back of attention on itself, in memory, as a technique for teaching students to realize and direct their capacities for self-restraint. And there is the drama of reversal, the teacher controlling his students by learning how to submit, at first, to their own power and pleasure.

10

"The heart must be cultivated"

It will not be enough to attend to the mere development and discipline of the intellectual powers—to initiate the juvenile mind into all the mysteries of the arts and sciences—no, sir; but on the contrary, the moral and religious feelings of the heart must be cultivated, as of paramount interest. In the education of our children, we must regard them as immortal beings who are rapidly hastening through this probationary state to the eternal world, and whose unchangeable destiny there, sir, will be according to the type of their characters here. O, then, how important is it, that while the tender age of our children is such as to render them most susceptible of moral and religious impressions—that while their characters and habits are being formed, and that, for the most part, for life, how important is it that they should be thoroughly indoctrinated in the principles and practices of our holy religion.

—WILLIAM WATKINS, *AN ADDRESS DELIVERED BEFORE THE MORAL REFORM SOCIETY* (1836)

At a "tender age," children are "most susceptible to moral and religious impressions." Their habits and ways are still in formation, still open to influence. The world is continually operating on the young mind and heart, shaping the child's character, and the men and women who hold the power to regulate this operation are obliged to ensure that the susceptible child will be "thoroughly indoctrinated," during this tender phase, "in the principles and practices of our holy religion." It is not enough for the guardians of the young "to attend to the mere development and discipline of the intellectual powers"; the feelings of the heart will have to be cultivated, if the soul is going to be saved.[24]

These remarks on religious instruction were delivered at the first meeting of a new organization, the American Moral Reform Society, in 1836, by the minister and schoolmaster William Watkins. Born to a free Black family in Baltimore, Watkins had received his early education at a local charity school, then founded his own, Watkins's Academy for Negro Youth, in the early 1820s. Under his leadership, the academy gained a reputation for strict discipline, blending a classical education with moral instruction, guided by the teachings of the African Methodist Episcopal Church.

When he was invited to deliver this address, Watkins may have been the most prominent Black teacher in the United States. He understood that his task was to lay out a vision for the kind of education that would serve the organization's mission of Black emancipation and uplift. Watkins and his fellow antislavery radicals opposed the enterprise of African colonization; they argued for immediate abolition and racial integration in North America. Both intellectual and moral instruction, Watkins proposed, were crucial to this future.

Watkins would not entertain the racist premise that Black children were naturally unfitted for moral discipline. The "source of ignorance and barbarism," he believed, was to be found not in nature but in culture, in "the neglect of the mind and morals" (3). Without a good education, any child would remain uncivilized; by way of a good education, any child might be lifted up. Watkins rehearsed the enlightened theory of human development that came to the United States from Britain and western Europe, and he simply took it for granted that the same theory applied to Black children as well. "While his infant mind is opening, it is continually receiving impressions from objects with which it is daily coming in contact" (4). Over time, Watkins explained, impressions shaped a person's habits, and in this way, one mind at a time, a whole population would acquire its distinctive character.

Watkins preferred to avoid religious controversy. He would not take sides in theological disagreements or promote the teachings of any particular Protestant denomination; he would not advocate that all Black children should be "baptized in, or proselyted to, the peculiar tenets of the different sects" (5). And he would not go so far as to claim that education alone could ever "change the heart from nature to grace," since salvation could only be "the province of the Holy Spirit." But Watkins would make the case that a good education, based on broadly shared Protestant principles, "is a powerful auxillary, under God" (6). Moral instruction prepared the disciple to receive God's grace, when the moment came.

Watkins's reasonable and chaste style of moral instruction hewed to a middle way, between the coldly rational and the fanatical. A good education would be a bulwark, Watkins believed, not only against a mercenary, atheistic self-interest but also against the wilder, more primitive styles of religious devotion. By cultivating the proper kinds of feelings in young people's hearts, he promised, "you banish from their religion that superstition, and from their devotional exercises that wild, ranting fanaticism, which are the legitimate fruits of ignorance" (14). The task was to distill a religion without superstition, devotional exercises without fanaticism. The method was a discipline of attention, regulating the impressions that would reach the tender heart.

Aside from a few passing remarks about the perniciousness of "neglect," Watkins spoke almost as if the most serious danger to Black children, in the middle decades of the nineteenth century, were the threat of a secular education that improved their minds without cultivating their religion. Elsewhere, over the course of his career, Watkins published severe, militant protests against the slave codes. A rigid traditionalist in morality, he was a radical in politics. As he delivered the address on education that became the most famous public statement of his career, however, Watkins was conspicuously quiet about the negation of Black life and thought under slavery.

"It will not be enough to attend to the mere development and discipline of the intellectual powers," Watkins pleaded to his colleagues in the reform society. He seems to have taken it for granted that at least on this occasion, in these circles, liberation was a shared hope—but he also worried that the movement for uplift and integration would fall into its own sort of distraction. He represented the modern schoolhouse as a secular institution in need of missionary outreach. And so, in calling his audience back to the question of devotion, Watkins brought a spirit of revival to the project of reform.

11

"You might see him looking steadily at something"

When his teacher said, "James, do you remember what I told you yesterday or this morning?" He would say, "Yes!" and then repeat it to her. Now what do you suppose the reason is, that you forget more easily than James? I will tell you—he attended very carefully to what was told him, and kept saying it over to himself. O I wish some of you could see him, when his teacher was repeating some little verse, or some story from the Bible. His eyes would be fixed on her all the time so carefully, that no noise would turn them away. Then when she had done, you might see him looking steadily at something, as if he was trying to retain in his memory what she had said.

—SUSAN PAUL, MEMOIR OF JAMES JACKSON, THE ATTENTIVE
AND OBEDIENT SCHOLAR (1835)

While the teacher reads aloud, she sees the boy fix his eyes on "something," as if to hold himself at anchor, then say the same words to himself in a low voice, apparently trying to memorize their sound and sequence. The student who attends most carefully when his teacher is reading poetry or Bible verses is the one who will be quickest to recall them and recite them, on request. His speech is a repetition, but it gives evidence of something new—it demonstrates his care, his cultivated receptivity.[25]

How do you describe a person who is paying attention? Attention is an act of the mind, so it can be hard to represent or picture. Here, the writer makes the effort—"O I wish some of you could see him"—and, with the same gesture, conjures up the spectral presence of the child whose death she is grieving.

The full title of this short, didactic biography identifies it as, in part, a eulogy: *Memoir of James Jackson, the Attentive and Obedient Scholar, Who Died in Boston, October 31, 1833, Aged Six Years and Eleven Months, by His Teacher, Miss Susan Paul.* The subject, James Jackson, was born December 5, 1826. His father and namesake died soon afterward, and James was left in the care of his mother, who began his education. When the boy was four, she enrolled him in Boston's public, segregated Primary School Number Six, where Susan Paul became his teacher. By Paul's account, James showed great intellectual and moral promise. He embraced his education, though it estranged him from other children. After his death from a sudden illness, his teacher composed his life story and shared it as an example for others to follow.

Susan Paul herself was the daughter of a prominent minister and a respected schoolmistress. Coming of age in Boston's free Back community, she made alliances in the Christian antislavery movement. (The radical publisher William Lloyd Garrison would print excerpts from her book in his abolitionist newspaper, *The Liberator.*) Paul's memoir describes a classroom conversation about the enslaved, who "live and die without ever going to school, or being taught by kind Sabbath school teachers"; the author notes of James that afterward, "in all his prayers, he remembered the poor slaves, and prayed for them" (89).

Paul's main concern in *Memoir of James Jackson*, however, is not enslavement in the South; it is the intellectual and moral instruction of Black children in the free states. Writing against the racist notion of a cognitive hierarchy fixed in nature, Paul wishes that her "little book" might assist in "breaking down that unholy prejudice which exists against color." Among children of color, she writes, there is "many a gem" that might be "brought out from among the rubbish and polished" (67). James Jackson stands for the combination of receptivity ("attentive") and submission ("obedient") that teachers might hope to cultivate, if they could secure the resources and the opportunity. His gift for attention makes him a candidate for reform.

In the memoir, Paul recognizes the young boy's talents right away. "He was so ready to obey all that she told him, and so attentive to what she taught," Paul writes, "that his teacher . . . loved him very much" (73). Over the course of his few years in the school, the bond between them grows closer. In the end she is almost like his second mother.

At the same time, James himself becomes more and more isolated from the other children in his neighborhood. When his mother tries to send him out to play, he refuses; the other boys are so wicked, he says, that he cannot stand their company. When he is on his way to school, they insult him and beat him up. "Sometimes he was attacked by these very wicked boys, and badly hurt, because he would not go with them," Paul notes (87). His love for his teacher and his school makes him an outcast on the streets.

As Paul considers James's gift for memorization, she seems almost to be trying to summon a community around him, in his image. Other children, sadly, are unlike him. For one thing, they lack his facility for recitation. The teacher would like to close the distance between them. She suggests that the gift can be learned and practiced, if they make the effort.

How can they learn from him, after he is gone? Paul's description moves into and around the empty place where James used to be. She wishes, she says, that the other children could see him. Creating a surrogate presence, she represents his posture, his expression, and the subtle movements he makes while he is paying close attention. She invites her readers to watch him listening to her voice.

The evidence is imprecise, and so is the representation. Paul qualifies her own remarks. "You might see him," she writes, and what you might see would be his way of "looking at something, as if he was trying," and so on. Paul's language marks her hesitancy, her unwillingness to make the leap all the way from observation to interpretation, from seeing the boy's actions to grasping his experience. The visible body gives every sign of the mind's attentiveness, but a description written by someone else can only go so far.

Paul's memoir is a didactic piece, sure of its own authority most of the time, but when the author approaches James's interior life, she exercises a measure of modesty and caution. "James loved to pray, and seemed to engage in it with proper feeling," she writes elsewhere, signaling her own uncertainty about his emotional state even as she praises him for it (88). The ritual was being executed, beautifully, but whether the boy's heart was really in it, only he and God could know for sure.

Paul's description of James in the act of listening and remembering is animated by a paradox that appears often in Christian devotional writing. Attention, enabling memory, shows itself in a performance of repetition, but the performance might always be merely mechanical, a form enacted without true conviction, even without comprehension. Maybe this is one reason why Paul, in composing the scene of intimate instruction, leaves the words themselves unrecorded. We see James listening, but we do not know what he is hearing. He repeats the verses, but his biographer does not.

12

"Their nobler faculties lie all undeveloped"

They are blind, and you are to be to them eyes; they are lame, and you are to be to them feet. In right of birth they are men, entitled to reason's large discourse; but their nobler faculties lie all undeveloped. They have been loved as the bear loves her cub; but the kindling influence of generous human sympathy has been withheld from them. They know not the power of emulation, and are strangers to ambition; their only hope having been to live as well fed animals. Your looks of kindness and your words of sympathy are to awaken them to a new life, and your generous counsel to strengthen them in its paths. Opening their gaze to the wide fields of human learning, you are to prepare them for strife with the world, and triumph over its temptations. They will be brought to you as pests of society, and you will qualify them for usefulness and duty. They will come to you heathens, and you will not part with them till you have taught them to bow the knee in grateful acknowledgments to God for blessings liberally bestowed.

—WILLIAM D. KELLEY, *ADDRESS DELIVERED AT THE COLORED DEPARTMENT OF THE HOUSE OF REFUGE* (1850)

A new juvenile reformatory, Philadelphia's House of Refuge for Children of Color, is opening its doors, and the "pests of society" are about to arrive. They come like malformed, broken creatures—blind and lame. They look uncivilized, like animals or heathens. But now their reformation can begin. Their keepers in the youth prison will give them new eyes, opening their gaze. Their teachers will strengthen their resolve against the world's temptations. Under lock and key, the creatures will be converted, the animals humanized, the pests made useful. Blessed with new capacities of strength and freedom, liberally bestowed, they will become capable of submission, learning "to bow the knee in grateful acknowledgments."[26]

The author of these lines, the reformer and judge William D. Kelley of Philadelphia, had watched with horror while his city fell into disorder. In a moral panic, he blamed profligate consumption. "Riot and tumult are the evils under which we groan. The wayward and restless youths who congregate in the street corners, hang about hose and engine houses, and throng the places of cheap and vulgar amusement in which the city abounds, are our terror at home and disgrace abroad" (13). Restless children were mobbing the scenes of low culture, indulging their appetites for "cheap and vulgar amusement," and respectable people like Kelley, a distinguished judge and activist, looked on with fear and shame. It was a disturbing picture of urban modernity.

It was, in other words, a scandalous representation of the social world that racial capitalism had made. As they developed their economies around industrial production and wage labor, Northeastern cities like Philadelphia had come to rely on thousands of hired workers, many of them recently immigrated or emancipated, without absorbing them into systems of domestic supervision such as indentured servitude. In their unoccupied hours, the working classes roamed the streets, making trouble.

A "free labor" economy was taking shape, and so was a free market of entertainment commodities. To Kelley and his collaborators in the reformist enterprise, the city was a bazaar of soul-corroding temptations. There were the theaters; there were the gambling tables and the sex workers; there were the dreaded "ardent spirits" on tap at rum houses and hotels. Merchants trafficked in tawdry and ephemeral pleasures, and underemployed, disorderly young people swarmed to the bait.

What was to be done? If a cityscape of vicious amusements and unruly mobs was the problem, what solution did it require? Kelley was here to talk to his fellow reformers about a reason for hope. His occasion was the opening of a new reformatory, the House of Refuge for Colored Children, an institution promising to restore law and order through disciplines of attention.

Philadelphia had opened its first juvenile reformatory a few decades earlier, in the 1820s, but that experiment was restricted. Although Pennsylvania was a free state, it was also a segregated one, and the city's first Refuge offered rehabilitation only to white children. Now the promise was going to be opened up, the experiment expanded, to a new population, aligning reform with a mission of racial uplift.

"The existence of a colored community in our midst is coeval with slavery," Kelley acknowledged. "Its members encounter not only the prejudice of color; but, go where they may, let their worth and ability be what they may, they are recognized as the descendants of slaves, and too often treated as though they deserved no better than their fathers' fate" (20). The Refuge was a scene of captivity, but Kelley defined its mission against the legacy of slavery. Its purpose was to prepare children of color for the rigors of free labor and a qualified assimilation into social and political life, under white Christian supervision.

Pennsylvania, with its traditions of Quaker pacifism and enlightened moral philosophy, had always been a leader in reform. Celebrating the latest stage in its advancement, Kelley placed the Refuge along the arc of civilization's progress in his home state. The story went back to the era just after the American Revolution, when reformers had done away with public hangings and tortures, replacing the gallows with modern institutions purpose-built for rehabilitation. Kelley celebrated the founders for "supplanting the whipping-post by the moral instructor" (5)—a phrase that could serve as a fitting slogan for the whole reformist enterprise.

Kelley recalled how the harsh justice of vengeance yielded to the softening influence of mercy. The age of enlightenment had dawned, he said, when reformers began treating common criminals with sympathy, as fellow human beings. Philadelphians had heard the story many times: a dawning recognition that every person, even the lowest, deserves a claim to civil rights and a chance at redemption; a movement from brute force to loving encouragement.

Sensing that the gravest threat to public order is the restlessness afflicting young people in a modernizing city, reform imagines that it can solve social problems by isolating selves, extracting them from the modern attention economy in order to rehabilitate them. The reformatory cell can become a scene of conversion—of the young offender's awakening—because it is first of all a "lonely" place where the impressionable mind lights only on good objects. The bare walls are designed to filter out wicked influences, letting only the benign ones enter.

Rather than hardening people, as older punishments—and the pernicious modern world at large—were likely to do, rehabilitation would open up the self to softening influences. It would educate the delinquents it held captive, quickening their intellects, and it would "impress and ennoble" them with religious instruction, exposing them to "the power and beauty of holiness" (5). Rehabilitation was a therapeutics of attention.

Kelley's account of criminal justice reform is a story of modern progress without being a story of secularization. In fact, Kelley sees the juvenile reformatory as a sign of Christianity's advancement. Reform happens when religion enters and transforms the criminal justice system. Kelley asked his audience to imagine the House of Refuge for Colored Children as a future monument to the triumph of religion. "Would that he who pronounced Christianity a failure were with us and would go hence to the courts and alleys, and of foul unfinished hovels, from which its future inmates will be brought!" (7).

Other writers, especially the advocates of secularism in statecraft (Jeremy Bentham, Thomas Jefferson, Benjamin Rush), had taken the opposite view. For them, the scaffold and the gallows were props of a benighted theocracy, and the point of reform was to rationalize punishment, rather than to Christianize it. But Kelley and his allies believed the opposite, that social order depended on religion. Reform would not expunge religion from punishment; it would invite missionaries into its classrooms and cells, using spiritual exercises in the campaign to rehabilitate delinquency.[27]

13

"Subdued and tender"

*The faithful instructions which Jacob received from the chaplain, were
followed by the exercises of the Sabbath-school, and the public preaching
of the Lord's day. To all these, he gave the most strict attention. Consider-
ing his age and his past habits of life, his improvement was really aston-
ishing. In nothing was his advancement so great as in the knowledge of
divine things. He was evidently taught of the Spirit, and daily grew in
grace and every Christian virtue. His temper, which had been uniformly
rough, and at times almost indominable, became subdued and tender.*

—A. D. EDDY, "BLACK JACOB," A MONUMENT
OF GRACE (1842)

An industrial prison becomes the scene for a Black man's conversion to Christian virtue. The prison chaplain guides him, faithfully,
in his private study of holy scripture. The Sunday School offers
him a moral education and some social reintegration. In the chapel, he joins a congregation in public worship. Religion goes to
work in rehabilitating his hardened character, and the ministers
overseeing his instruction are almost astonished by how rapidly
he improves.[28]

Jacob is an old man living out the late stages of a rough, wicked
life. His past habits and crimes are some of the worst, and he has
suffered through hard, grinding punishments. In spite of all his
misery, though, he is not beyond the reach of benevolent influences.

His capacities of attention are strong, and so is his discipline; he is showing signs of knowledge, growth, and reform.

The passage comes from a pamphlet, *"Black Jacob," A Monument of Grace*, written by the minister A. D. Eddy and published in 1842 by the American Sunday School Union, a powerhouse of evangelical printing. *"Black Jacob"* adapts the old conventions of Protestant conversion narratives to antebellum debates over race, crime, and moral reform. It is a story of one man's life, but it is designed to prove a claim about populations and the proper use of punishment on a much larger scale. Eddy's argument is that crime is an effect of historical conditions, not innate depravity— and that the right kind of prison system can transform criminals, including African American criminals in the free North, into subdued and tender Christians.

The author understands himself to be addressing a skeptical public. There are many racists in his world who doubt that Black men, especially those who have committed acts of violence, can ever be brought into the fold. Eddy accepts the premise that African Americans in the nineteenth century are a degraded class, but he wishes to demonstrate that their degradation is not unalterable. They might still become useful workers and responsible members of the community, if the right techniques are applied.

"Though this numerous class of men, as a body, have improved but little for many generations," Eddy writes in his preface, "there have been occasional exceptions to their general ignorance and degradation, which show what they might become, under influences more favourable to their physical discipline" (iii–iv). He composes the life story of Jacob Hodges as one of these exceptions, an example to demonstrate the possibility that disciplinary institutions might redeem the future of his race.

Reconstructing the story of Hodges's life through interviews with his subject and the ministers who knew him at New York's Auburn State Prison, Eddy traces Hodges's origins back to Pennsylvania, where he was born in 1763 to a free Black family "living in ignorance and poverty." The child receives no formal schooling or religion, and when he is ten years old he ships as a cabin boy on a schooner bound for the West Indies. Eddy makes no attempt at subtlety in arguing that Hodges is a creature of bad circumstances. He is born with some gifts—"a native dignity and a noble carriage"— but no benevolent institution shelters him, and he is turned wicked by the streets and the sea (7). A history of violence makes him.

Hodges spends decades aboard ships, first as a servant and then as a common sailor. His travels take him around the North Atlantic, from the Caribbean to several European ports. He travels from the New World to the Old World and back again while the great Atlantic revolutions (American, French, Haitian) inaugurate their new regimes. It is a career of exceptional cosmopolitanism and freedom of movement, but in Eddy's telling it is a school of vice: "In this situation, well calculated to perpetuate his ignorance and to confirm him in every vicious propensity, and farther removed than ever from the means of education and moral improvement, he soon became distinguished for every species of wickedness" (4). *This situation*: Hodges gets caught up in the motley unruliness and rootlessness of seafaring life in the Atlantic, where mixed-race crews operate without the constraining influence of moral instruction. Cut loose from any tutelage and confirmed in vice, he would appear to be bound for the prison, the gallows, or worse.

When the War of 1812 interrupts shipping and trade, Hodges finds himself on shore in New York City with no money and no means to support himself. By 1819 he has wandered upstate, where he falls in with a gang of bad characters who enlist him to help them with a murder, apparently motivated by a longstanding property dispute. Hodges is reluctant at first, but the conspirators persuade him with money, sex, and liquor. The bad habits he acquired at sea make him available to their manipulation. Unable to govern himself, Hodges becomes an instrument in other hands: he plays his part in the killing.

Arrested in New York City while trying to make his way back to sea, he soon offers a full confession. (Eddy notes that Hodges would maintain a consistent story for the rest of his life, more than twenty years, up to the point of a conversation between the two men in 1841.) Hodges describes being lured into the conspiracy, and he admits to firing a pistol at the victim, but he claims that his shot was not lethal; another man finished the job with the butt of the gun. As the trial unfolds, more evidence appears to corroborate his story.

A trial court convicts Hodges of murder and sets a date for his hanging. Before the sentence is executed, however, there is a political intervention. The investigators acknowledge that Hodges's cooperation was valuable to them in securing convictions for the ones who were really behind the murder plot. Authorities note that his expressions of remorse have been consistent and sincere. Perhaps he is not entirely unredeemable. The legislature is persuaded to commute Hodges's sentence. He will go to prison, not to the noose.

"These gloomy walls he now enters, a wretched outcast" (22). Eddy has spent some time with the details of the crime and the trial, but his true topic is Hodges's punishment—that is, his experience in confinement—and what prison discipline does to his character. For the first time, Hodges is inside a state-run institution whose effects on his behavior can be examined as a matter of public policy. This is the problem that Eddy's pamphlet really wants to take on: If one world, the world of the low-born and the loosely governed, the world of ships on a lawless sea and criminal conspiracies on land, has turned Hodges into a murderer, what might another world make of him? How might a calculated discipline work to reform his character?

Before Hodges can get there, he has to pass through one more crucible. Eddy organizes the central sections of "Black Jacob" around a stark contrast between two penal institutions. The prison to which Hodges is first admitted, in New York City, remains unreformed (and, in Eddy's pamphlet, unnamed). Its cells and practices are relics left over from an era when "the idea of making [prisons] nurseries of education, means of moral reform, and sanctuaries for moral and religious culture, was not entertained"; behind its gloomy walls, "but little attention was paid to the habits, education, or moral improvement of the inmates" (22–23). Hodges gets tough, unsympathetic treatment here. The racist guards see him as defiant and unsalvageable. If this dungeon has any effect on his character, it is only to harden him.

But then comes another intervention. After some time, Hodges is transferred out of the city and makes his way upstate, probably by boat—on the water once again—via the Hudson River and the canal system. He has already lived a long and strange life, riding the currents of modern history. Now he will enter the scene where another new system of law and order is being forged, the birthplace and model of industrial penal discipline in the United States, the world-famous Auburn State Prison.

As Hodges's story was being written, the prison where he had served his time was becoming one of the most famous institutions in the world and the prototype of industrial prison discipline all across the United States. The basic facts and dynamics of Auburn's rise are well-known to historians. Opened in 1816, it became the international standard-bearer for a distinctive new brand of prison discipline, known as the "New York system." Its crucial innovation was putting incarcerated men to work in proto-industrial workshops, leased and run by private contractors. This arrangement offset the state expense of building and managing a large-scale correctional institution—but it also exposed some contradictions in reform's program. Work discipline had to be enforced with the lash and other tortures, raising doubts about the prison's claims to enlightenment and, no less controversially, the state's relation to free labor.

In 1829, when Pennsylvania opened the monumental Eastern State Penitentiary, it introduced a serious rival to Auburn. In the "Pennsylvania system," also known as the "solitary system," every convict was held in an isolation cell, having contact only with prison officials and approved visitors, especially those from religious organizations. This was a big investment, especially because the solitary system could not be adapted to factory-style production. Its advantage was moral, rather than fiscal. Eastern State was beautifully designed for solitary reflection, stripped of virtually all distractions, the purest imaginable architecture for self-correction. It was associated with Pennsylvania's Quaker traditions (pacifism, a belief in each soul's "inner light"), but its solitary cells and its discipline of compulsory spiritual exercises also recalled the ascetic customs of the earliest Christian monks.

In the pamphlet war between two camps of reformers, Auburn had to answer the challenge. It found its defenders in evangelical Congregationalists from upstate New York and New England— ministers like Thomas Eddy, prison chaplains like Auburn's Jared Curtis, and prominent missionaries like Louis Dwight of the Boston Prison Discipline Society. These champions of the New York system would emphasize the rule of silence in Auburn's workshops, which prevented all communication among the incarcerated men. Silence was not just a security measure, they explained; it was a technique for preserving spiritual isolation in a group setting. In the prison workshop, each worker maintained a solitary cell within his mind.

The reformers expanded literary and moral instruction, Sunday schools, and services in the chapels. There were still many reports of brutality and disorder, but there were also accounts of remarkable conversion. Improbable as it may sound, the famous prison had become the means of an alliance between the religious mission of evangelicalism and the politics of free labor. The reformers who promoted it could understand themselves as strong opponents of slavery even as they promoted large-scale captivity and forced labor in chains.

In *"Black Jacob,"* Eddy has little to say about the notorious harshness of Auburn's discipline or its signature techniques for extracting labor. The minister's main interest is in rehabilitation—or, to use his own keyword, education. "Every thing was here arranged for the purpose of cultivating among the prisoners a desire for education, the means of an honourable support in life and the maintenance of correct morals" (24). Under the enlightened regime at Auburn (so Eddy's story goes), the inmate has the new experience of being addressed with dignity and sympathy. "For the first time in his life, Jacob was treated like a man" (24–25). This is

a commonplace of prison reform rhetoric, but it has special resonance in the case of someone like Hodges. Unlike the plantation,
Eddy means to show, the prison recognizes the humanity of the
African American captive. Force proved impotent to subdue him,
but love may do the trick.

It is not only the sympathy of the keepers at Auburn that goes
to work on Hodges's character. It is also the architecture. "No
sooner had Jacob entered this prison and seated himself in his narrow cell, than he found a Bible by his side and himself alone. This
was something new. He had never been in solitude before, where
all was silence and solemnity. Here he had nothing to do by night
but to review his life, to think alone upon his melancholy state and
what might be before him" (25). *This was something new*: it is as if
the prison's solitary cells have been designed not simply to break up
conspiracies and disable riots, but rather to eliminate distractions
and to cultivate attention. *Nothing to do by night*: not simply for
security but also for self-examination.

Eddy takes some pains to represent Hodges as a character suited
by nature, though not by history, to a disciplined concentration. "The
chaplain was forcibly struck with his fixedness of attention" (26).
By way of fixed attention, grace lends itself to rehabilitation. Once
"almost indominable," the condemned man emerges from his conversion with a new temper, "subdued and tender." All of his formi-
dable power has been redirected inward, where it has been put to
use in softening his heart.

The minister who composed these lines was facing a peculiar
kind of rhetorical challenge. His main task was not to justify the
brutal violence of incarceration against humanitarian protests. It
was to demonstrate that even someone as degraded as Jacob
Hodges could be redeemed. Eddy took it for granted that rehabilitation was a blessing. He meant to persuade his readers that African Americans should be allowed to receive the gift of their
own imprisonment. He would do so by exploring their capacities of
attention, their openness to reforming influences, the powers of
submission that made them capable of self-control.

14

"If he wanted to kill time"

Those was the dark and lonesome days when the convict had no library books to read, nothing but his bible and tract, and if he wanted to kill time during the long summer days, he must take his bible or tract from his shelf and wear away the long and lonesome hours that came a hanging on him like a heavy weight by reading them. The convict had no slate and pencil to kill time with, nor did he dare to have a knife in his possession to whittle time away. Ah, Reader, those was the dark and cruel days when young Plume was stripped stark naked and laid across the bench with his hand tied to the floor, and received such a severe punishment with the cats that he expired a few days after. Them was the days when the prisoners' backs was cut and lacerated with the cats till the blood came running down their backs. Many was the nights that the prisoners returned to their cells with their backs cut and hacked up with the cats, and cursing and damning their makers and uttering hard and horrible oaths.

—AUSTIN REED, *THE LIFE AND THE ADVENTURES OF A HAUNTED CONVICT* (1858)

In the middle years of the nineteenth century, a man of color who calls himself a Haunted Convict gives an account of his days and nights at Auburn State Prison. He composes sentences about time, about the time that is his sentence, giving the hours weight, the days a dark and lonesome feeling. Lacking the instruments to kill time, he remembers wishing for a knife to whittle it away. He finds, in prose, another way of shaping it.[29]

Midway through, with a cry—"Ah, Reader"—the writer makes a turn, moving from the lonesomeness and tedium of life in a solitary cell to the violence of prison discipline. He remembers, as he expects his reader to remember, the scandal of a death in the institution, when the keepers beat to death a young man named Charles Plumb ("young Plume"). The author recollects how the notorious lash, the cat-o-nine-tails, cuts into men's bare backs, drawing blood. He notes that the prison's rule of silence is broken by the hard and horrible oaths of the ones subjected to its punishments. Violence does not subdue them. When it does not kill them, it hardens their hearts, provoking their curses.

As he makes his turn from the pain of lonesomeness to the cut of the lash, though, the writer is not so much changing his topic as drawing a connection between two kinds of suffering. In the solitary cell, where he has no access to distraction—"no library books to read, nothing but his bible and tract"—time seems to acquire punishing, physical properties. It hangs on him, a heavy burden: a wooden time that makes him wish he had a knife.

Likewise, when the Haunted Convict writes about whipping, he dwells in its rhythms, marking the interval between the beating and the death, measuring the duration between the cut and the running blood. Mere confinement, passing time alone, is an embodied experience, and violence, too, takes time.

The author of this passage, Austin Reed, was born around 1823, in Rochester, into a free family of color. He had never seen a Southern plantation, but he had traveled a long circuit through other scenes of captivity and forced labor. The first institution that took hold of him, perhaps, was something of a relic. After his father died, Reed was indentured as a servant in a farming village to the south of his home city. This was a bondage secured by contract: for a period of years, he was supposed to provide his labor in exchange for room, board, and a basic education. The contract would expire when he came of age and entered the labor market.

Indentured servitude had been in place in New York since the colonial era. It placed the children of the poor in the homes of landholders and businesspeople, where their discipline could be handled domestically, without police or courts, as it was under the slave codes. Reed had been born into circumstances of relative privilege and security before the trauma of his father's death, and he did not take well to servitude. On the farm, he lamented his condition and refused to work. When he was whipped for his idleness, he responded to the indignity by setting fire to his master's house. He was arrested and convicted of arson. The state took him into custody in 1833, when he was ten years old.

The court sent Reed to New York City, to serve a term at the House of Refuge, the nation's first juvenile reformatory. If indenture was an old-fashioned, paternalistic kind of unfreedom, the youth prison was a new invention, an experiment in rehabilitating the children of an unruly population. Domestic servitude was part of the fabric of an older agrarian and mercantile economy; the House of Refuge took shape within a new industrial order, with its fast-growing population of dislocated and immigrant workers. The reformatory was a designated scene of capture and discipline within a society where "free labor" was becoming the new norm.

Reed was raised and educated at the House of Refuge. He learned to read and write and act on the stage. He received moral, as well as intellectual, instruction. When the reformatory opened a separate dormitory for children of color in 1835, he was almost surely moved into racial segregation, but by his own account he still worked and played alongside his Irish friends. The experimental institution— part prison, part factory, part school—continued to be shaken by controversies. Reed documented many instances of whipping and other violent punishments. In 1839 the original structure was destroyed by fire, probably an arson from the inside.

After a short time at large, Reed was arrested for a robbery and sentenced to a term at Auburn State Prison. He would spend most of the next decade and a half behind its walls, serving sentences for a series of minor property crimes. While he was there, the prison was carrying on its rivalry with Philadelphia to determine the future of modern prison discipline. At the same time, there was a factional division within the New York system itself, as evangelical reformers waged a Christian missionary campaign against hard-line wardens who cared only about security, obedience, and productive labor.

Writing around 1858 in a memoir that remained unpublished during his own lifetime, Reed would recognize, in a measured and ambivalent way, that reformers had made life at Auburn less miserable by introducing a gentler discipline. He draws a contrast between their styles of rehabilitation and the prison discipline that was in place during his first days of confinement. *Those was the dark and cruel days.* He recalls the restrictions on reading and writing and, with vividness, the violent techniques of work discipline and prison security. The cell, stripped down to the bare essentials, was supposed to remove all distractions, but in Reed's telling the effect is not a better style of attentiveness; it is a sense of emptiness, of loneliness, that makes him long for a pencil or a knife. The tract and the Bible itself are reduced to time-killing diversions.

When Reed does finally get his hands on the tools of expression, he uses them to document his suffering—but also to develop his artistry in prose. This passage is much more than a catalogue of institutional problems. There is poetry to be heard in its metrics, for instance in the almost military rhythm of the phrase "uttering hard and horrible oaths." And there is a sophisticated patterning in its structure, its ways of returning to and modifying a phrase—"Those was the dark and lonesome days," "those was the dark and cruel days," "them was the days"—like a motif in the composition.

Behind this pattern is a certain experience of time, a phenomenology of life within an institution that imposes austerity on attention. When every day is more or less the same as the one before, the same as the hundred or the thousand before, then even a small variation makes a meaningful difference.

At first glance, Reed's passage seems to imagine reading in one of two ways, either as a distraction from real life or as a tedious kind of moral work. The convict who is deprived of "library books," which are good for killing time, has no choice but to study his Christian "bible or tract." Like many nineteenth-century reformers, Reed thus appears to see idle distraction and disciplined attention as the two modes available to readers, each suited to a certain genre—sensational entertainment on one hand, moral literature on the other. And yet Reed's own writing does not neatly conform to either of these two paradigms.

He crafts his work with subtle artistry, inviting his reader to notice details and the patterns that they make. He teaches a certain kind of moral lesson, exposing the cruelties of industrial prison discipline. At the same time, his prose displays a self-conscious, writerly discipline. He directs his own perceptions and shapes his experience into ambivalently meaningful designs. He speaks not only for himself but also for others he has known inside, including their "cursing and damning," their "hard and horrible oaths." Reform has come to Auburn, and Reed has turned its disciplines of attention to his own purposes.

PART III

Revival

Strange as it sounds, the contemporary American landscape of digital media and twenty-four-hour commerce seems to be fertile ground for a spiritual revival. The most spectacular example is evangelical Christianity. Once marginalized by members of the wealthier, more influential "mainline" churches, white American evangelicals have now allied themselves with right-wing politicians, law enforcement, major television networks, and big business. Their movement has seized political power, not to mention wealth, while continuing to imagine itself as a righteous popular insurgency against what it calls the establishment. In a time when mainline churches are losing members and prestige, the evangelicals, with their mass media campaigns and their visions of being born again, are thriving in a deregulated marketplace. The inheritors of the Protestant missionary campaign whose open-air camp meetings, itinerant ministries, and pamphlet distribution networks produced a "Great Awakening" almost two centuries ago are engineering another one in today's attention economy.[1]

The evangelicals are not the only ones, however. The revivalist impulse makes itself felt elsewhere, too, even among artists and free spirits who would never join a church. It seems almost as if a steady diet of distraction is bringing on a craving for better, more sustained, more transcendent styles of attentiveness. The poet Christian Wiman sees the signs of a quiet but far-reaching change:

> All my friends are finding new beliefs.
> This one converts to Catholicism and this one to trees.
> In a highly literary and hitherto religiously-indifferent Jew
> God whomps on like a genetic generator.
> Paleo, Keto, Zone, South Beach, Bourbon.
> Exercise regimens so extreme she merges with machine.[2]

In "All My Friends Are Finding New Beliefs," traditional faiths and novelty diets intermingle, Catholicism next to Keto, like branded products on a shelf. One believer's God is a gadget, whomping like a generator. Another, something of a cyborg, merges with her exercise machine. Spiritual exercises all but devolve into commodities. Asceticism partakes of the shallow, worldly consumerism that it only pretends to leave behind.

Wiman's lines are comic, but they have some sadness in them, too. The poet begins by cataloguing the spiritual conversions experienced by "hitherto religiously-indifferent" people. He ends up discovering that the real heart of the matter is not in the substance of any particular belief. It is in *regimens*, the self-imposed programs that organize a convert's life. Whether the regimen is going to confession or cutting carbs, it is about paring things down, regulating consumption to restore some kind of focus. The sadness comes from the slow, accretive recognition that all our friends are hurting; everyone is lost.

For his part, though, Wiman invokes his cast of seekers not only with a comic wistfulness but also with big-hearted sympathy, acknowledging the authentic need that motivates their searching. The list of regimens could go on and on: transcendental meditation, martial arts, and long hikes in the woods. A full tally would also include contemplating works of art, for instance reading poetry. Fittingly, Wiman composes his lines in a loose but recognizable pentameter. Rather than availing himself of free verse—the form associated, since Walt Whitman's *Leaves of Grass*, with modern, democratic self-expression—Wiman chooses the enabling constraints of a more traditional poetics. Elsewhere, he has testified that writing poems, for him, requires "a monkish devotion to their source, and to the silence within you that enables that source to speak."[3] The poet, along with his friends, identifies his discipline.

In the nineteenth century, as in our own time, there was a great proliferation of "new beliefs" on the American scene. Then, as now, evangelical Christianity swept over the land, bringing in new converts in mass numbers, partly by exploiting new technologies and distribution networks. Evangelical organizations like the American Tract Society sent out legions of itinerant hawkers, carrying their pamphlets and Bibles from town to town, from door to door.

In the 1840s and 1850s, ATS colporteurs made contact with half the country, selling and giving away millions of copies of their publications. The organization's executive committee described the effect: ATS tracts, the committee announced, "have fallen like snow-flakes over the land."[4] This image mystified the real machinery and work that launched so many printed pages into circulation. Evangelical distribution, as its engineers described it, was not commercial traffic, powered by the steam press and the locomotive; it was a mighty work of nature or of God. Whitman played a similar trick when he called his printed poems *Leaves of Grass*. Just as religious literature appeared to be drifting directly down from the heavens, mystical poetry seemed to be springing up, wild and green, straight from the fecund dirt.

Along with the evangelical media campaign, there were also massive, motley gatherings in person, on the ground. While the presses churned out pamphlets by the millions, missionary crusades fanned out across the country and the globe. At camp meetings, in crowded churches, or under the open sky, they tapped into new sources of intensity. Itinerant ministers traveled their circuits. New prophets claimed that God was speaking through their mouths. The poor and disenfranchised took their places not only in the pews but also in the pulpits.[5]

Nineteenth-century Christian revivals created a spectacle and a scandal. As the evangelicals knew, some religious and social conservatives looked down on them as unrefined, maybe even dangerous. Were revivalists reclaiming the country from the secular forces of economic and technical modernization, or were they hustling in the marketplace of diversion? What kind of liberty were they interested in, and what kind of discipline were they trying to impose? If distraction signified a torpor of the mind, then it could seem to call for a great awakening; if the problem was a deadness, then a revival might be a good solution. At the same time, though, all this fire and drama looked distracting too. Seeking out intensities might carry the believer away from the quieter, humbler practices of true religion.

In his monumental study of U.S. churches and sects, *Religion in America* (1844), Robert Baird responded to these conservative anxieties about evangelicalism and produced his own elegant defense of the revivals. Distraction and attention were Baird's major themes. He described the modern masses as undisciplined creatures, badly needing supervision: "Their minds are so wandering," he explained, "that most of the time they give to contemplation is wasted in chaotic thought."[6] Even those who felt powerful stirrings in their souls, even some who had been born again, were liable to backslide into their old, bad habits.

The problem was to sustain the common people's faith and concentration. It was not "sufficient," in Baird's view, "when their attention is awakened, to send them to their Bibles and their closets"; on their own, struggling to pray without pastoral guidance, they would only fall into distraction once again. "They need, at every step, the assistance of an experienced mind to *hold them to the subject.*" To reclaim wayward souls for good, religious conversion called for steady discipline, over the course of days or even weeks, not passing hours. "Here, then," Baird decided, "is the great principle of revivals."[7]

Baird imagined evangelical revivals as programs for capturing and guiding attention. No prison guard or schoolmaster would bar the door. Everyone was freely invited, and anyone was free to leave. But the revival, like the reform school, was designed to awaken the attention of the unconverted and, once they answered the call, to keep their minds on task. Revivalists drew a distracted crowd; they converted it into a devout congregation.

This kind of Christianity seems to accept, if not to celebrate, the development of industrial capitalism and the free market; at the same time, it also serves to shore up certain social hierarchies that economic changes might otherwise disturb. For these reasons, nineteenth-century Christianity has always been a target of secular critique. "The criticism of religion is the premise of all criticism," Karl Marx announced in 1844, just as Baird was publishing his theory of revivals.[8] By religion, Marx meant Christianity. By criticism, he meant the philosophical work of dispelling mystifications, emancipating people's minds from the authority of priests and ministers. In the nineteenth-century United States, too, Marx's contemporaries developed their own criticisms. Freethinkers like Frances Wright exposed the church's role in the subjugation of women.[9] Antislavery radicals like Frederick Douglass denounced the hypocrisies of Southern evangelicals who performed devotion while holding property in souls.[10]

Academic historians have picked up and elaborated the same arguments. In a classic study of religion and labor in Upstate New York's burnt-over district, Paul E. Johnson describes evangelicalism as "a middle-class solution to problems of class, legitimacy, and order generated in the early stages of manufacturing."[11] Mining the same vein, Charles Sellers argues that Christian ministers made themselves the servants of capital by adapting to the morality of a nineteenth-century market economy. As older systems of enslavement and indenture gave way to wage labor, Johnson and Sellers explain, evangelical and other "crypto-New-Light" theologies promoted a freewill gospel and a discipline of personal culpability. In

Boston in the 1850s, one long series of prayer meetings called itself the "businessmen's revival."[12]

Baird's *Religion in America* itself has become a key piece of evidence in critical histories of white evangelicalism and Christian nationalism. As the cultural historian Tracy Fessenden argues in *The Culture of Redemption*, Baird's work "subtly aligns religious identity with political identity," securing the benefits of religious freedom for evangelical Christians while justifying persecution and state violence against people of other faiths.[13] Even this apologist for the evangelical movement, however, wanted to ensure that the revivals did not go too far. Relations between revivalism and the nineteenth-century free market were unstable. Improperly supervised, a revival might devolve into a carnivalesque scene of thronging and subversion. Motley and undisciplined communities might take shape at camp meetings. Even violent rebellions might be inspired by exhorters in swamps and clearings, under the open sky.

Beyond the fringes of evangelical Protestantism, too, nineteenth-century revivalism expressed itself in many other weird regimens and new beliefs. What Adrien Rouquette called the "age of machines and money" was also an age of penitents and revelators. There were mesmerists, spiritualists, and Mormons on the scene. There were experiments with Vedic mysticism and animal magnetism. There was the Transcendentalist movement in Massachusetts and, a little later, a transatlantic cult devoted to the worship of Walt Whitman.[14]

"There will soon be no more priests," Whitman wrote in the first edition of his *Leaves of Grass* (1855). "Their work is done."[15] The result, however, was nothing like the end of faith or ceremony. Instead, every kind of worship, from Calvinism to vitalism, now offered itself up to the modern seeker:

> My faith is the greatest of faiths and the least of faiths,
> Enclosing all worship ancient and modern, and all between
>   ancient and modern,

Believing I shall come again upon the earth after five
    thousand years,
Waiting responses from oracles. . . . honoring the gods. . . .
    saluting the sun,
Making a fetish of the first rock or stump. . . . powowing
    with sticks in the circle of obis,
Helping the lama or brahmin as he trims the lamps of the
    idols,
Dancing yet through the streets in a phallic procession. . . .
    rapt and austere in the woods, a
    a gymnosophist,
Drinking mead from the skull-cup. . . . to shasta and vedas
    admirant. . . . minding the koran,
Walking the teokallis, spotted with gore from the stone and
    knife—beating the serpent-
    skin drum;
Accepting the gospels, accepting him that was crucified,
    knowing assuredly that he is
    divine,
To the mass kneeling—to the puritan's prayer rising—
    sitting patiently in a pew,
Ranting and frothing in my insane crisis—waiting dead-
    like til my spirit arouses me . . . [16]

Whitman's catalogue is like and unlike Christian Wiman's. In
"All My Friends Are Finding New Beliefs," each person seems to
discover their own church or devise their own cult. In Leaves of Grass,
a single practitioner takes up a multitude of faiths. He samples all
the world's historical religions, "all worship ancient and modern,"
without fully buying into any of them. He is never permanently
absorbed; his participation is buffered and provisional.[17]

    In his own way, Whitman joined the evangelicals in hoping that
the collapse of an older, more unified religious order would en-
liven the American spirit. But he also loosened the ties that bound
revivalism ("til my spirit arouses me") to conversion, repression,

and social deference. He put spiritual fervor on the side of liberation, rather than restraint. Thus did he froth in his insane crisis. In the
passages that follow, I look into the strange visions that took shape
when markedly old-fashioned styles of worship were revived—
both recollected and reinvented—in self-consciously modern
social situations. Revivalism often enforced a kind of acquiescence
to economic realities, tempered by conservative morality. It also
inspired militant austerities and atavistic passions.

15

"All attention to the last sermon"

My Brethren,
   An occasion so melancholy as the present, viewed in all circum-
stances, hath rarely, if ever, fallen under our notice. This numerous as-
sembly, of all orders and characters, will attend with reverence to the
counsels that may be brought from the word of God. Especially is it to
be hoped, that he, whose tragical death is to succeed this solemnity,
may be all attention to the last sermon he will ever hear. I have ever
considered that I preached to mortal men; but was never called to
preach to one doomed to death by public justice, and but a few hours
before his launching into eternity.

—JAMES DANA, *THE INTENT OF CAPITAL*
PUNISHMENT (1790)

Preaching before a hanging in New Haven in 1790, the minister
James Dana begins with hopes and fears about attention. This is
no ordinary sabbath, where the minister might be in danger of
losing his congregation to daydreams or other restless drifting. All
eyes are on the spectacle; everyone is wide awake.[18]

But if the preacher does not have to work very hard to summon
attention, he does betray some worry about the style and qualities
of the attention that his listeners are paying to the scene. An execution draws a mob, "all orders and characters," and around the gallows strange appetites are stimulated. The motley crowd may be
hungry for a sensational thrill, not the moral lesson Dana intends

to deliver. Its potentialities are not easily predicted or controlled. And so, the minister calls the gathering to "attend" to his words "with reverence." This "numerous assembly," came to watch someone die, but it is going to hear a sermon first.

The occasion is the hanging of Joseph Mountain, a Black man sentenced to hang for the rape of Eunice Thompson, a thirteen-year-old white girl, toward the end of the eighteenth century. Mountain was a stranger in the region, and as his case played out, local authorities had tried to piece together the story of his life. Who was the figure "whose tragical death is to succeed this solemnity"? What was he supposed to mean to the Christian people of New England?

According to a sensational pamphlet, prepared by a local attorney but rendered in the first person, in the condemned man's own voice, Mountain had been born in Philadelphia in 1758. He identified his father as Fling Mountain, a "Molatto." He gave no name for his mother, but he mentioned that she had been enslaved until the age of twenty-one.[19]

Mountain spent his childhood as a servant to an elite family. "My master was industrious to instruct me in the Presbyterian religion which he professed, teach me to read and write, and impress my mind with sentiments of virtue," he confessed. "How grossly these opportunities have been neglected, the following story will too fully evince."[20] The narrative of his life, he promises, will demonstrate how he failed to benefit from the early intellectual and religious instruction that was offered to him, a child in servitude.

At seventeen, Mountain sailed for England where, in time, he joined a circle of thieves. The company of "highwaymen" and "footpads" suited him. Mountain had been born into racialized subordination, but in the English underworld he won respect and made a fortune "notwithstanding the darkness of his complexion." Coming of age in an era of revolutions, he fashioned himself as an adventurer—robbing merchants and humiliating aristocrats, rioting at Parliament and storming Newgate Prison, traveling around the Atlantic on slave ships and other vessels. Such a creature terrified the New Haven ministry; he appeared to embody virtually all of the most destructive forces of secular modernity.[21]

In 1789, for reasons that remain obscure, Mountain returned to the United States. He was passing through Connecticut, on his way from Boston to New York, when officials arrested him, drunk on "ardent spirits," and confined him to the local jail. Mountain pled not guilty, but the Supreme Court convicted him and sentenced him to die. His request for clemency was denied. He would die by hanging on October 20th, 1790, watched by a crowd of ten thousand spectators.

Before Mountain went to the gallows, though, he went to church on the town green, where he heard Dana's sermon. The minister—a Harvard graduate, patriot in the revolutionary cause, and antislavery advocate—had taken over New Haven's First Church just a year earlier. Because of theological divisions among the New Haven Congregationalists, Dana's appointment had been a matter of controversy. Delivering a sermon before the execution of a notorious criminal was a significant event in his career, an occasion to secure his position.

Dana took it seriously, addressing an urgent legal and religious question: the legitimacy of the state's power to kill. In the wake of the Revolution, some American reformers had begun to call for an end to the death penalty. In their view, the gallows stood as a relic of tyranny, an offensive site in a Christian republic devoted to the sovereign rights of its people, and executions were dangerous occasions that warped the public's capacities for sympathy, rather than instilling reverence for law and order.

Answering these challenges, Dana turned his ministry to the purposes of justifying legal violence; he defended civil authorities' right to secure their communities by taking an offender's life. His title, after all, was "The Intent of Capital Punishment." The sermon serves not only the Christian mission of devotion, then, but also, with a special urgency, the civil project of deterrence. And deterrence calls for a certain choreography of attention.

"Examples of public vengeance," as Dana puts it, "naturally strike terror into others, whose lusts and passions might inspire them to the same, or as great evil, were it not for this warning" (12). The minister is in the act of administering this warning from the pulpit, and he wants to be sure that it will be received in the proper spirit, with the right kind of terror. The punishment of one offender must demonstrate to many others, to all those tempted by crime, that they will receive the same harsh penalty if they do not restrain themselves.

The restraining power of deterrence requires an act of imagination, a provisional identification between the observer and the condemned man: if I do not supervise myself, if I give in to my lusts and passions as he did, I will suffer as he does. But the same requirement—that the spectators, in their own imaginations, put themselves in the convict's place—also opens up some other, more dangerous possibilities. What if the crowd identifies with the offender in the act of transgression, not in the passivity of his suffering? What if it identifies with the executioner, with the act of inflicting pain and death, not as a solemn duty but as the indulgence of a vengeful passion?[22] The very spectacle designed to secure civil order might produce the opposite, a disposition toward crime and violence.

Dana's effort to control the crowd's attention therefore tries to ward off these threats. "Melancholy," "reverence," "tragical," "solemnity": proliferating terms for seriousness (and, intriguingly, for the genres of serious literature), he would chasten the people's appetites and bend them to reverence. The sermon is a supplement to the spectacle, an effort to shore up its lessons by disciplining the crowd's attention and turning it inward, to the examination of each person's own transgressive tendencies.

"Ravishment is such an outrage on humanity, an injury so great and irreparable, a crime so baneful and dangerous to society," Dana preaches, "that civilized nations have agreed to protect female honor from violence by making death the penalty for this crime" (9). Mountain has committed a special kind of crime; his violation represents an outrageous kind of scandal in his home country. In American rituals of sovereign violence, it is not just any criminal but a racialized, sexually pathologized one whose spectacular killing by state authorities will serve to reconstitute the lawful, Christian community of the living. It is a matter of civilization, and therefore, in the United States in the decades after independence, it is a matter of race.

Around 1790, Connecticut elites like Daggett and Dana were involved in fierce debates over the abolition of slavery. Many of them, on both sides of the question, feared that Black freedom, especially without the restraint of religion, would devolve into what Dana called "licence" and "lust." Were Black men capable of self-discipline, or were they by nature a threat to social order? Like many other authorities, both civil and spiritual, Dana took up the question. "'Can the ethiopian change his skin, or the leopard his spots? then may those who have been accustomed to do evil, learn to do well.'" Dana uses these lines, adapted from the Book of Jeremiah, to bind Mountain's crime to his skin (26–27).[23]

Dana's discourse, then, is in many ways a classic text of American racial terror. In this sermon, the minister of an established church justifies the state's right to kill by rallying his audience around the cause of a white girl's virtue, invoking the awful figure of a "bold and shameless" rapist. The minister presents the condemned man as one beyond rehabilitation in this world, hardened to the civilizing influences of kindness and virtue. He argues that the state's only choice is to take Mountain's earthly life and remand his eternal one to God's judgment.

Even as Dana sanctions the hanging, he holds out that hope for redemption. The minister takes care to insist that his listeners should witness more than a ceremonial killing. Mountain's "unimbodied" soul, he says, is hanging in the balance. From the beginning of his sermon, he speaks not only to the congregation but also, with special directness, to the "one doomed to death by public justice."

Dana imagines that the condemned man, hardened in life, might be moved, just before his death, into a softer attentiveness. In the scene his sermon creates for its audience, Mountain stands alone, apart from the community, already an outcast, but Dana speaks a prayer that would awaken even this doomed soul's powers of concentration. Dana's hope, strange as it seems, is that Mountain might achieve a pure receptivity—"all attention to the last sermon he will ever hear."

If such a transformation could be worked, then Mountain's body, an object of vengeance and an ongoing threat to the social order, would virtually disappear. His "ethiopian" shell, hardened and darkened by crime, would fall away. What would remain would be his capacity to hear a message, his availability to the preacher's influence. The offender, before being punished for his violent action, would be converted into a passive instrument. The preacher extends, to the very last second, the opportunity for penitence made possible by the magic of attention.

16

"The power of fixed and continuous attention"

The power of fixed and continuous attention in deepening the impressions of any subject is one of the most familiar principles of mental science. To nothing, however, does it apply with so much force as religion, whose objects are at once so vast, so remote, and so repulsive to the natural heart. Men must look at their condition and ponder it deeply, before they can feel the extremity of their wretchedness and guilt. It is the first step in turning to God; and one reason, no doubt, why so many sit from year to year under the ordinary preaching of the word, moved and affected, in some degree, almost every Sabbath, and yet making no progress in divine things, is, that the impressions produced are not followed up and deepened during the subsequent week. On the contrary, even when a person feels but slightly moved, if his mind can be held to the subjects in steady and prolonged attention, while every object is excluded that can divert his thoughts, and the whole field of vision is filled with clear and vivid exhibitions of divine truth, it is surprising to see how rapid, in many cases, the progress of conviction becomes.

—ROBERT BAIRD, *RELIGION IN AMERICA* (1844)

In this serpentine passage from *Religion in America*, Robert Baird brings "mental science" to bear on the problem of religious conversion. He asks: Why is the progress of conviction so slow, even for those who find themselves moved and affected, briefly at least, in church on Sundays? Why does the divine truth not take a more lasting hold? What psychic conditions make it so hard for people to reckon with their own spiritual wretchedness and turn to God? The science of attention provides some answers to these questions.[24]

The trouble, Baird thinks, has to do with something called *impressions*. The mind is a receptive thing, open to various influences. The objects it observes and the messages it receives leave marks (impressions) on the mind, sculpting its character. The way to form a self—or to convert one—is therefore to control these forces, protecting the vulnerable mind from bad influences and ensuring that the right things make the strongest impressions. If preachers are failing to convert their congregants to an enduring, life-transforming faith, their ministry must be making fleeting, shallow impressions. So feebly grasped, the people will backslide.

Religion, Baird acknowledges, is "repulsive to the natural heart." We creatures of desiring flesh and tainted blood are quick to turn away from its demands. Its objects are so vast and so remote that they make weak claims on our interest. Worldly things impress themselves on us more easily, with quicker pleasure. We are given to distraction, naturally.

Missionaries therefore have to develop the art of "deepening the impressions"; the "impressions produced" on sabbath days have to be "*followed up* and deepened during the subsequent week." How will this effect be obtained?

Baird finds the secret in "the power of fixed and continuous attention." The crucial task is to grasp and direct this power. But since religion exerts such meager attraction on the natural heart, since it is a disadvantaged competitor for people's attention, it cannot accomplish its mission within the space of just a few hours on Sundays. It has to change the whole environment, transforming the attention economy where it conducts its business.

Baird comes with good news: by improvising and experimenting, evangelicals have devised a mechanism for reordering religious space and time. It gives them the power to hold minds in steady, prolonged attention, and to deepen good impressions. The mechanism is called a *revival*.

By the time he wrote *Religion in America*, Baird had seen his share of camp meetings and conversions. He was a graduate of Princeton Theological seminary who became a prominent Presbyterian minister and missionary. As an agent of the American Sunday School Union, he had distributed religious pamphlets among the poor. As an activist for education reform, he had helped to modernize Pennsylvania's schools. As an itinerant preacher, he had traveled over New England and into the South, organizing churches and gathering in souls. Along the way, he learned about nineteenth-century America's attention economy.

In the early 1840s, Baird was living in Geneva, one of Protestantism's capital cities, discussing ministry with European preachers and scholars who looked skeptically on the American scene. To the uninitiated, the revivalists' peculiar methods—thronging camp meetings that lasted several days at a stretch, mass conversions acted out with convulsions and tears—looked wild. Baird set out to explain, in civilized and sensible terms, just how they worked. He produced the American evangelical movement's most sophisticated "theory of revivals."

Revivals, Baird argues, "are not seasons of mere excitement and fanaticism, but might reasonably be expected, from their consistency with the great laws of human action, to produce those great and lasting reformations with which they have actually blessed the American churches" (467). Baird tries to reconcile faith and knowledge, demonstrating the reasonableness of evangelical techniques. In particular, he shows how revivals cultivate Christian devotion by working on the human "mental constitution."

A camp meeting, as Baird represents it, is no regression to savage passions; it is a rational procedure for managing thought and action. Evangelical ministers and exhorters are no rabble-rousers, no traffickers in false enthusiasm. They are moderns, using psychological principles to expand their churches and convert the multitudes.

What keeps some people from experiencing the depths of religious transformation, Baird explains, is distraction. The revival is designed to pare away diversions and to fix the mind on the divine truth. "The ordinary *amusements* of life, which interest the feelings and divert the attention, are at such periods wholly laid aside" (211). Revivals, in Baird's view, work efficiently to arouse religious desire; to quicken expectation; to cultivate sympathy; and to awaken a spirit of inquiry. But the key to it all, "the great principle of revivals," is attention.

It is easy to think of nineteenth-century evangelicals as old-school reactionaries, recoiling from the shocks of scientific progress and liberal politics. They could be fierce critics of any cold rationalism that left the heart unmoved. Sophisticated discourse, with its paradoxes and its detachment from common sense, oftentimes made them restless. But Baird's work shows how well evangelicals could swim with the currents of modernity.

Preachers were already mastering the machinery of the mass press, so crucial to their missionary enterprise. They could also learn enlightened mental science, with its concepts of impressibility and attention. And they could come to terms with liberal commitments like the freedoms of conscience and the will. The revivalists were bidding for souls in an open market, where anyone at all might be addressed, but every passing stranger would be at liberty to decide whether or not to answer the call. How else had the evangelicals become such savvy operators in the attention economy?

Among historians of American religion, Baird's work has become a classic source. *Religion in America* gives an expansive survey of the nineteenth century's many faiths, but it also marks a change in the meaning of religion itself. Revisiting Baird, scholars notice how he explores various types of congregations, movements, and devotional styles while tacitly accepting certain relatively narrow Anglo-Protestant premises about what counts as a legitimate faith, or true religion. For instance, Baird emphasizes sincere belief over ritual performance, and he values the liberty of conscience, not government enforcement of religious observance.

These commitments lead Baird—and many other conservative and moderate Protestants like him—toward certain liberal political conclusions. Baird understands religion primarily as a matter of private faith, and so he supports the freedoms of conscience and expression. At the same time, he describes a pluralistic society where much of public life is transacted among people of differing religious convictions. Baird argues that religion flourishes best when it is freely chosen by the faithful, not imposed by the state, and he isolates religion, as a private affair, from other types of knowledge and commerce. For these reasons, *Religion in America* has come to be understood, paradoxically, as contributing to a secular worldview.

For most of his career, Baird had worked in the wake of disestablishment. By the 1830s, all of the states in the union had severed their formal alliances with established churches. (The Congregationalists in Massachusetts, great-grandchildren of the original New England theocrats, held out longest.) At first glance, Baird acknowledged, this development looked like a loss of power, a decline into secular conditions. Abandoned by the state, religion seemed consigned to a narrower sphere of voluntary associations and family relations, a matter of private conscience rather than an affair of state. As Baird saw it, though, disestablishment turned out to be a gift to evangelicals.

Of course, religion's enemies, the atheists and freethinkers, had advocated disestablishment. For them it was a matter of survival. They associated religion with state tyranny, secular reason with personal liberty. They staged a rebellion against the outmoded, illegitimate styles of domination that found expression in witch trials and inquisitions.

What may still seem surprising is that nineteenth-century evangelicals, too, came to embrace the separation of church and state. The new arrangement, where government would take the part of no official church, freed Baptists and Methodists to pursue their own ways, to stage their revivals and launch their missions.[25] What they discovered was that making religion voluntary did not always loosen the ministers' grasp on churchgoers' minds and souls.

Instead, an appeal to the free will might enlist believers in the work of perfecting themselves, affirming their own submission.

True religion, the nineteenth-century evangelicals believed, was voluntary. True Christians came to their faith, as Baird wrote, "always from free impulses, without any outward coercion."[26] The conversion of a nation of believers without outward coercion: this was the evangelical vision, which in the early nineteenth century seemed to be taking shape as a reality. But the phrase "outward coercion" would be redundant unless its author recognized its counterpart, *inward* coercion, a self-discipline endowed with the power to control bodies and correct defects of character. A vast conformity that felt, to the faithful, like the spontaneous expression of self-determining people.

Religious liberty in the nineteenth century was a Protestant cause in this sense: it extended the freedom of worship mainly to those whose practices complied with a Protestant definition of what a true religion looks like.[27] Revivalism combined inward coercion, an effort to capture and redirect the will itself, with a profession of freedom. And thus, it both exercised and disavowed its will to dominion, recasting its disciplines as self-disciplines, attributing to its subjects the very power it wielded over them. In this exercise of power, attention was both its instrument and its alibi.

17

"The relations of business and religion"

The relations of business and religion need to be more fully developed. Men must be taught to bring their worldly avocations within the pale of religion. They must be educated into the belief that laymen and ministers are to live and labor for ONE *and the same object, though it the matter of directness there exists a difference in accomplishing that object. It must be shown to them that secular pursuits may be made sacred,—that any legitimate calling, if pursued in a proper manner, and with right ends, is rendered, in the best sense of the term, a "sacred calling,"—and that unless it is rendered such, it is pursued in a manner unworthy of the Christian's high vocation.*

—HENRY CLAY FISH, *PRIMITIVE PIETY REVIVED, OR THE AGGRESSIVE POWER OF THE CHRISTIAN CHURCH* (1855)

In Boston, 1855, the Congregational Board of Publication held an essay competition. An anonymous donor had contributed two hundred dollars for the prize, to be awarded to the best piece dealing with "*the more perfect exemplification in Christian life of the doctrines of the gospel.*" The charge was to revive faith "as an energizing and all-conquering *principle,* actually subordinating earthly things to heavenly," and to show, along the way, "the true sense of self-denial required by Christ as essential to discipleship." The benefactor was worried about backsliding and a weakening of piety; the competition would contribute to a renewal of devotion.[28]

The prize was claimed by the Reverend Henry Clay Fish, a Baptist preacher from Vermont who had settled into a pastorate down in Newark, New Jersey. Fish's essay promised fire. Judging by his title, *Primitive Piety Revived, or The Aggressive Power of the Christian Church*, readers could fairly expect a jeremiad.

And Fish delivered one, in his way. He began with the conventional lamentations about a general decline of faith. American Protestants in the 1850s, he observed, were making fortunes in manufacturing and trade, but they were growing poor in spirit. "Business is too often a perfect thralldom, where all the energies are exhausted in the drudgery of mammon, and where the religious affections are welnigh stifled and destroyed" (48). Too many promising young men were pursuing careers of worldly success while the churches lacked capable ministers. Too many were spending their money on liquor and tobacco while the foreign missions scraped for funds.

Fish did not spare his brothers in the ministry from his scolding. He accused the churches themselves of yielding to the seductions of worldly wealth and fashion: "We may perfect the machinery as much as we will, may improve our Sunday school, educational and missionary organizations,—build commodious and tasteful sanctuaries for ourselves and others,—may remove errors and imperfections from our articles of faith, and church-discipline; and yet, behind this complete organism, there must be the mighty motive power of *a hidden interior life*, or all is fruitless and vain" (31–32).

Fish's choice of "figure," the image he uses to represent a church that has lost its way, is a revealing one. He speaks of "machinery." Religious institutions have become modern contraptions, "commodious and tasteful" in their form but hollow in spirit. There is a streak of anti-modernism in this lamentation. It hungers for a *primitive* piety—stripped down, unadorned, uncorrupted, plainer in its surfaces and driven, first of all, to cultivate the inner life of devotion.

Thus, the Baptist preacher of 1855 calls back to the Puritans who built the Congregationalist Church in Massachusetts and, beyond them, to the earliest disciples. But then, midway through his discourse, Fish returns to his own scene, the bourgeois world of investors and professionals in the industrializing North.

What might it look like, the revival of primitive piety in modern times? This was the Christian's duty, as Fish imagined it, and as he was rewarded for imagining it: to occupy one's proper station in the world, to go to work, to obey the law (answering a "legitimate calling"), even to accrue wealth—in short, to participate in secular business—but to do all this in the service of God. The disciple must not renounce work or profit. Whatever Fish means by "primitive piety," he does not intend the asceticism of the legendary anchorites and mystics. His ideal, instead, is the creature he calls "a *business Christian*" (50).

The business Christian is a capitalist who uses worldly wealth and influence to promote Protestant conversion, faith, and order: "The Lord blessed him richly, and made him, by his consistent and active usefulness, a rich blessing to others" (51). Despite its title, *Primitive Piety Revived* preaches a prosperity gospel for nineteenth-century American Protestants. Fish represents himself as a voice for old-time "primitive" Christianity in a country that has abandoned spiritual concerns for worldly ones. He calls his readers to put their faith above their private interests. He reminds them that all their labors should be dedicated to God's service, and that all their blessings come from Him. For all Fish's fiery words, though, he is really excusing his readers from any ascetic self-denial and authorizing their pursuit of wealth. Undertaken in the proper spirit, "secular pursuits may be made sacred."

18

"My mind was powerfully wrought upon"

I was now about nineteen years of age, and had become quite steady. I attended meetings again quite often, and my mind was powerfully wrought upon. At this time my heart was susceptible of good impressions. I would think upon the varied scenes of my life—how often the Lord had called me, and how for a season I attended to that call—of the blessed and happy times I had experienced in the house of God, and in secret devotion; and the days of darkness and nights of sorrowful anguish, since those days when the spirit of God breathed upon my soul. Then, I enjoyed happiness in a pre-eminent degree! Now, I was miserable, I had offended God—violated his laws— abused his goodness—trampled his mercy under foot, and disregarded his admonitions. But still he called me back to the path of duty and of peace.

—WILLIAM APESS, *A SON OF THE FOREST*
(1829, REVISED 1831)

After years of wandering, a young Christian feels the Holy Spirit working on his mind and touching, once again, his still impressionable heart. He recollects the old times when worshipping the Lord, whether at church or in solitude, used to bring him happiness; he looks back over the early season in his life, the blessed occasions when he attended to the call.[29]

In the light of this good memory, in the presence of a divine voice, the penitent's recent life of adventure and indulgence looks miserably hollow. He sees that he has strayed from the path of righteousness, and a sense of remorse sets in. Shaken, he makes a series of confessions: he acknowledges that he has violated God's laws, that he deserves to suffer for his sins.

At the same time, in his wretchedness, he hears his Lord's call, renewed. For all his crimes, he is not yet hopelessly hardened; his heart is still "susceptible of good impressions." There remains an opportunity for redemption, if he will attend.

William Apess, a self-styled "son of the forest" who became a Methodist preacher and a militant in the struggle for Native self-determination, was born in Massachusetts in 1798. His parents were mixed-race people affiliated with the Pequot community; through his mother, Apess claimed a kinship to the legendary King Philip. As a young boy, he was left in the care of his hard-drinking, abusive grandparents, then indentured to a white family. His new mistress, a pious Baptist, treated Apess kindly, almost like one of her own children, and introduced him to religion. "The conversation and pious admonitions of this good lady made a lasting impression on my mind," he wrote in tribute to this benefactor (19). For the rest of his life, Apess would align himself with the fiery evangelical Christianity of common people.

Dignified Presbyterianism, with its formal rituals and its conspicuous displays of erudition, left him cold: "It did not arouse me to a sense of my danger," Apess recalled (37). But the evangelicals, with their camp meetings and their intensities of feeling, stirred him up. When they began to preach, he avowed, he "listened to the word of God with the greatest degree of attention" (26). Hearing a Methodist sermon on the crucifixion, Apess felt himself awakening to a new kind of faith: "I felt convicted," he remembered, "that Christ died for all mankind—that age, sect, colour, country, or situation, made no difference" (41). This doctrine gave Apess a good deal of joy, an assurance that the way to salvation was open even to himself.

It also afflicted him with a new sense of guilt. If the lamb of God had made "a free-will offering for my unregenerate and wicked soul," promising Apess the possibility of redemption, then the same offering "removed every excuse" (41). With the freewill gospel came the condition of personal culpability. "My spirits were depressed—my crimes were arrayed before me, and no tongue can tell the anguish I felt." Even as Apess saw the gates of heaven opening to him, then, he began to appraise his own thoughts and conduct with a less indulgent eye, to judge himself more harshly. He measured, as if for the first time, the true weight of his transgressions, and the anguish hung heavy on him.

For weeks, in secret, Apess wrestled against the devil and tried to get his own wayward, stricken heart under control. He gave up all the ordinary comforts and consolations of the life he had known up to this point. He prayed for grace. "I now hung all my hope on the Redeemer, and clung with indescribable tenacity to the cross on which he purchased salvation for the 'vilest of the vile.' The result was such as is always to be expected, when a lost and ruined sinner throws himself entirely on the Lord—*perfect freedom*" (45). This was Apess's conversion: by way of his complete abjection, the liberation of his soul.

When he wrote that the "result" of his penitence was "such as is always to be expected," Apess meant that his conversion experience conformed to a familiar pattern. "There was nothing singular . . . in my conversion," he acknowledged. He meant that what happened to him was generic, not special; the same thing might happen to anyone who felt their own depravity so deeply that they abandoned themselves entirely to Christ's mercy. In this way, Apess offered himself up to the reader as a token of a type. If he could be converted, so could multitudes.

Such a claim, as Apess understood it, had implications for the future of civilization on the continent. "A most sweeping charge has been brought against the natives," he wrote. "It is this, that they are not susceptible to improvement" (72). Apess took it upon himself to demonstrate that North American Indians were capable, in fact. "Many of them have been converted to God, and have died in the triumphs of faith," he testified. There was no hierarchy of races fixed in nature. There was only the great divide between the lost and the redeemed.

In the hands of some preachers, this message had served a settler colonial mission, legitimating conquest. For Apess, conversion's universal promise opened up other, more subversive possibilities. Working from the premise that Christ died for everyone, Apess attacked the hypocrisy of white New Englanders who professed religion while they displaced and dispossessed the indigenous population. But Apess understood that evangelical commitments could also animate principled acts of civil disobedience, even militant resistance against imperial expansion. During a sojourn on Cape Cod in the 1830s, Apess would help organize the uprising known as the Mashpee Revolt, fighting for indigenous control of land and resources, along with more religious liberty.

On his way to Christian militancy, Apess took a long and winding path. Not long after his childhood conversion, he began to wander far from home. Escaping from his master's house at fifteen, he rambled through the towns of the northeastern United States and southeastern Canada, taking on odd jobs and committing petty crimes. For a while, he joined a New York militia and fought for the United States in the War of 1812. By his own account, the government refused to compensate him for his service because he was an Indian, and so Apess was left to fend for himself. "I was also exposed to some temptations, as I met often in the road the veriest wretches that defile the earth—such as would forget the dignity of human nature so far as to blackguard me because I was an Indian" (76–77). He hired himself out as a laborer, pursued some further adventures, and drank a lot of rum.

A conflict with a new master, called Mr. Geers, brought Apess to a turning point. "I served him faithfully," Apess wrote, "but when I wanted my pay, he undertook to treat me as he would a degraded African slave, he took a cart-stake in order to pay me; but he soon found out his mistake, as I made him put it down as quick as he had taken it up. I had been cheated too often that I determined to have my rights this time, and forever after" (79). In this test of wills, when his master threatens to beat him instead of paying him for his labor, Apess feels not only the physical danger but also the indignity. To be battered and insulted, as he imagines it, is a kind of blackening—the sort of treatment that might be inflicted on "a degraded African slave." Against the white master, and against the specter of racialized abjection, Apess holds his ground. He is determined, he says, to have his rights.

This act of self-assertion, along with the decent payment it secures for him, leaves Apess feeling "quite steady" on his feet. Nineteen years old, settling into a secure life for the first time in several years, he returns to religion. God seems to be calling Apess back into the fold, and he seems ready to attend. The time has come for his rehabilitation.

Attending to God's voice, Apess begins the work of penitence. He looks over his life, and he sees a terrible series of crimes. "I had offended God—violated his laws—abused his goodness—trampled his mercy under foot, and disregarded his admonitions." A long time ago, he had been acquainted with the sweetness of grace, but in the meantime he has passed through "days of darkness and nights of sorrowful anguish." For the second time, he grasps the full weight of his own wickedness. For the second time, he wrestles with the devil and mortifies himself in search of grace.

Slowly, painfully, Apess finds his way back to God. A Methodist camp meeting helps him along; among the Methodists worshipping in the open air, Apess remembers, "I found some comfort, and enjoyed myself tolerably well" (84). Soon afterward, he leaves the white community.

"I went among my tribe," Apess writes. He moves into the house of his aunt Sally George, in Groton, and the two of them begin to organize informal Christian services, a series of three-day revivals. "These seasons were glorious," Apess writes. "We had no house of divine worship, believing 'That the groves were God's first temples,' thither we would repair when the weather permitted. The Lord often met with us, and we were happy in spite of the devil" (85). Having experienced his own evangelical conversion, Apess begins to organize a new series of revivals, open to all.

19

"I began to direct my attention to this great object"

It had been said of me in my childhood by those by whom I had been taught to pray, both white and black, and in whom I had the greatest confidence, that I had too much sense to be raised, and if I was, I would never be of any use to any one as a slave. Now finding I had arrived to man's estate, and was a slave, and these revelations being made known to me, I began to direct my attention to this great object, to fulfil the purpose for which, by this time, I felt assured I was intended. Knowing the influence I had obtained over the minds of my fellow servants, (not by means of conjuring and such like tricks—for to them I always spoke of such things with contempt) but by the communion of the Spirit whose revelations I often communicated to them, and they believed and said my wisdom came from God. I now began to prepare them for my purpose, by telling them something was about to happen that would terminate in fulfilling the great promise that had been made to me—About this time I was placed under an overseer, from whom I ran away.

—THE CONFESSIONS OF NAT TURNER (1831)

In chains, in a Virginia jail cell, in the last days before he goes to the gallows, a rebel prophet recollects his life. His story goes back to his early education, the days when he learned to read and pray. Showing signs of giftedness, he was told by his elders he would never be suited for slavery. Sure enough, as he came of age, his master's will ran more and more against the will of his creator. In time, the day arrived when the young man felt he had to choose between the two. Which one would he serve?[30]

The passage is attributed to the inspired leader of American history's best-known slave insurrection, in that event's most controversial document, *The Confessions of Nat Turner*. The pamphlet was prepared by a Virginia attorney, Thomas Ruffin Gray, based on his jailhouse interviews with Turner. The one who appears to speak in its pages is the rebel exhorter himself.

The document interweaves two kinds of confession, the legal and the religious. As an acknowledgment of criminal guilt, it serves as evidence against the speaker, justifying his punishment. As a spiritual autobiography, like Augustine's *Confessions*, it testifies to Turner's devotional practices. It is an account of his crimes, but it is also the story of his visions, his ascetic self-discipline, and his rise to religious authority among the enslaved.

Ever since *The Confessions of Nat Turner* first began to circulate, readers have argued about its authenticity and its effects. Gray said he wanted to encourage stricter white vigilance against the enslaved population, but the passages featuring Turner's voice were taken up in many ways, some of them subversive and incendiary. Few readers of the *Confessions* have paused to notice, or take seriously, how attention matters to its plot.[31]

"I began to direct my attention," the prisoner confesses, "to this great object, to fulfill the purpose for which, by this time, I felt assured I was intended." Attention sets the events in motion. Attending is a deliberate act, and it turns the speaker against his white master—yet it is also an act of devotion to another power. The speaker becomes an implement, under the direction of this other agent, for whose "purpose" he believes he is "intended." Even his rebellion entails a kind of submission.

The next step is assembling a crew of militants. Turner dilates on the source and nature of his influence over other minds. They trust his authority, and not because he manipulates them with "conjuring and such like tricks"; he holds such hoaxes in contempt.

The other servants follow Turner because they believe his wisdom comes from God. He is the vessel of a divine truth, not of his own making. When they listen to his voice, they hear the Spirit.

"I now began to prepare them for my purpose," Turner says. It is a turning point. Just a few lines earlier, he identified himself as one called to fulfill another's "purpose." Now the purpose is his own. The other servants are becoming his implements, weapons under his control. To prepare them for the task—the "work of death" (11), he calls it elsewhere—he introduces a new economy of information and attention. He quickens his listeners' vigilance by disclosing his design in stages, little by little. "Something was about to happen"—something, a placeholder word, a blank space to be filled in when the right time comes. They are not to know, not yet, just what he is preparing them for. They are just supposed to attend, vigilantly, waiting for the sign.

The promise has been made; Turner and his accomplices ready themselves for its fulfillment. But then, abruptly, Turner interrupts himself. Before the sign can be given, before the work of death gets underway, the prophet finds himself grasped by other forces, watched by supervising eyes. "About this time I was placed under an overseer," he says, shifting back into the passive voice as he describes his transformation into an object of disciplinary attention.

In the next breath, with wonderful casualness, Turner reclaims his subjectivity—"from whom I ran away." In another kind of narrative, the whole drama would be here, in the fugitive's escape. In Turner's confessions, though, the flight is only a distraction. After three days in the woods, he returns to the plantation. No slave-catcher drags him there. Instead, he follows a holy voice.

Turner explains himself this way: "The reason of my return was, that the Spirit appeared to me and said I had my wishes directed to the things of this world, and not to the kingdom of Heaven, and that I should return to the service of my earthly master" (10). It is the most traditional Christian reprimand, an injunction to turn his mind from earthly concerns to heavenly ones, and it leads Turner into a lonely period of spiritual exercises. "I now withdrew myself," he recalls, "from the intercourse of my fellow servants, for the avowed purpose of serving the Spirit more fully." Again, devotion creates a contradiction of purpose, where the act of willful self-assertion is also one of self-denial and submission.

In Turner's confessions, the discipline bears fruit. Practicing his renewed austerity, Turner begins to receive his revolutionary visions. He sees drops of blood on the corn, hieroglyphics on the leaves of trees. He watches as white and black figures war against each other in the Virginia sky. Finally, a solar eclipse seems to give the signal that Turner has been waiting for, and he gathers his little congregation in the woods. There, in the open air, he reveals his prophesies and speaks his exhortations. "From a Camp Meeting about the Dismal Swamp," a Richmond newspaper reported, "the slave rebellion emerged."[32] After his return from wandering, Turner's plot unfolded in this sequence: devotion, revival, insurrection.

20

"Hear me now, love your heart"

"Here," she said, "in this here place, we flesh; flesh that weeps, laughs; flesh that dances on bare feet in grass. Love it. Love it hard. Yonder they do not love your flesh. They despise it. They don't love your eyes; they'd just as soon pick em out. No more do they love the skin on your back. Yonder they flay it. And O my people they do not love your hands. Those they only use, tie, bind, chop off and leave empty. Love your hands! Love them. Raise them up and kiss them. Touch others with them, pat them together, stroke them on your face 'cause they don't love that either. You got to love it, you! And no, they ain't in love with your mouth. Yonder, out there, they will see it broken and break it again. What you say out of it they will not heed. What you scream from it they do not hear. What you put into it to nourish your body they will snatch away and give you leavins instead. No, they don't love your mouth. You got to love it. This is flesh I'm talking about here. Flesh that needs to be loved."

—TONI MORRISON, *BELOVED* (1987)

A congregation gathers in a clearing in the woods. They arrive from elsewhere, from "yonder," where they are despised. Out there, in situations overseen by white masters and slavecatchers, Black people are not loved; they are worked to exhaustion, killed, and consumed. Here, in the clearing, they are called to love and care for themselves, beginning with their flesh. Hatred atrophies their bodies, but loving attention promises to bring them, piece by piece, member by member, back to life.[33]

Though this passage tells a story from the 1850s, it was published in 1987. Toni Morrison, like other writers seeking histories of Black experience under slavery, understands that the nineteenth century's documentary archives can hide and distort as much as they disclose; she uses the resources of imaginative fiction to pursue the truth by other means. The sermon in the clearing is her fabulation of what a Black revival, unseen and unrecorded by white authorities, might have sounded like.[34]

The one who speaks in Morrison's novel is an "unchurched preacher," formerly enslaved, called Baby Suggs (102). Like many other preachers, Baby Suggs draws a stark opposition between two realms. The two she has in mind, however, are not the eternal and the secular. In her exhortation, there are two places, two theaters of life. She points to them with the words *there* and *here*. There are also two communities, *they* and *you*. The living world itself is segregated, Baby Suggs knows, and in this segregated world the old religious subordination of the flesh to the spirit has been racialized.

As she preaches, Baby Suggs draws from and recomposes a familiar passage from the Book of Psalms:

> They have mouths, but they speak not: eyes have they,
>   but they see not:
> They have ears, but they hear not: noses have they, but they
>   smell not:
> They have hands, but they handle not: feet have they, but
>   they walk not: neither speak they through their throat.
>   (115:5–7)

The psalm is describing "heathens" who worship idols made by human hands, neglecting the true God. It portrays them as lifeless bodies, made of organs that do not sense and limbs that do not work. Their fixation on worldly things becomes a kind of blinded incapacity; they have been created for a higher purpose, but they remain detached from it, inattentive and silent.

In Baby Suggs's revision, the imagery is of white neglect and violence toward Black flesh. White people are unloading their ancient fears about desire, the wickedness of the body's needs and appetites, onto Black lives, then repressing and dismembering them, murderously. "O my people they do not love your hands. Those they only use, tie, bind, chop off and leave empty." A terrible asceticism turns self-mortifications outward, against the other; white people destroy the Black bodies they hold captive and exploit, as if to punish the wickedness of their own dependency.

The revival in the clearing, as Morrison develops it, is a ceremony for healing the wounds inflicted by this pathological economic and social relation. Baby Suggs reclaims and revivifies the bodies of her listeners, one part at a time. This preacher is a genius of *deixis*, the linguistic act of referring to the circumstances of a speaker's copresence with her audience—"here," "in this place," "this is flesh I'm talking about here," she says, summoning and awakening them. She is speaking commands, but she is also activating their own powers of perception, their capacity for care. She is calling their attention to the very worldliest parts of themselves, to their own flesh, taking it out of other hands. Love is her word for this reanimating act of attention to one's own organs of sensation and expression.

21

"Read these leaves in the open air"

This is what you shall do: Love the earth and sun and the animals, despise riches, give alms to every one that asks, stand up for the stupid and crazy, devote your income and labor to others, hate tyrants, argue not concerning God, have patience and indulgence toward the people, take off your hat to nothing known or unknown or to any man or number of men, go freely with powerful uneducated persons and with the young and with the mothers of families, read these leaves in the open air every season of every year of your life, re-examine all you have been told at school or church or in any book, dismiss whatever insults your own soul, and your flesh shall be a great poem and have the richest fluency not only in its words but in the silent lines of its lips and face and between the lashes of your eyes and in every motion and joint of your body.

—WALT WHITMAN, LEAVES OF GRASS (1855)

In this passage from the prose text known as the preface to the first edition of *Leaves of Grass*, Walt Whitman lays out some guidelines for the conduct of life. "This is what you shall do," he begins, moving into a sequence of imperatives and prohibitions: *love, despise, give, stand up, devote, hate, argue not.* In all, there are fourteen (two times seven), a fitting number for a devotional work, if you count the last one—"and your flesh shall be a great poem"—though this particular line reads less like a rule, more like a promise or a prophecy.[35]

Whitman calls his followers to free themselves from conventional authorities and trifling concerns. He instructs them to hate tyrants, not to take their hats off to their social superiors, to go freely with the lowly and the wild. He invites them to forget what they have learned from other, less worthy sources. He tells them to give their money away. Practice these principles, Whitman says, and you will be transformed. Your flesh will become a great poem. The shapes and movements of your body will partake of some rich fluency.

But here, as elsewhere—and as he made himself famous for doing quite flagrantly—Whitman contradicts himself. He exhorts his disciples to refuse all gestures of submission, yet he makes up a list of prescriptions, telling them what to do. He casts himself as a liberator, but he plays the lawgiver, too. Is this hypocrisy? At least one modern scholar proposes that Whitman's true ambition was to become not just a famous poet but the founder of a new religion.[36] Can readers really be commanded to refuse submission, summoned to disobedience in the imperative mode? Does Whitman reject the authority of churches and schools, or is he trying to take their place?

What makes the difference, for the author of *Leaves of Grass*, between the tyrant who imposes an imperial code and the poet who says, "This is what you shall do"? The first (as Whitman himself and many other nineteenth-century Americans imagined it) is the voice of oppression, demanding compliance. The second would appeal to the listener's own inborn sense of generosity, dignity, and self-respect. The tyrant confronts you with a choice between submission and resistance. Whitman's directives, by contrast, stand or fall with the powers that you recognize in yourself. They exert none of what nineteenth-century evangelicals called "outward coercion"; they are simply speech acts, with no police power to enforce them. Your willing acquiescence is the condition of their felicity. And so, saying *yes*, as Whitman invites you to imagine it, is not an act of compliance, not a surrender. It can be an expansion of yourself.

"Think not that I am come to destroy the law, or the prophets," Jesus preached in Matthew 5:17. "I am come not to destroy, but to fulfil." His sermon on the mount took the form of a series of revisions. It cited and transformed the commandments of the ancient prophets in order to give them new life, new force in directing belief and conduct. "Ye have heard that it hath been said, An eye for an eye, and a tooth for a tooth. But I say unto you, That ye resist not evil: but whosoever shall smite thee on thy right cheek, turn to him the other also" (Matthew 5:38–39). Christ quoted the traditional scripture and then rewrote it, but He called His new text the fulfilment, not the erasure, of the older one.

Introducing *Leaves of Grass*, Whitman in his own peculiar way is following the sermon's example. He invites the faithful out of their closets and into the open air. His mission is not to found a new spiritual kingdom over which he will preside with sovereign authority. It is to renew their spirits and reanimate their bodies by displaying his own beautiful example. In this way Whitman tries to reconcile a practice of willing submission with a sense of undomesticated freedom.

It seems fair to say that *Leaves of Grass* aspires to be something more than literature in the narrow sense; it is not a volume of poems lending themselves to aesthetic appreciation or to scholarly analysis. (All readers of Whitman will notice his hostility to anything approaching an academic style of thought or comportment.) And in fact, Whitman's *Leaves* did find this reception, a Whitmanism that flourished less in schools than in queer networks of so-called "Whitmaniacs" whose first encounter with Whitman felt, to them, like a conversion. They held gatherings on riverbanks and read his poetry aloud together; season after season, they returned to it. For these readers, Whitman's discipline did not mortify the flesh. It sharpened the senses and exposed the body—undraping it, leaving it unprotected against pain but also intensifying its capacities for pleasure.[37]

"Each moment and whatever happens thrills me with joy," Whitman sings elsewhere (30). Not in his propositions but in his modes, not in the content of his beliefs but in the genres of his speech acts, he is a revivalist. The effect, as he imagines it, is a habit of intense wakefulness—a burning, sensuous receptivity to the world. His wild abandonment to desire entails its own discipline of attention.

Afterthought

Around the turn of the twentieth century, the Irish poet Edmond Holmes wondered about the uses of Christian devotional literature in a modern world that was liberating itself from dogmatic and repressive authorities. Holmes turned his mind especially to the widely influential fifteenth-century devotional manual known as De Imitatione Christi. For centuries, it had guided Christians in practices of self-purification, detaching them from worldly concerns and lifting them up toward God. "In the Imitation of Christ, the growth of the soul is entirely upward," Holmes observed. "Of sympathy with outward Nature; of the expansion of the soul in the direction of art and poetry, of knowledge and action; of interest in political, in social, in domestic life . . . there is not a trace."[38]

Holmes, who thought of himself as a pantheist, could not accept such a stark, self-mutilating way of life. He found this "austere inwardness" hostile to the true needs of the human soul. To develop in harmony with its own nature, Holmes felt, the soul could not simply ascend from the world into "sublime solitude." It also needed to expand outward, to make contact with others and the world. The soul craved not only "self-denial" and "submission to discipline" but also "love (in the human sense of the word)." And what was true for the soul was true for society, too; people needed intimacy as well as order, relations to nature and each other as well as to divinity.[39]

Holmes wanted to counterbalance asceticism with a healthy love for the world, to supplement the "aspiring inwardness of medieval monasticism" with "the exultant naturalism of modern democracy." He found just the text that he was looking for in Walt

Whitman's "Song of Myself." In this "extraordinary work (poem I
cannot call it)," Holmes said, he had discovered the pure expression of "democratic equality" and a profound attachment to ma-
teriality, life, and nature.[40]

Holmes's Whitman was the anti-monk, the counterbalance to
ascetic self-denial. The old devotion looked to heaven. Everything in Whitman moved the other way; he spilled outward, into
the world, and strained horizontally, toward comradeship. "So far
as he liberates us from our ordinary selves, he does so by carrying
us outside ourselves into the life of outward Nature, and into the
social life of mankind." There was an intensification of self-
consciousness without any constraint of self-discipline, social
"adhesiveness" without distinction of rank, erotic "amativeness"
without idealization.[41]

Thomas à Kempis and Walt Whitman, the preacher of self-
sacrifice and the poet of animal desire—"the two conceptions,"
Holmes wrote, "are vehemently and fundamentally antagonistic
to one another." And yet there was some kind of affinity, too, between *The Imitation of Christ* and what Holmes called the "Song of
Myself." "Both are passionately in earnest. Both have a strong
sense of reality. Both have a deep contempt for 'the world.' Both
are impatient of conventionality, of fashion, of opinion."[42]

Even Holmes understood that these were banal statements,
impressionistic rather than analytic. Serious readers, he thought,
would have to penetrate beneath the trivial similarities to discern
the deep conflict between the two works, between the ascetic's
devotion to eternal life and the poet's appetite for carnal joy.

But what made it possible for Holmes to place the two works
alongside each other in the first place was another kind of kinship
between them. It was not a matter of their passionate attitude or
their "strong sense of reality," whatever that might mean. It was
that *Leaves of Grass* and *The Imitation of Christ* offered themselves
up as manuals for self-cultivation, guiding their readers through
spiritual exercises and training them in the arts of attention.

Holmes was feeling his way toward this insight when he said that he could not call Whitman's work a poem. "Song of Myself" was not a poem in the modern sense, a work of art available to aesthetic judgment and critical analysis. Whitman drew from and revised such religious genres as the creed, the manual, and the spiritual autobiography. "I am the man, I suffer'd, I was there," he wrote. *Leaves of Grass* was, like the *Imitation of Christ*, a devotional.

PART IV

Devotion

Composed midway between Henry David Thoreau's lifetime and ours, the journals of the philosopher Simone Weil give beautiful expression to a familiar wish: "We have to try to cure our faults by attention."[1] Though she was born into a bourgeois family, Weil was a militant critic of modern capitalism. She was too radical for most of the organized religions and therapeutic regimens that presented themselves to her in wartime Europe and the United States. Rather than withdrawing into a convent or a cabin in the woods, she went to work in factories for a year, to learn the ways of industrial wage labor.

Weil's search for a more sustained, ethical attentiveness drew her back to the most austere spiritual traditions. She studied practices developed centuries earlier by Christian mystics and ascetics. "Attention, taken to its highest degree, is the same thing as prayer," she wrote in her private notebook.[2] She was trying to find, in disciplines of attention, a way out of exploitation and waste—a way to be in, but not of, the distracted world.[3]

Since her death in 1943, Weil's writing has become canonical, inspiring exegetical reading in its own right, and Weil herself is now revered alongside Thoreau as one of attention's patron saints. The essayist Susan Sontag wondered how a writer who was given to such extreme self-abasement could attain, paradoxically, such vast "personal authority" in American intellectual culture. Sontag concluded ambivalently: "In the respect we pay to such lives, we acknowledge the presence of mystery in the world."[4]

The singer and memoirist Patti Smith recalls making a pilgrimage to an English cemetery, looking for Weil's grave. As the traveler nears the shrine, in Smith's account, the atmosphere turns faintly mystical. "There were larks and sparrows, a small shaft of light that appeared, then disappeared," Smith writes. "I turned my head with no exalted pause and found her, in all her modest grace."[5] The passage comes from a short book where Smith, an American Romantic who came of age in the urban counterculture of the 1960s, reflects on her own inspirations and practices. In tribute to Weil and other heterodox seekers, Smith chooses a title that evokes ancient spiritual exercises; she calls her book *Devotion*.

Devotion is sometimes used as a synonym for religion itself, but the term refers especially to ascetic practices of attunement and fidelity. In contrast to a camp meeting or a mass, devotion is usually undertaken in quieter, private settings—a monastic cell, for instance, or an isolated hermitage. Devotion was often learned under the pastoral guidance of a priest or minister; eventually, the disciple was expected to master its arts well enough to perform it alone. Among the Puritans who settled the lands that they called New England in the seventeenth century, it was common to build houses with a small chamber, a "closet," designed for solitary prayer. And yet devotion promised intimacy, not isolation. It was about experiencing a transcendent love, and it sometimes opened into ecstasy.

The tradition of Christian devotional literature is full of pious exhortations and shame-faced confessions of sin. It also includes passionate expressions of desire. "Speak so that I may hear," Saint Augustine prays in his *Confessions*. "See the ears of my heart are before you, Lord. Open them and 'say to my soul, I am your salvation.' After that utterance I will run and lay hold on you. Do not hide your face from me."[6] Full of longing, it is a promise of readiness. The author's heart waits, all attention, for a whisper from the one he loves.

In 1843, Elizabeth Palmer Peabody brought out a new, American edition of Augustine's classic work. The available English printings were too expensive, Peabody explained in her preface, and the *Confessions* "should be within the reach of every Christian."[7] American readers and seekers in the nineteenth century might also have been familiar with early modern devotional manuals such as Thomas à Kempis's *Imitation of Christ* (circa 1420) and the *Spiritual Exercises of Saint Ignatius* (1522–24). Many of them certainly studied the English writer and reformer Hannah More's popular *Book of Private Devotion*, which was reprinted by several American publishers after More's death in 1833.

As for Peabody, she was a liberal, cosmopolitan thinker, hosting intellectual salons and promoting the work of her literary friends. At her innovative school for girls, she experimented with the latest European and American theories of education. At her bookshop, she offered not only Christian devotional works but also mystical and unorthodox writings from around the world. Augustine's work, as Peabody understood it, belonged in this expansive company.

"One especial advantage, in a practical point of view, which this work has over most devotional books, written since the Reformation, is the absence of the technology then invented to serve the purposes of the controversies of the day," Peabody wrote. What gave the *Confessions* its particular value for readers in the 1840s was its freedom from the factional concerns that divided Christian communities against each other. For hundreds of years, devotional literature had been burdened by a cumbersome "technology" that restricted its scope, dividing Catholics against Protestants, Old Lights against New, Congregationalists against Methodists, and so on. Augustine seemed to transcend these divisions.

Augustine had "apprehended," according to Peabody, "that God made the earth as well as the heavens, the darkness as well as light, the waters below the firmament as well as those above." Augustine's work, as Peabody read it, opened up a devotional practice that could attend to creation as well as divinity—that could find its way to God through the world. The movement of his thought was out of division, toward resolution.

Along with many other writers and experimenters in the arts of the self, Peabody was shaping a culture of devotion beyond church institutions. Devotional practice, as she imagined it, should not reinforce the believer's identification with this or that sect; it was not a matter of correcting doctrinal errors or accepting a certain belief. Instead, the aspiration was to tap into the mystical currents of what Peabody called the "Energy of Love."

Thus, Peabody used Augustine to repair the historical rupture between Protestant and Roman Catholic devotional traditions. By doing so, Peabody authorized herself to import Augustine, along with other archaic devotional works, into a society where modern market capitalism and evangelical Protestantism were the prevailing forces on the rise. On one hand, this was a peaceable operation: Peabody was making such literature seem less exotic, less threatening to "every Christian" in nineteenth-century New England. On the other hand, though, Peabody was also resisting Protestantism's effort to establish itself as the single moral authority in her culture.

Peabody's remarks show how nineteenth-century writers were coming to imagine devotion as a specialized but nondenominational kind of spiritual discipline. Devotion cultivated certain modes of attention and experience that were not locked in to any particular religious doctrine or belief. Devotion opened onto strange, unorthodox transports and intimacies. You could practice devotion to the Christian redeemer, but you could also pray to the Energy of Love. What mattered was the quality of devotional practice, not the particular god that it addressed. By putting Augustine's work into circulation, Peabody was also offering his extremely rigorous, self-searching discipline as one standard against which nineteenth-century Americans should measure their own faith. Here, as elsewhere, attention was undergoing a double transformation: its theorists were expanding the range of attention's legitimate objects while trying to intensify and refine the experience of attention itself.

In our own time, scholars and critics in American universities have taken a renewed interest in devotional reading. In *Devotion:*

Three Inquiries in Religion, Literature, and Political Imagination,
Costance M. Furey, Sarah Hammerschlag, and Amy Hollywood
make a collective effort to revive the tradition. "Reading is a form
of interconnectedness that can itself be transformative," they write.
"It can amplify and sometimes alter our vision of reality, focus our
attention on how we relate to one another, and, indeed, bring new
modes of sociality into being."[8] The authors feel no contradiction
between the private scene of reading and the public arenas of social and political life; they see devotion as a withdrawal, but only
a provisional one, preparing the practitioner to return to the world
with an expanded sense of what it might become.

Among literary critics, the effort to cultivate better attention to
our objects has given rise to a movement known as "postcritique."
Postcritique imagines the work of literary criticism as a single,
sustained encounter between the text and the reader's mind. It
describes its methods not in terms of research, analysis, or even
interpretation but as different styles of "reading"—reparative reading, surface reading, affirmative reading, and so on. Such reading
practices, as Rita Felski puts it, display "a willingness to attend
rather than to analyze."[9] Stephen Best and Sharon Marcus are explicit in defining their approach as a discipline of attention: "Many
dismiss surface reading as obvious, but find themselves unable to
sustain the slow pace, receptiveness, and fixed attention it requires."[10] Along the same lines, Heather Love calls for "practices
of close attention . . . rely[ing] on description rather than interpretation" and pointing the way to "an alternative ethics."[11]

It is true that many readers struggle to sustain "fixed attention"
as they read; it has been true for at least two hundred years. When
nineteenth-century reformers looked into the sources of this weakness, some of them pointed the finger at the devil, and others
speculated about the natural inferiority of certain stigmatized populations. But many nineteenth-century writers also saw how their
own historical conditions were making distraction more extreme.

The manifestos of postcritique do not share this analysis of
their own political economy. Instead, they argue against other

critics, especially those whose literary interpretations are informed by histories of money, sex, and power. Such historical concerns, from a postcritical point of view, are distractions from the text, which calls for closer, more ethical attention. But it is hard to imagine studying histories of money, sex, and power without exercising attention. For this reason, the critic David Kurnick has argued that the rhetoric of postcritique "offers an impoverished account of what it means to pay attention to texts."[12] Despite the high value it appears to place on attention, its definition of attention is unnecessarily narrow and contentious. Just as Peabody used Augustine's devotional vision to transcend the sectional divisions within American Christianity, literary criticism now enlarges the purview of attentive reading to overcome a methodological conflict within the discipline.

In this section I reflect on passages about nineteenth-century devotional practices, including the reading and writing of devotional literature. Most of the passages that I have chosen to examine stage a person's withdrawal from the world into a position of relative seclusion. None of these practitioners of devotion, however, comes to rest in solitude. Each finds a way back to some kind of intimacy with other people and contact with the world beyond a life of hermitage.

As for my own attention, it shifts back and forth between receptivity and detachment. Sometimes I move with the writer's thought; sometimes I move against it. Each of my reflections is informed by modern theories of the human mind and by some knowledge about nineteenth-century history. Each was drafted and revised over time. In other words, my "readings," like most others, are really pieces of writing. The person who appears to attend to the passages here is something of a fiction. By shaping my own writing in relation to someone else's words, I compose myself, in retrospect. In this way, the attentive reading mind might really be the effect, rather than the source, of a sustained performance of attention on the page.

22

"Noble sentiments of devotion"

"In the country, we seem to stand in the midst of the great theatre of God's power and we feel an unusual proximity to our Creator. His blue and tranquil sky spreads itself over our heads, and we acknowledge the intrusion of no secondary agent in enfolding its vast expanse. Nothing but Omnipotence can work up the dark horrors of the tempest, dart the flashes of the lightning, and roll the long resounding murmur of the thunder.

How auspicious such a life to the noble sentiments of devotion! Besides, the situation of the farmer is peculiarly favorable to purity and simplicity of moral sentiment. He is brought acquainted chiefly with the real and native wants of mankind: employed solely in bringing food out of the earth, he is not liable to be fascinated with the fictitious pleasures, the unnatural wants, the fashionable follies and tyrannical vices, of more busy and splendid life.

Still more favorable to the religious character of the farmer is the circumstance, that, from the nature of rural pursuits, they do not so completely engross the attention as other occupations. They leave much time for contemplation, for reading, and intellectual pleasures; and these are peculiarly grateful to the resident in the country."

—AN ANONYMOUS WRITER (J. S. BUCKMINSTER),
AS QUOTED IN ANN PLATO, "A RESIDENCE IN
THE COUNTRY" (1841)

In the country, where work and trade do not "completely engross the attention," devotion flourishes. Undistracted by the "fictitious pleasures" and "unnatural wants" of urban life, the farmer encounters the works of God, unmediated—or rather, the sky itself becomes the "great theatre" where thunderstorms play out their mighty drama. Such conditions favor a contemplative life.[13]

The original source of this passage is an 1807 Thanksgiving sermon by the Boston preacher J.S. Buckminster. Entitled "The Circumstances, in the Situation of Our Country, Favorable to Moral and Religious Eminence," the sermon considered the future of Christianity in the United States. Buckminster described a thriving new country, beautifully set up for piety. The United States in 1807 had not yet developed industry or cities on the scale of England's, and a nation of farmers working their own land seemed likely to maintain strong habits of devotion.[14]

Buckminster was a bright star in early nineteenth-century New England's culture of letters. After his death in 1812, his works were taken up by intellectuals like the Transcendentalists and by reform-minded educators.[15] Excerpted, liberally revised, and reprinted, his Thanksgiving reflections on the virtues of rural life made their way into several textbooks for children, including Noah Worcester's *Friend of Youth* (1822) and Samuel Putnam's *Analytical Reader* (1831).[16] Buckminster's thoughts became part of a curriculum that combined intellectual and moral lessons, in the key of Christian nationalism.

It was probably in one of the textbooks that a revised extract from his sermon came to be studied, with something like devotion, by Ann Plato. A teenaged student training for a career as a teacher in Connecticut, Plato was also an aspiring writer. Without citing Buckminster by name, Plato incorporated several paragraphs from his sermon into her own essay, "A Residence in the Country," which appeared in 1841.

What did Plato make of this discourse about the virtues of American farmers? The passage she quoted came from a Thanksgiving sermon, but it did not mention the indigenous people killed and displaced by New England's first European settlers, and its vision of agriculture ignored plantation slavery. Over the decades since 1807, meanwhile, its picture of a quiet, rural nation had become more and more outdated. Plato, who was probably descended from both Native and African Americans, was keenly aware of these histories. War, slavery, and urban capitalism had shaped her early life and work.[17]

In Plato's book, the violent histories that Buckminster represses are recalled by other voices. One of Plato's longest poems, "The Natives of America," stages a monologue by a defeated chief, mourning the massacre of his people and the theft of their land. "Our country is cultur'd, and looks all sublime," he says of the United States, but he understands that this appearance is an illusion. Beneath the cultivated surface, there lie unmarked graves. This territory was once a "land serene," but then Europeans invaded, and the "strangers destroy'd / The fields." The poem grieves the losses of Native lives and ways: "We were crush'd: / Into the dark, dark woods we rush'd / To seek a refuge" (110–112). Plato, by way of this other speaker, acknowledges how aggression clears the way for white civilization.

Elsewhere in Plato's book, a different figure appears, this one invoking slavery and its racist ideologies. James W. C. Pennington, the formerly enslaved minister of Hartford's Talcott Street Colored Congregational Church, provides the volume's preface. Pennington describes Plato's writings as evidence for the intellectual and moral capacities of Black children. Plato's hope in publishing her work, he writes, is "to accomplish something for the credit of her people." The piety and grace of her compositions will "show the fallacy of that stupid theory, that *nature has done nothing but fit us for slaves, and that art cannot unfit us for slavery!*" (xviii).[18]

Pennington's tone is fiery, defiant. Plato uses a more tender voice. With titles like "Obedience" and "Benevolence," her compositions rehearse familiar tenets of American reformism; they promote the disciplining of attention. "When you are in school," she writes, "give your time and thought to the employment which is marked for you by your teacher" (48). The line appears to address a student younger than herself. The rhetorical situation is really otherwise, however. It is an exhibition—or, in Pennington's word, a show. Plato is giving this command in the presence of the reading public, which has been invited to judge her performance. Pretending to speak to an inferior, Plato displays her own internalized training.

When she takes up Buckminster's ideas in "A Residence in the Country," too, Plato plays the part of the student who has learned her lessons well. Despite all that she knows about colonization and slavery, she seems to accept Buckminster's idyllic account of the American countryside. His sermon describes the rural Christian's reverent attitude toward nature, and Plato models the same attitude toward his text. Her treatment is never openly defiant or even critical; it is rather devotional.

Still, Plato's devotion is not strictly repetition. In her essay, she recalls observing, among country people, a special "quietness of mind" which "seemed to proceed from a sense of justice." *Justice* is her own word, not Buckminster's. She explains that she means people "doing their duty even to inanimate things; for we owe a duty to every article in our possession" (65). She imagines possession in terms of obligation, not extraction or mastery.

In the 1840s, a young writer stands against colonial warfare and racism while also answering a white minister's call to a distinctly American kind of Christian moral conduct. There is no real contradiction here. It is the way of reformism, whose disciplines of attention offer promising children like Plato a limited assimilation into the nation. At the same time, though, Plato uses devotion to create some dissonance. The authorities assembled in her book—Buckminster, Pennington, the unnamed Native elder—do not speak in the same voice or for the same communities. Plato moves among these figures ambivalently, sometimes opaquely, almost like someone putting on masks. She writes both with and against them, showing how serial acts of devotion allow for detachment and distance. Her identification with any one of them is only provisional, nonbinding.

23

"Savoir attendre"

"Ce que nous voyons de plus grand a rarement eu de grands commence-ments; le grain de sénevé *n'est past tout-à-coup devenu un* grand arbre, *où les oiseaux puissent s'abriter et bâtir leurs nids. Rarement la nature et la grâce franchissent les abymes où brisent les anneaux inter-médiaires; l'année a son printemps avant son été, le jour a son aurore avant le lever du soleil; tout procède avec gradation, de progrès en progrès, allant du moins parfait au plus parfait, jusqu'à l'achevèment, où se trouve le repos dans l'unité.*

Il faut donc savoir attendre: *l'impatience, la précipitation est la grande faiblesse de notre siècle; une sorte de fièvre l'agite; il semble qu'aujourd'hui on veuille tout faire mûrir en* serre-chaude; *et que l'on regarde comme* irréalisable *tout ce qui n'est pas* réalisé a l'instant même."*

[What we perceive as great has rarely come from great beginnings; the mustard seed *did not all of a sudden become a* mighty tree, *where birds could shelter themselves and build their nests. It is rare for nature and grace to leap over an abyss or break the middle links in a chain; the year has its spring before its summer, the day has its dawn before the sunrise; everything proceeds gradually, step by step, going from less perfect to more perfect, until completion, where peace is found in unity.*

We must therefore learn to wait: *the great weakness of our age is impatience, a panicked haste, an agitation like some kind of fever;*

today, it seems, we wish to ripen everything in a hothouse; and we regard as unachievable *anything that cannot be* achieved in a moment's time.]

—ADRIEN EMMANUEL ROUQUETTE, *LA THÉBAÏDE EN AMÉRIQUE, OU APOLOGIE DE LA VIE SOLITAIRE ET CONTEMPLATIVE* [THE THEBAID IN AMERICA, OR IN DEFENSE OF THE SOLITARY AND CONTEMPLATIVE LIFE] (1852)

A creole mystic, living among the Choctaw people near Lake Pontchartrain, just north of New Orleans, taps into the ancient tradition of spiritual exercises. The Louisiana wilderness, he imagines, might become a space for monastic withdrawal and self-purification, just as the Egyptian desert had been to the first Christian hermits. The priest finds, in this landscape, the right environment for a therapeutic slowing down, a remedy for hothouse haste and hurry. The Thebaid in America: a territory outside civilization, virtually without history, where time moves in step with nature and grace. Rouquette recovers the natural capacity *to wait*, or in his first language *attendre*.[19]

The author of this Catholic book of devotion, the Abbé Adrien Rouquette, also known as Chahta-Ima, was born in New Orleans in 1813. His parents were wealthy slaveholders, occupying a colonial mansion on the outskirts of the city. As a young boy, Rouquette often slipped away into the woods with his closest friends, the children of Choctaw traders who sold herbs and other goods in New Orleans markets. Rouquette was educated in Kentucky, Pennsylvania, and France, but in time he returned to Louisiana, where he pursued a long, strange career as a priest, a man of letters, and a missionary.[20]

Like many other people of faith in the middle decades of the nineteenth century, Rouquette recoiled from the mercenary, secular styles of thought that seemed to come along with industrial capitalism. The "cold and calculating rationality" of the modern "age of machines and money," as he saw it, was estranging men and women from divinity. One conspicuous effect was the unleashing of "animal passions," a peculiarly modern style of regression to base nature. But the remedy for this affliction was not to be found in American civilization. The pathway back to God, as Rouquette imagined it, went through the wilderness.

An ordained priest, Rouquette bound himself to chastity, but like other ascetics he crafted his self-discipline to make himself available to ecstasy. "The chaste man," he wrote in *La Thébaïde en Amérique*, "is like one intoxicated and exalted by the superabundance of life that floods his heart and flows through his veins; he feels the *sacred fire* of divine love smoldering inside him" (28). Practicing spiritual exercises was like drinking at the tap of holy fire. Compared to such transports of rapture, the pleasures of the consumer marketplace were shallow and frigid.

The writings of this Louisiana hermit mix Catholic and Romantic mysticisms, renouncing worldly pleasures for an encounter with primitive experience. Earlier, in a volume called *Wild Flowers: Sacred Poetry* (1848), his only book in English, Rouquette avowed that a mysterious power had moved him to write in a language he hardly understood—"a mystic and inwrapping spirit, breathed within me; and my soul was sweetly wrought into a kind of rapture." Rouquette called this mystic spirit his "wild muse."[21] He was not so much the author of his poems as the amanuensis of the breathing spirit that inspired him.

Rouquette wrote mainly in French, but he made connections with American poets writing in English who shared his fantasies about wildness. He corresponded with Henry Wadsworth Longfellow, the author of *The Song of Hiawatha* (1855), and he appears to have collaborated with Walt Whitman on a collection of Choctaw folk tales for a local paper, the *New Orleans Bulletin*.[22] Rouquette probably never met Henry Thoreau, but a copy of *Walden* reached him in Louisiana, and he read it with delight. Soon afterward, Rouquette sent Thoreau a letter and copies of three of his own books. Among them was his manifesto for a solitary, devotional life in the woods, *La Thébaïde en Amérique*, published two years before Thoreau's, in 1852.

In his preface, Rouquette anticipated hostile questions from his nineteenth-century audience. *"Who was this book written for? Why was it written at all?"* (v). The author did not expect to find many sympathetic readers. The modern public, he believed, craved flattery and easy pleasures. It had no patience, no discipline for reading a book that demanded slow attentiveness. "This book is not addressed to you, men and women of the world," he wrote. "You'll never understand."

Rouquette dedicated his work, instead, to a small circle of seekers and believers who were not entirely "of the world." He wrote for people who wished to transcend the conditions of modernity. To them, he proposed that the wildernesses of America offered the right conditions for a renewal of primitive mysticism. In the woods, along the shores of lakes and rivers, they might take up a solitary and contemplative life.

By withdrawing from the city and following a regimen of spiritual exercises, disciples might learn once again how to attend, bringing their souls back into alignment with the natural rhythms of the seasons and the days, composed by God. Rouquette's word for patience is *attendre,* usually translated into English as *to wait.*

In French, *attendre* connotes readiness and care, the responsiveness of an attendant, and some of the poetry of Rouquette's writing comes from his ways of bringing out this latent meaning. Waiting, in this passage, has nothing to do with idleness or killing time; waiting requires vigilant alertness, an attunement of the self to slow, unfolding processes. It is an act of the will, under spiritual discipline. Done right, it heals the afflictions—the weakness, the feverish agitation—that the author associates with the cityscapes of his modernity.

24

"The greatest exercise of mind"

It may be necessary to inform the public, that the author of the following work is fully aware that other productions of a similar character, written by able and experienced men—together with many other weighty considerations—might very properly lead him to abandon the design of publishing his own writings: but all these circumstances, as well as all personal considerations, are neutralized and overcome by the physical condition of the author, and the consequences flowing therefrom. Having been visited by a severe paralysis, which has partially disabled and rendered him incapable of much bodily effort, his thoughts naturally were turned inwardly, resulting in the greatest exercise of mind, in proportion as he found that the physical world was withdrawn from his view. The question, under these circumstances, naturally occurred to his mind, how he could best accomplish the two-fold end of becoming useful to his fellow-men, and, at the same time, contribute to his own support. The result will be seen in the religious poetry herewith offered to the public.

—ANONYMOUS ("A FRIEND"), INTRODUCTION TO
ABRAHAM JACOBS, *SPIRITUAL MEDITATIONS,*
WRITTEN IN VERSE, ON PASSAGES SELECTED
FROM THE SACRED SCRIPTURES (1848)

Suddenly afflicted in his body, withdrawn from the world, a simple Christian practices a great "exercise of mind." He composes devotional poems by the hundred. This is the story of Abraham Jacobs of Cumberland County, Pennsylvania, in the middle years of the nineteenth century.[23]

The son of a farming family, Jacobs received a modest education and found work teaching at a local common school. He was a pious Christian, fond of edifying literature, especially verse. He had made a tranquil life for himself, but then he suffered a severe paralysis, apparently the effect of a stroke.

Unable to continue teaching, Jacobs withdrew into a private life on his family's farm. He cast his mind toward God, spent time with his Bible, and began to write. He would publish his *Spiritual Meditations, Written in Verse, on Passages Selected from the Sacred Scriptures* in 1848. The book received little notice then, and almost no one today remembers these hundreds of devotional poems or their author. A few copies survive in rare book archives, preserved as historical curiosities.

Jacobs made no claims to be an important poet or even a good one. He addressed himself to readers who cared more about renewing their faith than appreciating a fine turn of phrase. He imagined that they might be people in a hurry, "without much time," or lacking the capacity for "deep, laborious, and lengthened perusals" (vii–viii). Jacobs had some sense of the nineteenth-century marketplace, where deep attention was in short supply.

Jacobs knew that his writing was unrefined, even rustic, but he felt no shame about it. The introduction to his book, by someone identified only as "a friend," explained: "The author makes no pretensions to learning, as he never enjoyed more than an ordinary education; but presents to the reader the sincere sentiments of his own heart, clothed in a simple habit, and expressing the most essential duties of christianity." It was a commonplace in Protestant discussions of rhetoric and poetics that stripped-down expression was more honest and, in its way, more beautiful than a fancy style. Plain garments, a "simple habit," suited the truth.

Still, the design Jacobs laid out for himself had a large, ambitious scale. He adapted his structure from a popular English devotional text, *A Spiritual Treasury for the Children of God*, by the Calvinist minister William Mason (1719–1791). Devotional books are often organized in relation to a plan of days. Many offer a reflection for each day in a four-week cycle, twenty-eight in all. Some double this number by including a prayer for each morning and one for each night. Jacobs took on a far bigger task. "It consists in a simple and practical paraphrase of various scripture passages, expressing the plain practical duties of the christian, and arranged for every day in the year." Jacobs included 366 poems in all, including one for leap day, the 29th of February. Each poem summarized and reflected on a passage he selected from the Bible.

Jacobs's practice of private devotion on his family's farm was a personal discipline of attention; having mostly withdrawn from the social world, he used reading, writing, and prayer to keep his thoughts with God:

> Jesus our attention claims,
> And his loving heart proclaims—
> "O ye weary and oppress'd,
> Come, and I will give you rest." (60)

From the opening pages of his book, Jacobs was answering the call. His meditation for New Year's Day was a vision of perfect, uninterrupted vigilance. He took his text from Genesis 16:13: "Thou, God, seest me." It was a passage about being the object of attention, about being watched. Jacobs used it to reflect on what it would mean to feel God's eyes on him all the time, unblinking. He imagined that living in mindfulness of this all-seeing eye would lead the believer to become more vigilantly watchful over himself.

Intriguingly, though, this devotional exercise, designed to cultivate submission to God, begins with a question about running away: "Jehovah, whither from / Thy presence shall I flee?" (1). The poet asks what lines of flight, what fugitive ways, might escape the Lord's field of supervision. Soon enough, he answers his own question: there is no way out.

Where'er I take my flight
O'er mountain, dale, or sea,
Or through the dreary wilderness,
Still, 'thou, God, seest me!'

God's purview encompasses every kind of landscape. This means that He can always be called, that His love is always available to the believer, even far from home. It also means that no sin can be concealed from his detection. No matter where the poet runs, no matter what he tries to hide, "Thy piercing eyes behold."

For Jacobs, there seems to be no contradiction between inexhaustible love and perfect surveillance. The work of the poet's meditation is to reconcile the two, and to reconcile the poet himself to living within the kind of eternal supervision that his poem is describing.

In the final stanza, Jacobs turns the tables, briefly, on the Lord. He becomes the subject, not the object, of attention, at least in his imagination:

Lord, may I always live
    As if beholding thee
With eyes of faith, and walk within
    Thy fear continually. (2)

The phrase "as if" does strange work in this prayer. It allows for a reversal of positions that is not quite a subversion of power relations. Up to this point in the poem, watching has been strongly associated with supervision. The one who sees is in a position to punish or forgive. But now the poet allows himself to occupy this place—or, rather, to live "as if" he occupied it. He prays to conduct himself as if he were the observer, with God in his sights.

After a line break, Jacobs qualifies himself. He requests to look with "eyes of faith," not with suspicion or with the prerogative to judge his God. When he thinks about looking at God, he thinks about restraining his doubts and suspicions.

This, in turn, leads the poet to a new way of thinking about the world, a different map of space. The craggy landscape of the mountain and the "dreary wilderness" becomes the zone of "Thy fear"—that is, the poet's fear of God. Jacobs prays for a constant, inescapable fear, because this terror is for him the same thing as peace of mind. It is the internalized terror of being judged, of losing God's love. This fear ensures his ongoing self-discipline.

All the while, the *Spiritual Meditations* are also performed before another audience, the reading public. The author recognizes that making a claim on public attention is a risky thing to do. Publication betrays a kind of pride, reserved for men of ability and experience, but at the same time it is an occasion of vulnerability and potential embarrassment, since it concedes to the public the authority to appraise the speaker's skill and make judgments about his character. Jacobs displaces the claim, performing a ventriloquist's act where God or Jesus, not the poet, makes the claim, and where rest, not pleasure or even knowledge, is the promise held out to the ones who answer.

The strangest, richest passage in *Spiritual Meditations* is not in Jacobs's poetry but in the framing introduction, attributed to the anonymous "friend." Did Jacobs write it himself? Who knows? Such authenticating and apologetic documents were common enough in nineteenth-century letters. So was their forgery.

"It may be necessary to inform the public," the passage begins. The mode of address is decorous and cautious. The writer appears to be taking on a duty, performing a required task. The "public" invoked here is a demanding one. It has little time to waste. It would not appreciate trifling authors imposing themselves on its attention. The introduction assures the public that the poet has anticipated some objections. "The author of the following work is fully aware"—in other words, Jacobs knows, and takes responsibility for knowing—that there is already a good deal of devotional poetry in the world, and much of it was written by "able and experienced men." Next to them, he will look like an amateur.

Such a demonstration of peaceableness, of self-censure reluctantly abandoned, implies a culture. The writer shows respect for a system of customs, recognizing an ordered distribution of authority. In the world of devotional literature, it seems, there is only so much space and time. To publish your writings in this world is to make a claim on public attention, a limited resource conventionally reserved for those of superior talent and ampler experience. When an unskilled, unknown poet like Jacobs decides to circulate his work in this marketplace, some diplomacy will be required.

And so, his *Spiritual Meditations* apologizes for its own entrance into the world. It is not the only book to strike such a humble pose. Nineteenth-century literature, religious and secular, makes this kind of gesture almost as a matter of course, especially when the author emerges from the lower social ranks. Ministers assure the public that conversion narratives are legitimate; public men and women of letters vouch for the accuracy of slave narratives. Prefaces and introductions justifying a work's claims on the public's attention are routinized, conventional documents.

In the case of *Spiritual Meditations*, though, there is no need to soothe suspicions about the volume's authenticity. Unlike the testimony of fugitives who would bring the public's judgment down against the slave system, Jacobs's professions of faith require no rigorous verification. What is in doubt is not his validity as a witness but his value as an artist. The questions seem to be simpler: why did he feel compelled to publish this book, and why should anyone buy or read it?

The anonymous friend gives two answers. First of all, Jacobs needs charity. Unable to continue working at the school or to contribute his labor on the farm, he is desperate to support himself. All the modesty and "personal considerations" that might have made him withhold his poetry "are neutralized and overcome by the physical condition of the author, and the consequences flowing therefrom." Poetry is all the work that he can do, and his book is the only thing he has to sell.

Even as the introduction conjures Jacobs as an object of pity, it is also making a second, subtler move; it is endowing him with a special kind of power. "His thoughts naturally were turned inwardly, resulting in the greatest exercise of mind, in proportion as he found that the physical world was withdrawn from his view." Jacobs's suffering has strengthened his mind. His cloistering has brought spiritual objects into clearer view. However faintly, the lines make a promise about second sight. Perhaps it really is Jesus, not Jacobs, who claims the public's attention in the *Spiritual Meditations*.

Watch closely here, and you will see that the introduction has executed a cunning reversal. What looks like an apology for Jacobs's entry into the public sphere of print has been spun into an alibi for his withdrawal into private meditation.

In Jacobs's Protestant world, there is no ready sanctuary for such a practice—no monastery, no hermit's anchorage. Good Christians are supposed to show their faith by cheerfully accepting their place, readily carrying out their assigned tasks. In other words, they go to work. Few can claim a space for spiritual exercises untouched by the concerns of labor and trade; for a man to desire such a space would be flirting with immorality. The nineteenth-century Protestant who takes up a truly ascetic way of life, unemployed except in his own meditations, courts the suspicion of preachers and the public.

But something unexpected and unbidden has happened to Jacobs. He has been "visited" by an affliction that becomes a kind of gift. "Naturally," though not quite willfully, he has turned away from his old life. Severe paralysis has opened up a career of spiritual labor and a vision of divinity. His injury authorizes both his appearance before the reading public and his disappearance from the world, into habits of devotion.

25

"A true sauntering of the eye"

I must walk more with free senses. It is as bad to study stars and clouds as flowers and stones. I must let my senses wander as my thoughts, my eyes see without looking. Carlyle said that how to observe was to look, but I say that it is rather to see, and the more you look the less you will observe. I have the habit of attention to such excess that my senses get no rest, but suffer from a constant strain. Be not preoccupied with looking. Go not to the object; let it come to you. When I have found myself ever looking down and confining my gaze to the flowers, I have thought it might be well to get into the habit of observing the clouds as a corrective; but no! that study would be just as bad. What I need is not to look at all, but a true sauntering of the eye.

—HENRY DAVID THOREAU, JOURNAL (1852)

In this passage from his journal, written between his two-year retreat to a cabin by the pond and the publication of *Walden*, Thoreau considers the problem of attention by reflecting on his own habits, sensations, and wishes. His mind turns especially to the question of observation, of how he encounters objects along his way. He finds that when he walks in the woods, he does too much looking and too little seeing. What is the difference? What kind of gift would it be to "see without looking"?[24]

It seems to have something to do with the will. *Looking* means directing the eye. The one who looks is one who studies. He goes to the object; he confines his gaze. But the one who *sees* relaxes his will and allows his eyes to wander. He does not strain. His senses are at rest. As if of its own volition, the object appears to come to him.

On this reading, seeing means a kind of surrendering. The observer would not take possession of an object, would not reach out toward it—*ad tendere,* the Latin root of attention—but would drift along, undirected. And the object, unchosen and unbidden, would find its way to him. Looking is searching; seeing is passive receptivity.

Drawing his distinction between two kinds of observation, meanwhile, Thoreau rejects another. The difference between seeing and looking matters more, he says, than the differences between flowers and stars. The point is not to choose a better object of attention, to look up from the earth to the heavens. The point is not to choose, that is, "not to look at all."

Thoreau is playing with and rejecting an ancient injunction: the Christian believer's call to give up attachments to worldly things and to seek out heavenly ones. For centuries, confessional and devotional writing had rehearsed the same exhortation. True penitents must not be distracted by the flesh or material goods; they must turn to higher concerns.

Thoreau makes light of this piety: "When I have found myself ever looking down and confining my gaze to the flowers, I have thought it might be well to get into the habit of observing the clouds as a corrective; but no! that study would be just as bad." Looking up from the ground to the sky is not enough to free your senses. As long as you are looking, up or down, you are lost.

It would be no corrective, then, "to get into the habit of observing the clouds." *Habit*—Thoreau uses the word twice in one short journal entry. He must have known that a habit is, among other things, the costume of a priest or a nun: the penitent, taking leave of this world, gets into a habit and lives in devotion to God. For Thoreau, though, the habit is no aid to prayer; habit is the problem, the hurt that needs some balm.

"I have the habit of attention to such excess that my senses get no rest." It is a curious, paradoxical phrase, isn't it? Habit and attention are hard to reconcile. We are accustomed to the idea that habit dulls perception; it renders the world familiar and thus all but invisible. And, in another sense, one closer to Thoreau's meaning, habit is said to overmaster the will. To have a habit to excess is to have a vice, like a drunkard or an addict. Attention, meanwhile, is usually understood as a matter of focused, heightened perception and, on most accounts, an exercise of will. *A habit of attention*—Thoreau seems to be saying, paradoxically, that the deliberate, disciplined regulation of one's senses can become an affliction, "a constant strain," in its own right.

Again, Thoreau is reworking an older asceticism. Christian penitents would exercise the will to govern their bodies, chastening the flesh. Thoreau, for his part, would liberate his senses from his own direction. He would "walk more with free senses," letting his body roam. What he has in mind is a passive kind of freedom, less a discipline than a therapy. At stake is not what Thoreau wills but what he needs, not action but release. In all these ways Thoreau's meditation on the habit of attention leads him away from any conventional asceticism. He virtually erases the distinction between the worldly and the heavenly; he releases the body from the will; he wishes not to labor but to wander.

And yet this beautiful passage about surrendering and sauntering, about releasing oneself from the direction of one's will, about freeing oneself from the impulse of correction, is written largely in the imperative mood. "Be not preoccupied with looking. Go not to the object; let it come to you." Who speaks these commandments, and to whom? Thoreau is taking himself as the object of address. He is laying out a regimen, prescribing for himself a set of practices.

As it turns out, the will is not abandoned. It is doubled, turned back against itself, becoming both the subject and the object of its own activity. In fact, the passage does not only exhort its author to a set of self-corrections. It enacts a series of revisions—reversals which are also repetitions—in its own prose. Although it comes from Thoreau's journal, not his printed works, the nominally private, even confessional scene of its enunciation is nonetheless an arena of supervision, discipline, and self-fashioning. Just when he is calling himself to let objects penetrate his organs, Thoreau's writing obtains its most radical reflexivity. The marks of his will are all over it.

The passage contains one obvious example of revision. Thoreau cites Carlyle's statement that "how to observe was to look," and then he offers his own version, or rather his own inversion: "I say that it is rather to see, and the more you look the less you will observe." Track the key verbs in this sentence: observe—look—see—look—observe. They make a palindrome. Thoreau's move against Carlyle is a correction, but it is a mirroring, too.

The entire journal entry has the same palindromic shape. The first sentence says, "I must walk more with free senses." The final sentence says, "What I need is not to look at all, but a true sauntering of the eye," rehearsing the idea in different, perhaps freer words. The same thing happens to the second sentence. "It is as bad to study stars and clouds as flowers and stones." This is Thoreau's rejection of the distinction between looking down at the earth and looking up at the heavens, and it returns (with a difference) in the penultimate sentence: "When I have found myself ever looking down and confining my gaze to the flowers," and so on.

Thoreau's critique of asceticism is a revision of the art of self-discipline in which the will itself—not the appetites, the flesh, or some other alien element—becomes the object of its own disciplinary correction. And this style of self-correction plays out in the prose of the journal, in a practice of revision which is also a habit of self-repetition.

With this journal entry, Thoreau came close to rejecting certain spiritual and writerly practices that he had been developing for many years. At Walden, he had begun by trying to undistract himself, to reawaken his own powers of perception and refocus his attention on natural, uncommodified objects of contemplation.

By doing so, he had hoped to free himself from the degrading cycle of labor and consumption that organized middle-class life under market capitalism. In the long run, though, he found that this very effort exhausted his senses and trapped him in a "habit of attention." Thoreau did not quite say so, but he had begun to feel the similarities between his self-discipline and the other, more coercive disciplines that he had hoped to leave behind. Now he dreamed of another kind of release, a truer sauntering, but even this fantasy of escape was neatly crafted on the page, its composition shaped by careful attention and reflection.

26

"If we do not guard the mind"

To be deeply impressed with a few fundamental truths, to digest them thoroughly, to meditate on them seriously, to pray over them fervently, to get them deeply rooted in the heart, will be more productive of faith and holiness, than to labour after variety, ingenuity or elegance. The indulgence of imagination will rather distract than edify. Searching after ingenious thoughts will rather divert the attention from God to ourselves, than promote fixedness of thought, singleness of intention, and devotedness of spirit. Whatever is subtle and refined, is in danger of being unscriptural. If we do not guard the mind, it will learn to wander in quest of novelties.

—HANNAH MORE, *THE BOOK OF PRIVATE DEVOTION* (1832 EDITION)

Here in a passage from Hannah More's "Essay on Prayer" is a miniature aesthetic treatise for good Protestants. More sets out to cultivate a certain style of taste, elevating the simple over the sophisticated, basic and familiar truths over elegant novelties. As she makes these distinctions, she subordinates all questions about beauty and pleasure to higher concerns about the believer's spiritual devotion. Meditation on an object is a moral act. Done right, it opens up the self to God.[25]

The path to holiness is a treacherous one, though, and myriad temptations lie in wait. More warns readers to guard against "whatever is subtle and refined." The pleasurable but pernicious "indulgence of imagination" will not bring the seeker to faith; it will "rather distract than edify." Other reformers who set out to guide the intellectual habits of modestly educated Christians might have pointed to the dangerous lures of sensational literature, with its romances of crime and erotic adventure. For her part, More has little to say about the wickedness of low culture. Her devil does not dwell in the gutter; he prefers the finer arts.

More was an evangelical, mentoring seekers in a practice of spiritual exercises, but she was also a writer. Her essay lays out some of the ideas that guided her craft, defining the virtues of her aesthetic school against the vices of other schools. Earlier in her career, More had written tragedies for the stage and moved in a distinguished circle of London intellectuals. But toward the end of the eighteenth century, she experienced a political and aesthetic conversion. She watched the French Revolution from a distance, troubled by the spectacle of violence and radical democracy, and she read with a sense of alarm as Romanticism staged its rebellion in the arts, conjuring a cult of beauty that looked wild and demonic in the glow of revolutionary fires.

More turned from high literary pursuits to practical endeavors, giving her money to charitable causes and her labor to reform. She took a special interest in the moral education of the poor. Her philanthropic enterprises meant to alleviate the worst of their suffering. Because she feared the consequences of unrest and discontentment, though, she also tried to reconcile them to their low station. In teaching everyone to know and accept their proper place in the world, not to hunger after liberties and luxuries reserved for their superiors, Christianity could be a consolation. More helped to organize a series of Sunday schools and wrote didactic literature, much of it published in the form of cheap tracts to be distributed among the lower classes, which won popularity on both sides of the Atlantic.

Her *Book of Private Devotion,* a selection of religious poetry and prose, accompanied by the introductory essay on prayer, was published in London, Boston, and New York in 1832; dozens of editions would appear over the course of the next several decades. A classic devotional text, it mentored its reader in the arts of reading and meditation, tending toward closer communion with God and the conduct of a more pious life. Its theology was liberal, but its politics were counterrevolutionary; its program of self-culture was also a discipline of self-restraint.

In the introductory essay, as More works out her distinction between elaborate inventions and "fundamental truths," she imagines a kind of force that might be steered in one of two directions. "Searching after ingenious thoughts" draws readers away from what centers them, weakening their attachment to God and setting them adrift. The action is a style of vagabondage. More calls it diversion, questing, wandering. The undisciplined, unguarded mind goes loose in the seductive world.

The alternative, "singleness of intention," feels more like being held at anchor. With the language of stillness—roots, fixity—More invokes a sense of proper emplacement. Attention tethers us where we belong. It is a practice of fidelity, and it keeps the mind at home.

Rather than venturing out on quests, then, good readers learn to play the host. They adopt a homely regimen that protects them by restraint. Their self-culture makes no shell around the heart. Instead, it allows the objects of their devotion to enter into them. Rather than becoming hardened characters, they soften to benevolent influences. The one who receives devotional literature in the proper spirit incorporates its truths, digesting them so that they may take root within. The effect, as More imagines it, is one of being "deeply impressed."

Impression: This figure of speech has become so conventional that it may be difficult to recover its original significance, but More and her contemporaries took it seriously, even literally. They imagined that attention allowed objects to enter into and reshape the mind. Like wet clay, the developing self takes its form from what presses onto it. The influences we encounter, especially when we meet them in a state of attentive receptivity, will sculpt us according to their own design.

This theory of impressibility entails an aesthetics of rustic simplicity and an ethics of disciplined self-culture. It makes character a matter not of inherited propensities or natural depravities but of human cultivation, traceable to a person's education and personal habits. As a way of picturing the soul's ongoing development, then, it marks its distance from rigid Calvinist visions of predestination; it holds a closer affinity to theologies that emphasize the will. It assumes our nature to be malleable, corruptible but also available to benign reforms. Beguilingly, too, it blurs the line between pastoral care and personal responsibility. It makes you the custodian of your own impressible self.

There is a paradox in More's ethical regimen: although the endeavor is to stay on guard against temptations that would "divert the attention from God to ourselves," the work requires careful surveillance of our desires and attachments, and its highest aspiration is to produce the right kind of character. Prayer becomes not so much a way to address God as a discipline of attention to oneself.

If you are an innocent apprentice, according to More's theory, you are also in training to become your own master. Like many other nineteenth-century writers on devotional attention, she divides the self into two parts. One is a passive, impressible surface; the other, its counterpart, is a vigilant and willful actor. The first is child-like, the second a protective guardian. Our mind, that vulnerable and exposed organ, needs watching over by a different, wiser agency. It must be educated to receive the impressing power of the sacred, not to be diverted by charming novelties, and we are the ones who have to become its teachers.

And how, according to this essay on prayer, does the reader come of age, morally, and rise to a state of self-mastery? By learning the essay's lessons so well, internalizing them so deeply, that they become the reader's own guiding principles. More's voice should grow so familiar to you that you seem to recognize it as your own. Enforcing its disciplines on yourself should feel like an exercise of your own free will.

The Book of Private Devotion is a classic of devotional literature, distilling a theory of the genre and giving its reader explicit direction in the mode of attention it expects. The author's tone is high-handed and imperious, calling for obedience. With a righteous confidence, she hands down her lessons in humility. And yet it is possible to detect an anxious undertone in More's commanding voice. This is a book that needs to initiate people into its ways, composed by a writer who cannot take her own authority for granted—who is trying to win, rhetorically, the power that she pretends to hold already.

From the beginning, *The Book of Private Devotion* understands itself to be competing against other books and other ways of reading. Even as More condemns those devilish works that enchant the reader with their subtleties and refinements, even as she preaches that the highest truths require no such craftiness, she is positioning herself and making strategic moves within an attention economy. The book displays a peculiar kind of artfulness, one that disavows itself, seeking to secure attention and acquiescence by appearing not to join the contest for them.

Afterthought

Evangelicals like More made a sophisticated analysis of their situation. They sensed that the world was changing quickly all around them. They could depend on just as much attention as their missionary works captured in a crowded marketplace, and they made it their business, first of all, to capture as much as they could. It might be said that this is what evangelicalism really was, at least in the eighteenth and nineteenth centuries—not a special theology, though it had its own commitments, and not an identity, as it would become in later decades, but the adaptation that Protestantism made within a modernizing attention economy. For all their reactionary exhortations against modern worldliness, the evangelicals played their part in making it so.

To circulate books in such a world is to send them on a mission, but it is also to put them at risk. Here is one reason why devotional writers like More go to such great lengths to provide instructions in how to read: Picked up by unknown hands, passing into situations that the author can hardly anticipate, much less control, the book exposes itself to all sorts of uses and abuses. If it is lucky, it might be read compliantly, according to its own guidelines, but it can also be treated in other, weirder ways. This is what happened, in at least one wonderful American instance, to *The Book of Private Devotion*.

In the 1830s, experts in New England and New York investigated the case of Lurena Brackett, a medium who displayed mysterious powers under the influence of animal magnetism. The investigators were trying to find out whether magnetism (also known as mesmerism, a forerunner to hypnotism) was a science or a con. Among the enlightened, the prevailing view was that mesmerists were frauds who manipulated the credulity of their patients and the public to enrich themselves.

For reasons that educated skeptics could not quite explain, though, popular interest in magnetism was on the rise, and marvelous accounts of its effects were going around. If there was any truth to them, it would have serious consequences for science and for trade. What if mesmerism really could cure disease? What if it could transfix workers in factories and on plantations, holding them fast to their assigned tasks?[26]

Brackett was a peculiar subject, even among mesmeric mediums, because she had recently been blinded in an accident. Her doctors were trying to cure her using ordinary therapies, and she was making halting progress. But when she submitted to magnetism she seemed suddenly, though only temporarily, to recover her sight. While the spell lasted, she spent whole nights reading. What she liked reading most of all, as it happened, was the devotional poetry of Hannah More.

Reporting on the case, the investigators published the following observations:

Unless she is magnetized she cannot enjoy the pleasure of reading, and this is one cause of her being so fond of remaining magnetized.

While she was residing at the mansion of Stanford Newel, Esq., she found there Hannah More's Private Devotions, a small work which has been printed since she became blind. This she took with her when she retired one night; and in the morning, before she was awakened from the magnetic sleep, she observed that she had been reading much of the time. One of the ladies of Mr. Newel's family soon discovered that by giving out the first line of several of the poems, she was able to repeat the whole, verbatim. In this manner she had learned at least twenty of the pieces. I have seen the book. It is the fine-type edition of Messrs. Crocker & Brewster; Boston, 1836. The exercise doubtless has a tendency to retard the progress of her cure; but the natural activity of her mind makes it difficult for her to sit idle.[27]

"I have seen the book," the witness testifies. The question is whether Brackett has seen it as well. The author emphasizes the publication date and the size of the printed text to insist that Brackett could not have learned the poems in any other way. If she has been able to make out the words in this small, fine-type edition, produced after the date of her accident, then there is persuasive evidence that mesmerism is in fact working to restore her power of sight.

In reality, Crocker and Brewster of Boston had published at least one edition of *The Book of Private Devotion* as early as 1832. If modern scholars wish to debunk More's performance, the likeliest explanation is that she had memorized the poems before she ever lost her sight or submitted to magnetism. It is also possible that she had heard the poems read aloud. For a study of attention, though, the antiquarian point about chronology matters less than the drama of antagonistic modes of reading and styles of power played out by Brackett and her observers.

Although the episode turns on a story about Brackett reading devotional literature, the report takes no interest in the truth (or falsehood) of that literature's Christian lessons. The investigators do not care whether *The Book of Private Devotion* is right or wrong about religion. As far as they are concerned, what matters is not the content of the work but the physical properties of the printed volume. In this encounter between Christian poetry and rational science, devotional reading finds itself absorbed into an experiment testing material, not spiritual realities.

Still, the investigators do need to know that Brackett herself is sincere—not that what she believes is true, exactly, but rather that she is a true believer. The report is documenting some hard facts, but it is also endorsing the credibility of a witness, and the validity of her testimony depends on her good faith. If she is an earnest Christian, animated by a real desire to internalize devotional poetry, then she is less likely to be a deceitful coconspirator in a mesmerist's hoax. True religion would restrain such wicked play.

While Brackett's story is about the persistence of religious reading in modernity, then, it is also about the emergence of other kinds of reading, other kinds of plots. Scrutinizing Brackett's case, skeptical, curious observers demonstrate their reason by talking about how she exercises her faith. Men's secular knowledge defines itself against a woman's religious faith, their worldliness against her bedroom devotions. They are the subjects of knowledge, and she is the specimen.

As it turns out, though, this gendered assertion of authority has some destabilizing effects. It does not reduce Brackett to a figure of Christian purity. Instead, it provides cover for thinking about her attractions and her restless impulses, "the natural activity of her mind." She is "so fond of remaining magnetized," the report supposes, because under the mesmeric influence she can "enjoy the pleasure of reading." Conscripting Brackett as an object of scientific investigation also entails casting her as a subject of desire, one who is willing to go against her doctor's counsel, to "retard the progress of her cure," because idleness does not suit her temperament.

To some moralists, this might look like an abuse of *The Book of Private Devotion*, repurposing religious verse as a source of embodied joy. Hannah More herself had warned readers against the "indulgence of imagination" and the hunger for "novelties" that would "divert the attention from God to ourselves." In the reports on Brackett's case, the prohibition is relaxed. The investigators, with their secular assumptions about why people read, namely as a source of amusement and diversion, have also discerned something about devotional literature that its authors sometimes concealed: these works could be used to cultivate, not to repress, the fervency of desire. Even Protestant poetry might enable an active, restless mind, awake in the night, to take its pleasures.

27

"The valves of her attention"

I've known her—from an ample nation–
Choose One–
Then—close the Valves of her attention–
Like Stone–

—EMILY DICKINSON, "THE SOUL
SELECTS HER OWN SOCIETY"

Valvae, in Latin, are folding doors. In English, in the nineteenth century, *valves* could also refer to shells, membranes, or parts of a machine. All were portals or enclosures; valves controlled what entered into protected spaces, and what was left outside.[28]

Dickinson's poem goes back to the oldest meaning. It opens with an act of closing: "The Soul selects her own Society—/ Then— shuts the Door." This is a story about going inside, shutting out the world. When the valves of her attention close, the Soul admits no outside influence; her stony surface receives no impression.

In a way, she disappears. The Soul, Dickinson writes, is no longer "present." Lofty, queenlike in her icy sovereignty, she refuses to acknowledge any suitor who comes calling. A chariot stops at her gate, and an emperor kneels at her threshold, but she remains "Unmoved." She has detached herself. Her doors are shut.

It is tempting to interpret this image as a self-portrait of the author. The legend of Dickinson's withdrawal from nineteenth-century society still has a hold on her readers. The first time that I tried to write about this poem, it still had a hold on me. I invoked the mythic "nun of Amherst" who refused marriage, declined social invitations, and turned away from the political conflicts that were shaking her country. I read this poem as a kind of manifesto for the author's ascetic life, a description of her self-imposed solitary confinement. I took "her own Society" to mean just the Soul herself, gone into isolation.[29]

What made me want to read the poem this way was not just the popular legend of Dickinson's anchoritic detachment. It was also Dickinson's other poems, which so often imagine imposing restraints on oneself, then finding power in confinement, even in suffering. *After great pain, a formal feeling comes.* It was the fineness of her observations, the compressed precision of her expression. *There's a certain Slant of light.* In her way, Dickinson did belong to the tradition of spiritual exercises. She practiced her own discipline of attention.

Coming back to this poem now, though, I see how it is not really about solitude. I think it is about a kind of intimacy, a single-minded love. The Soul here chooses "One," but she chooses someone else, not self-isolation. She selects her companion, the single object of her complete devotion. Nothing else seems to touch her anymore. No traffic or entreaty moves the Soul away from the attachment she has chosen. She is in her chamber, with her "One," with no attention to spare for the rest of the "ample nation."

The One might be a lover or it might be a god. What is happening behind closed doors, whether it is sex or prayer, the poem does not say. From the poem's point of view, it does not really matter. The poet is watching from the outside, knowing that the valves are closing, seeing the impressionable surface turn to stone.

There is a solitude in this poem, but the solitude is not the Soul's. It is the stunned, excluded feeling of someone who observes her from beyond a boundary—the door, the gate, the valve. I think this sense of being left outside, of paying close attention to a Soul as she turns her own attention to someone else, is the true source of the chilly loneliness in this poem about intimacy.

28

"Aroma finer than prayer"

I believe in the flesh and the appetites,
Seeing hearing and feeling are miracles, and each part and tag
*   of me is a miracle.*

Divine am I inside and out, and I make holy whatever I touch
*   or am touched from;*
The scent of these arm-pits is aroma finer than prayer,
This head is more than churches or bibles or creeds.

—WALT WHITMAN, *LEAVES OF GRASS* (1855)

"I believe," Whitman begins, and if you grew up in the right kind
of church you might recognize, already, the familiar rhythms of a
creed. *Creed*, from the Latin *credo*, "I believe"—a ritualized avowal.
Your mind might begin to fill out the rest of the line from memory,
"I believe in one God, the Father almighty," and so on, down
through the verses, to *amen*.[30]

The creed is a script. The ones who speak it are not, ordinarily,
its authors. They affirm, in public, their belief, but the words are
not their own spontaneous expression. They are going through the
motions of a rote performance learned, internalized, in devotional
practice. This can be troublesome. The creed may become one of
the empty forms that Protestants regard with so much suspicion.
Like an oath or a pledge, it may be spoken in a state of dissociation,
without conscious intention, almost mechanically. You can say the
words, you can rehearse the creed, even if your heart isn't in it.

How would anyone know? As usual, ritualized worship introduces disturbing questions about sincerity and attention.

By writing his own vows, Whitman solves some of those problems, but his credo raises other, graver ones. His faith is no generic, common script, approved by church authorities. It is a new expression, in his own voice, full of commitment and intensity. But his oath is also wildly blasphemous—defiant, even diabolical. Whitman affirms his belief not in some remote divinity but in his own flesh and appetites. He says yes to carnal desire. More devilishly still, he sacralizes the living body. As the churches affirm Christ's resurrection, the poet acknowledges the "miracles" of his own sensation. The seat of this belief is not the mind or the soul but the physical "head."

It was a special task of creeds like the Nicene and the Apostolic to avow the believer's faith in the trinity: Father, Son, and Holy Ghost. Whitman does not partition divinity in the conventional way, but he does write in sets of three. One of his ways of revising religion's scripts is by making light of its institutions (bibles, churches, creeds); one of his ways of professing sensuality is by sacralizing the senses (seeing, hearing, feeling). There is imitation of Christ in Whitman's verses—"I am the man, I suffered, I was there"—but the endeavor is never to detach the disciple from the world. Something like the opposite is happening here, something like an incarnation.

Whitman was not the first poet to write devotional verse that engaged the senses and expressed erotic intensities. *Batter my heart, three-person'd god.* Much religious expression, as modern philosophers like to demonstrate, is shot through with masochistic longing. Even the seventeenth-century New England Puritans, who by Whitman's time had come to be remembered as the very archetypes of repression (look at what they did to Hester Prynne), had imagined their own private devotions as ways of overcoming low appetites so that they could ascend to a more incandescent desire. At its best, it felt like being ravished by the Lord.

For his part, Whitman is not simply opening a space for erotic intensities in religious practices. He is moving in the opposite direction, finding religion by observing and feeling the world. It is through the organs of perception, first of all, that he makes his way to faith in the divine. ("I believe in you my soul," he writes elsewhere in "Song of Myself," again revising the script of a creed, but immediately he appends a word of caution to this affirmation— "the other I am must not abase itself to you" [15].) The contact of flesh with the world is a sacrament: "I make holy whatever I touch or am touched from." Whitman's devotional practice never represses. It turns the body on.

This brings him to the startling, beautiful line, "The scent of these arm-pits is aroma finer than prayer." The stink of the body is the incense in Whitman's house of worship. It is not just that he prays with, or even prays *to*, his body. More, his body expresses itself while he observes and bears witness. Whitman's verses are profane in the strict sense; they unsettle the boundary between filth and sacred purity. Whitman's creed defiles. One of its games is to flirt with disgust.

Still, for all its spectacular defiance of religious codes of belief and comportment, the poetry somehow *feels* religious. Doesn't it? To tell the truth, we modern readers, unlikely to be offended by Whitman's blasphemies, may find ourselves more embarrassed by his enthusiasm. Who is this reeking exhorter, this wild self-appointed prophet, worshipping the parts of himself? In appraising Whitman's contribution to American literature, Ezra Pound has this to say: "His crudity is an exceeding great stench."[31] Pound wants craft and refinement from a poet, not raw nature on the page. It may not be our concern that Whitman violates orthodox doctrine, but he also breaks the rules of secular literature. Exposing himself, he asks too much of his readers.

"I stop somewhere waiting for you": the final line of "Song of Myself" begins with an I and ends with a you. Are you the one is he waiting for? He wants you to lay down all the armor that you bring to your reading. In school, or somewhere else in a secular culture, you have learned to divide yourself while you read. One part of you enjoys, vicariously, the intensities of represented experience, but all the while another part of you holds back, protected, analyzing and judging the quality of the experience. Whitman would disarm you of your critical detachment.

Whitman extracts the creed from its fixed place in a ceremonial order, then, but he does so in order to reanimate its power. Rather than rebelling against religion, he is staging a reformation, and his technique for it is revision, writing new life into an ossified form. This is why, blasphemous and carnal as it may be, Whitman's poetry still feels strangely religious: because it sets itself against the protocols of secular reading. It does not mean to amuse you or to impress you with its artistry; it calls you, evangelically, lovingly.

Afterword

Imagine a person coming out of isolation. Maybe he has been locked down in quarantine, suffering from some kind of illness. He is feeling better now, though, and he is finally allowing himself to be with other people again, in public spaces. He finds a nice little table at a café. There is a newspaper in front of him, but he just looks out the window, people-watching, letting his mind wander.

This is how Edgar Allan Poe begins his classic tale about the modern cityscape, "The Man of the Crowd" (1840). As the story gets underway, an unnamed narrator sits in a London coffee house, enjoying his return to urban life. After his convalescence, he is in one of those "moods of the keenest appetency, when the film from the mental vision departs." He feels wide awake, his senses sharp. He gazes through the window as people move along the thorough-fare outside, a motley, spectacular pageant.[1]

He begins to amuse himself by playing a kind of sociological game. He calls it "scrutinizing the mob." Studying the clothes and attitudes of passers-by, he places them in categories. Some of them, in his appraisal, belong among the "men of leisure," some the "tribe of clerks," some the "race of swell pick-pockets," and so on. From his seat behind the window, he is breaking the crowd into components, then arranging them into a hierarchy. Thus, the "mob" becomes a picture of society, ranked from the comfortable top to the desperate bottom. The well-heeled gentlemen who seem to be "conducting business upon their own responsibility," he admits, "did not greatly excite my attention." Rather than admiring the upper classes, he lets his imagination linger with gamblers, hustlers, and sex workers.

Interrupting this amusing game, an unclassifiable stranger appears. "Suddenly there came into view," the narrator recalls, "a countenance which at once arrested and absorbed my whole attention." Among so many faces in the street, why is this the countenance that captivates him? The effect, he feels, has something to do with "the absolute idiosyncracy of its expression." The passerby is making a face whose meaning is hard to grasp because it seems to have no precedent. "Any thing even remotely resembling that expression I had never seen before." All the other faces belong to some recognizable, classifiable type, but this one looks inscrutable, and so its mystery takes hold of the observer's whole attention.

The watcher at the window is excited and disturbed. His thoughts turn, briefly, to some famous paintings of the devil, but the comparison does not solve his riddle. The man in the coffee shop, looking at the man in the street, thinks of "expression," thinks of "pictural incarnations of the fiend," and thinks of books; he speculates about the wild history that might be "written" in the stranger's heart. While he tries to "form some analysis of the meaning" of the passerby's countenance, his head fills up with confused, paradoxical ideas. He is having an interpretation crisis, struggling to read.

"I felt singularly aroused," the narrator confesses, and a "craving desire to keep the man in view." Before his chance is lost, he grabs his hat and cane and hurries down into the street. He is in stealthy pursuit, not cruising for a face-to-face encounter. He follows the stranger "closely, yet cautiously, so as not to attract his attention." Without quite recognizing what is happening to him, he is becoming a stalker.

He wants to keep watching without being seen, but it is a tricky operation. At first, the narrator was just an observer, safe behind his window. Now he has stepped out from behind his pane of glass, and he needs to be careful about managing his distance. Down in the street, everybody is exposed to everybody else's eyes. Like other stalkers, vigilantes, and agents of surveillance, this one knows that there is a certain power in being the subject, rather than the object, of an attentive gaze.

At the same time, though, the observer senses that the situation is not entirely under his own control. His attention, as he puts it, is "arrested and absorbed," as if he had been stopped by the police or soaked up by a sponge. Rather than charting his own course through the city, he finds himself copying the stranger's moves. Is this attention, or is it really distraction? Is he the hunter, or is he being dragged along? If you happened to be watching both of these men from a distance, it would be hard to determine which of them was making the decisions. As often happens, attention blurs the line between agency and submission, unsettling any clean distinction between its subject and its object.

Soon the two men are moving quickly, surfing on "the waver, the jostle, and the hum" of the city's human currents. They make their way from one crowded scene to another, then another. This goes on all night. When it gets late and everything else shuts down, they end up in a bar. When morning comes, they circle back around to the more respectable shops and businesses. Eventually, the truth becomes clear: the stranger has no final destination. He is just going wherever the largest gatherings are happening, wherever business is hottest at any given hour. A saloon is just as good as a bookshop to him, as long as it is buzzing.

Finally, exhausted and confused, the narrator gives up his chase. He has not entirely solved the mystery of the stranger's expression, but he has seen all that he can handle. Unlike some other detective stories, this one offers no climactic revelation of the criminal's identity. In fact, what it investigates is not a crime, just a weird activity. Rather than the secret motives of a killer or a thief, the inquiry diagnosis a compulsion.

"He refuses to be alone. *He is the man of the crowd.*" This new human "type," as the narrator understands him, is a crowd-addict who needs to be among the masses, both surrounded and ignored. The man of the crowd will never find his way home. Instead, he is chasing the experience of crowdedness, taking his shelter in the crowd itself, around the city and around the clock. As for the narrator, who started out trying to read a peculiar kind of expression, he ends up just wandering from site to site, following the traffic, wasting all his precious time.

———

"The crowd—no subject was more entitled to the attention of nineteenth-century writers," according to the critic and philosopher Walter Benjamin.[2] In his remarks on Poe's tale, Benjamin all but ignored its convalescent narrator and its title character, the man of the crowd. Benjamin thought the story's real action was in the crowd itself. He wanted to understand Poe's swarms of people in the street, with their bizarre, inhuman "gesticulations." What kinds of creatures move this way? "For Poe," he wrote, the crowd "has something barbaric; discipline just barely manages to tame it."[3] As Benjamin revisited Poe's tale in 1940, a century after its first publication, this monstrous image interested him. It seemed almost like a prophecy.

"Poe's text," Benjamin continues, "makes us understand the true connection between wildness and discipline."[4] This is an intriguing promise. By "the true connection between wildness and discipline," Benjamin does not mean what Thoreau and other Romantics might have meant—he is not saying that practicing self-discipline is, paradoxically, the best way to shake off the corrupting effects of civilization and recover one's natural, wild freedom. Rather, Benjamin means that what looks like "wildness" in

Poe's city dwellers, with their grotesque fidgeting and flailing, is the effect of a distinctly modern "discipline" that they have learned in factories and shopping centers.

Poe's "pedestrians act as if they had adapted themselves to the machines and could express themselves only automatically," Benjamin explains. The rhythms of the industrial market economy have reconditioned their reflexes. "Technology has subjected the human sensorium to a complex kind of training."[5] Thus Benjamin's reading of "The Man of the Crowd" becomes a meditation on the broader problems of attention and distraction in an industrialized environment.

As pedestrians move along busy thoroughfares, he thinks, the city's messages and stimulations come at them so fast, with such intensity, that their conscious minds can never process all the noise. Their attention is overwhelmed. Most of what they see and feel—most of what Poe calls "the waver, the jostle, and the hum"—gets screened out of consciousness along the way. They forget it before they arrive at their destinations.

According to Benjamin, most of what happens to people in the street influences their behavior without making a lasting impression on their minds. That is, they are being affected by the sights and sounds around them, and they are reacting, but they are not really absorbing or processing a sequence of isolated, memorable experiences. They are probably not even aware, for instance, of how they are constantly adjusting their pace, dodging traffic or keeping up with it. This is because they have learned how to navigate the city's circuits and rhythms unthinkingly, dissociating while other topics—their jobs, their families, or whatever—occupy their conscious thoughts.

Poe, for his part, introduces his tale as a drama of attention, where an observer tries to remain undetected while seeking out the mystery of another man's heart. In Benjamin's reading, those dynamics barely matter. What Poe really described in "The Man of the Crowd," Benjamin decides, is something Poe himself was not quite prepared to understand or reckon with: the modern, industrial masses, chronically distracted.

Crucially, though, Benjamin rejects Poe's reactionary attitude toward the crowd. As the critical theorist Paul North notes in *The Problem of Distraction*, "There is something about the quality of 'Masse' that Benjamin likes."[6] Benjamin, unlike Poe's narrator, refuses to indulge in any nostalgic fantasy about going back to some older, more integrated and orderly kind of community. Such fantasies, as Benjamin understood them, had nightmarish political effects in Europe in the twentieth century, when fascist cults were feeding on widespread popular anxieties about spiritual decay and social disorder. Reactionary nationalists depicted the masses as pathologically distracted, decadent, and uncivilized; they stirred up fears about cultural degeneration, and they used the moral panic to justify violent forms of social discipline and genocidal purging. Fascism, as Benjamin saw it, was attempting to gather a heterogeneous and absentminded population into a single, militarized, national subject by summoning the people to attention, then weaponizing them.

For these reasons, Benjamin thought that modern distraction created a dilemma for critics of the arts. In his most famous essay, translated into English as "The Work of Art in the Age of Mechanical Reproduction," Benjamin proposed that critics had to choose between two starkly different points of view. Either they could indulge in a reactionary nostalgia for older media like literature and painting, suited to sustained, solitary contemplation; or else they could embrace new media, especially cinema, which popular audiences experienced in a state of distraction.[7]

Benjamin was trying to push his thinking beyond what he called a "commonplace," namely the old-fashioned "lament that the masses seek distraction whereas art demands concentration from the spectator."[8] Unlike other critics, Benjamin was not interested in complaining about his culture's slide away from better, more traditional styles of attentiveness. Instead, he investigated the aesthetic and political possibilities that came along with mass distraction.

Against painting, therefore, Benjamin took the side of cinema, which, like Poe's cityscape, overstimulated the crowd with its abrupt, mechanized rhythms. "The painting invites the spectator to contemplation," Benjamin notes. By contrast, "the film makes the cult value recede into the background" because it "requires no attention." This new kind of popular art, Benjamin imagined, would be "useless for the purposes of Fascism."[9] His hope was that the jarring rhythms of modern life, whether in the factory or at the movie theater, might inoculate the public against right-wing nationalist sorcery. Distracted people would not be easily converted or conscripted; they were unfit for any cult.

————

Benjamin wrote beautifully about the aesthetic and political possibilities of modern distraction.[10] Today in the United States, though, it is hard to share his faith. The American right-wing nationalists of the twenty-first century make only confused, half-hearted gestures toward what they call the tradition of Western literature and thought. They have no real patience for high culture. Their attacks on critical race theory and cultural Marxism are more and more transparently racist, reactionary efforts to delegitimate, dismantle, and privatize the whole infrastructure of higher education, especially the critical humanities. They still align themselves with religion, mainly with evangelical Christianity, but they also exploit mass media diversions like reality television and online disinformation campaigns.

As a matter of experience, for a lot of us, distraction does not feel like a way out of power's grasp. It more often feels like being manipulated, losing time to technologies and systems we can barely understand, much less control. To tell the truth, from where I sit behind my screen, the cityscape that Poe describes in "The Man of the Crowd" looks less like a movie house and more like the Internet.

The man of the crowd might be some kind of devil, as Poe's narrator suspects, but he is also a finely calibrated tracking device. Drawn to interaction for its own sake, he identifies the sites where the crowd's activity is most intense. Like an algorithm, he registers the surges and cycles of heavy traffic. He tells you exactly what is hottest, "trending now," at any given time. Meanwhile the convalescent narrator cannot resist the man of the crowd's prompts to flit from one random site to another. He does not contemplate any object of beauty or of interest; his investigation arrives at no conclusion; he cannot read. He just surfs anxiously along.

Was Poe describing life in an attention economy? It seems anachronistic at first, I know, to speak of such a thing two centuries ago. The phrase gained currency only with digital technologies and the Internet. It refers to an economy where attention, not goods or services or even cash, has become the most desirable kind of currency. In this economy, the kind of attention that holds the greatest value is not the sustained, steady focus of a reader or a viewer, absorbed in careful study. It is the fleeting but intense attention of the maximum audience, the crowd, clustering out of a global dispersal.

According to the digital attention economy's early theorists, who developed the concept around the turn of the twenty-first century, Internet-based news and entertainment sources were not simply competing with other, more established platforms to sell the same old kinds of content. Instead, online enterprises were in the business of attention itself. Just as a premodern agricultural economy had become a modern industrial one, it was said, and just as the industrial one had given way to a consumer economy, now the age of buying and selling goods was over; the new trade was in attention, not commodities.[11]

In reality, farming, industry, and shopping were still going on, and Internet commerce included credit card transactions, not just clicks. New media companies were devising ways to profit from, or *monetize*, their users' attention. They found that if they summoned a big audience, they could sell whatever they could make of it. Like broadcast media, internet companies tried marketing their users' attention to advertisers, at first. Before a website would display a video or an article, for example, it required the user to watch a short commercial. Rather than paying money for your content, you had to pay a little bit of attention to some content that you did not choose.

This kind of transaction was not such a radical innovation. In fact, it was probably first conducted in Poe's milieu, the nineteenth-century newspaper and magazine trade. At least one recent study, Tim Wu's *The Attention Merchants*, traces the origins of our attention economy back to that hustling scene. Wu starts his chronicle in 1833, when an enterprising New York printer named Benjamin Day began selling his newspaper at a price below his own production costs. Day was willing to take this gamble because he expected to make his profits from advertising, rather than subscriptions. He was not going to sell papers; he was going to sell space in them.

Day knew from the start, however, that the space had little value on its own. Businesses would only pay to place their ads where lots of people would see them—that is, in a paper with a mass audience—and so the entrepreneur did all he could to grow his circulation numbers. He charged just a penny for a copy of his paper, all but giving it away, and he sensationalized the news to catch the public's eyes. In the process, he transformed his readers from his customers into the product that he sold. Day was gathering and marketing a new resource, the crowd's attention.[12]

Eventually, in the digital era, engineers developed more sophisticated techniques for capturing, monitoring, and selling attention. By tracking users' behavior online, they generated detailed information about what people liked and shared. They harvested data about personal tastes, habits, and connections. To do so, they relied not just on clicks and screen time but also on the words and images that users published on their sites. Cunningly, with an almost imperceptible sleight of hand, online platforms had turned nonpaying consumers into unpaid producers. The users were not normally paid for their contributions, but they were given the chance to get attention from their friends, their followers, and far-flung strangers. It came in quick bursts, and it turned out to be a strong incentive.[13]

Social media invited users to treat its sites as forums of their own self-expression. It offered them platforms for sharing their feelings and arguing their points of view. As a business, though, it was more or less indifferent to the user's own self-image. The novelist Zadie Smith wrote mournfully in 2019, "to the technological mo-nopolies that buy and sell your data—and for whom your daily input of personal information is only raw data, to be traded like orange juice futures or corn yields—you reveal yourself not so much in your views or hot takes as by the frequency of your posts or tweets, their length or syntax, the pattern of their links and fol-lows."[14] The platform's managers concerned themselves not with beliefs or expressions but with metadata, quantitative information that could be severely at odds with the stories people told them-selves about who they were and what they valued. Like Poe's man of the crowd, then, the attention business moved beyond con-scious motives, beyond interiority; it sought out interaction for its own sake.

For all these reasons, it makes sense to imagine the attention economy as an environment that people move around in, not just a type of transaction. The philosopher Yves Citton has introduced the term *attention ecology* to describe how attention is paid and received within particular kinds of large-scale systems, like habi-tats.[15] The insight is helpful, but the neologism is not really neces-sary, since the word *economy* already connotes a dwelling place. The root word, *oikos*, means a household, with its contending forces and resource management systems. This is why Thoreau, when he described his homemaking in *Walden*, called his first chapter "Economy."

The cityscape of "The Man of the Crowd" is the image of an en-vironment where everyone is moving, often clustering, but no one is at home. Like Poe's narrator, we might find ourselves flitting from site to site, following a lure or a prompt whose algorithmic character we do not quite understand, becoming more and more uncertain about where we are going and why, more and more uneasy as the minutes and the hours tick away.

Poe was acutely sensitive to the fickleness and fleetingness of public attention. He had to be, since he was hustling to make a living as a magazine writer and editor. He became a master of sensational genres like detective fiction and the horror story, catering to the public's appetite for quick intensities. His "crowd" was, among other things, an image of the reading public whose attention he craved and whose distraction he resented, often spitefully. He saw mass distraction as a social pathology, and some part of him longed for older, more contemplative kinds of aesthetic and spiritual culture. In this way he belongs to the heterodox assembly of writers, religious thinkers, and social reformers whose works I have gathered in the pages of this book.[16]

———

Before there were digital machines, there was already distraction. Turning away from the noise of industry and the urban marketplace, Ann Plato imagined a residence in the country, and Adrien Rouquette set up a hermitage on Choctaw lands. Emily Dickinson and Abraham Jacobs withdrew into their families' homes, writing poetry. But even at the edge of town, behind closed doors, it was not easy to disconnect from the circuits of business. The sound of the steam engine shook Henry Thoreau in the middle of the night. There was no perfect sabbath, no perfectly isolated hermitage. Rehabilitating distracted minds was not just a matter of finding some quiet place to rest. It called for discipline.

Devotion's cabins and cloisters, revivalism's tents and meeting halls, reform's schools and correctional institutions—these were the semi-enclosed sites that nineteenth-century writers, preachers, and social reformers designed to rehabilitate attention. These scenes were sometimes described as out of sync with the times, either preserving a "primitive" faith or previewing a more enlightened future. They were frequently depicted as asylums, or "houses of refuge," spaces apart from the hustling world of modern work and consumption. In reality, that very world created them, and they belonged to it.

Rattled by new systems of production and consumption, nineteenth-century people of letters drew from the cultural resources available to them, especially from the traditions of religion, literature, and moral philosophy. Thus, a society that was becoming larger, more diverse, more violent, more openly committed to making and spending money as fast as it could was also creating semiprivate settings for spirituality, aesthetic experience, and moral discipline. Some writers who practiced and promoted disciplines of attention were fierce critics of their civilization, especially of slavery and imperialism; even so, they tended to recast large-scale economic and political problems as private ones, as damage to the individual's psychological and moral character to be addressed through regimens of personal rehabilitation. This was the only way that they could imagine for their cultural work—mainly the disciplines of reading, writing, and teaching—to make any difference in history, and this is the predicament that we humanists inherit from them, unresolved.

Still, the refuge was not always, not even most of the time, a site of permanent capture. Even as the keepers justified their institutions by promising to turn delinquents into submissive workers and docile consumers, they were also cultivating powers of self-discipline and capacities for loyalty that could be turned to other purposes. It happens all the time in churches and schools, as well; disciplines of attention become practices of radical analysis, civil disobedience, strange artistry, and even militant resistance. Detachment is never complete, and devotion is never pure. Because attention's sanctuaries are not entirely sealed off from this world, it is hard to foresee what might emerge from them to touch and change it.

In "The Pond in Winter," a late chapter toward the end of *Walden*, Thoreau once again finds himself peering down through the surface of the pond, watching creatures in the still, cold depths. Here, though, what he glimpses is not a torpid snake but a school of fish, and what he feels in their presence is not uneasy distraction but a radiant calm. Kneeling—"to drink," he says, though he knows that kneeling is also a posture of devotion—he sees that down there, in the clear water, "a perennial waveless serenity reigns as in the amber twilight sky, corresponding to the cool and even temperament of the inhabitants. Heaven is under our feet as well as over our heads."[17] Earlier, Thoreau and the fish had both been rattled by the locomotive, carrying commodities to market; now there is no traffic, and they meet in stillness.

To arrive at this transcendent encounter, Thoreau never had to turn his eyes upward from the water to the sky. He had to transform himself and his own habits of perception, and he had to use his axe. He remembers cutting his way "first through a foot of snow, and then a foot of ice." He is talking about digging for his drinking water in the dead of a New England winter, but he is also describing the effect of his spiritual discipline. He has cleared away the cold layers that used to shroud his vision. This is the end of an errand that started early, in the first light of a winter day, with a silent act of self-composure:

Then to my morning work. First I take an axe. . . .

ACKNOWLEDGMENTS

While I was making this book, things kept falling apart. Disasters played out at every scale—the planetary, the political, the personal—and they all seemed connected to each other. Fires in the West, troubled waters in the East: For a long stretch of days one summer, I watched hundreds of menhaden fish floating dead in the poisoned currents of the lower Quinnipiac River, near Long Island Sound. Gulls and crows picked at their bellies, then littered the shores with carcasses, all silvery and sickle-curved, for bugs to finish off. It was a feast for scavengers. In time, the tides lapped away the bones.

No place is entirely insulated from such bad weather, and these days hardly any optimism feels uncruel. (Lauren Berlant, I miss your relentless mind.) One thing I try to respect in this book, therefore, is people's wish to find some consolation and some small-scale, sustaining intimacy within a vast, churning calamity, even when they might despair of changing anything more structural than themselves. When I look around and realize what generous friends and fellow travelers have kept in touch with me in these unraveling times, I feel lucky. I am grateful for your gifts.

Thank you, Katie Lofton and Paul North, my local sister and brother, for all those beautiful hours devoted to walking, drinking, and talking together, and thanks most of all for showing me grace, even if that's not your word for it. In a time when I needed it, y'all were my Fair Haven.

Thank you to the friends from work who spent time with me elsewhere: Michael Warner in his garden and in the green mountains, Jonathan Kramnick on the Sleeping Giant trails, Greta LaFleur on the roof deck around sunset, David Kastan among the dunes on the Atlantic side, R. John Williams at the pool hall, Noreen Kahwaja at some bar, reminding me that the word *accomplice* is more interesting than *complicity*.

Thank you, Joshua Bennett, Tracy Fessenden, and Kyla Schuller for gathering, virtually, to read a whole draft of my manuscript; your good ideas helped guide me in the late stages. Thank you, D. Graham Burnett, Joanna Fiduccia, and the Friends for keeping faith in attention, and thank you John Durham Peters for your belief in discipline. Thank you, Nancy Levene and the Working Group on Religion and Modernity for raising the stakes. Thank you, Rachel Kushner for twenty years of thinking together about writing, institutions, and ideas; you called this my "Book of Distraction," a good name for it.

Thank you to the many people who read pieces of my work in progress: Elizabeth Anker, Theo Davis, Richard Deming, Leslie Jamison, John Modern, Emily Ogden. Thank you to my brilliant critic friends and teachers who made all kinds of impressions on these pages over the years: Charlie Altieri, Max Cavitch, Brigitte Fielder, Lisa Corrigan, Nan Da, Josh Dubler, Merve Emre, Tom Ferraro, Harris Feinsod, Virginia Jackson, Sandra Macpherson, Meredith McGill, Anahid Nersessian, Kyla Tompkins, Marianna Torgovnick, Nate Wolff.

Thank you to my students, especially the ones in the graduate seminars I called "Reading, Attention, and Distraction" and "Transformations of the Confession." Thank you to the people in the archives where I went to study, including the Beinecke, the Huntington, the American Antiquarian Society, and the New York State Archives. Thank you to the hosts who invited me to share some parts of this work, and to the audiences who came to hear it, at the Dartmouth Summer Institute for American Studies, Georgetown University, Johns Hopkins, Pomona College, UCLA, UC Irvine, the University of Colorado, and the University of Toronto. Thank you to my collaborators in the Yale Prison Education

Initiative: Zelda Roland, James Jeter, Roderick Ferguson, and company. Thank you, Wendy Strothman and Anne Savarese for expertly handling the business of turning these several reflections into a book that people can hold.

Van Smith, little bird, while I was finishing my writing, you were just learning how to read, but being with you these six years has changed my mind in all kinds of ways, not least the way I think about distraction and attention.

Sarah Mesle, you are in my eyes. Like the book says, the sun's a morning star. Let's go!

NOTES

Introduction

1. Thoreau's axe was not his own. By some accounts, it belonged to Ralph Waldo Emerson; by others, it came from the educator Bronson Alcott; Ellery Channing also made a claim. See Henry David Thoreau, *Walden: A Fully Annotated Edition*, ed. Jeffrey S. Cramer (New Haven, CT: Yale University Press, 2004), 39, n. 213. On Thoreau's life and relationships, I draw from Laura Dassow Walls, *Henry David Thoreau: A Life* (Chicago: University of Chicago Press, 2017). On the religious significance of Thoreau's anecdote, see Paul Williams, "The Borrowed Axe: A Biblical Echo in *Walden*?," *Thoreau Society Bulletin* 83 (1963): 2.

2. Thoreau, *Walden*, 40.

3. Thoreau, *Walden*, 40.

4. Thoreau used the terms *snake* and *serpent* as synonyms, and he clearly knew what these creatures symbolized in the Christian tradition. See, for instance, his discussion of local snake species in "The Natural History of Massachusetts," where he imagines becoming "as wise and wily as the serpent." Henry David Thoreau, "The Natural History of Massachusetts," in *Essays: A Fully Annotated Edition*, ed. Jeffrey S. Cramer (New Haven, CT: Yale University Press, 2013), 20. See also his depiction of the carnal appetites as reptilian in a later chapter of *Walden*, "Higher Laws": "We are conscious of an animal in us, which awakens in proportion as our higher nature slumbers." Thoreau, *Walden*, 210. In an essay on Thoreau's symbolism, Barbara Johnson cites the passage about the "striped snake" as "a somewhat atypically explicit analogy" in *Walden*. According to Johnson, Thoreau's symbols are usually obscure, but in the case of the snake, by contrast, he offers a more "conventional" or "classical" kind of "analogy between the natural and the human worlds." To make this point, however, Johnson removes Thoreau and his broken axe from the scene: in a block quote, Thoreau's lines about the wedge are cut and replaced by an ellipsis. Ignoring Thoreau's self-representation in the passage, Johnson treats it as a fairly straightforward, conventional one, where Thoreau writes in the mode of "the moralist, the evangelist, the satirist, and the lyric poet." But the passage is stranger and more reflexive than Johnson's brief reading allows. Thoreau's position here is not one of

judgment from on high. He diffuses himself, especially his shame, into his symbols. Barbara Johnson, "A Hound, a Bay Horse, and a Turtle Dove: Obscurity in *Walden*," in *A World of Difference* (Baltimore, MD: Johns Hopkins University Press, 1987), 49–56, 54.

5. Henry David Thoreau, "Life Without Principle," in *Essays: A Fully Annotated Edition*, ed. Jeffrey S. Cramer (New Haven, CT: Yale University Press, 2013), 347.

6. Thoreau, *Walden*, 119.

7. Thoreau, *Walden*, 50.

8. Sharon Cameron, *Writing Nature: Thoreau's Journal* (Oxford: Oxford University Press, 1985), 34. Theo Davis, *Ornamental Aesthetics: The Poetry of Attending in Thoreau, Dickinson, and Whitman* (Oxford: Oxford University Press, 2016), 40. Alda Balthrop-Lewis, *Thoreau's Religion: Walden Woods, Social Justice, and the Politics of Aestheticism* (Cambridge: Cambridge University Press, 2021), 183. On Thoreau and attention, see also Stanley Cavell, *The Senses of Walden* (Chicago: University of Chicago Press, 1992); and Branka Arsić, *Bird Relics: Grief and Vitalism in Thoreau* (Cambridge, MA: Harvard University Press, 2016). Cavell's remark about Thoreau's prose style captures its complicated attachment to and disavowal of New England's religious traditions: "The more deeply he searches for independence from the Puritans, the more deeply, in every step and every word, he identifies with them—not only in their wild hopes, but in their wild denunciations of their betrayals of those hopes." Cavell, *Senses of Walden*, 10.

9. Hannah Arendt, "Civil Disobedience," in *Crises of the Republic* (New York: Harvest Books, 1972). On the paradoxes of Thoreau's individualism, see also Milette Shamir, *Inexpressible Privacy: The Interior Life of Antebellum American Literature* (Philadelphia: University of Pennsylvania Press, 2006). For a reading of Thoreau as an early fantasist of suburban self-culture, see Maura D'Amore, "Thoreau's Unreal Estate: Playing House at Walden Pond," *New England Quarterly* 82, no. 1 (March 2009): 56–79. For a critique of Thoreau's relation to New England's indigenous communities, see Mark Rifkin, "Loving Oneself Like a Nation: Sovereign Selfhood and the Autoerotics of Wilderness in *Walden*," in *Settler Common Sense: Queerness and Everyday Colonialism in the American Renaissance* (Minneapolis: University of Minnesota Press, 2014). By contrast, Elise Lemire in *Black Walden: Slavery and Its Aftermath in Concord, Massachusetts* (Philadelphia: University of Pennsylvania Press, 2009), explores how Thoreau engaged with the multiracial working-class community that inhabited Walden Woods before and after his arrival.

10. Lydia Maria Child, "Conversation on Attention," *Juvenile Miscellany* 1, no. 1 (1826): 72–87. Thanks to Stephen Krewson for introducing me to this text.

11. Joseph Stevens Buckminster, "Sermon XII: The Circumstances, in the Situation of Our Country, Favorable to Moral and Religious Eminence" (1807), 374–388 in *The Works of Joseph Stevens Buckminster: With Memoirs of His Life*, vol. 1 (Boston: J. Munroe, 1839), 381, quoted without attribution in Ann Plato, *Essays: Including Biographies and Miscellaneous Pieces, in Prose and Poetry* (Hartford, CT, 1841), 66.

12. Adrien Rouquette, *La Thébaïde en Amérique, ou Apologie de la Vie Solitaire et Contemplative* (New Orleans, LA: Méridier, 1852), 20–21. My translation. When Rouquette discovered Thoreau's work, he sent him a letter and copies of three of his own books, two of them in French. Thoreau's reply is interesting: "Though I have not had time to peruse your books attentively—I have looked far enough to be convinced that not all in your section of the union any more than my own, are devoted to trade alone." Thoreau to Adrien Rouquette, Nov. 13, 1854, in *Correspondence of Henry David Thoreau*, ed. Robert N. Hudspeth, Elizabeth Hall Witherell, and Lihong Xie, vol. 2, *1849–1856* (Princeton, NJ: Princeton University Press, 2018), 272. Corresponding with Rouquette, Thoreau had matters of attention and devotion on his mind.

13. Thoreau, "Life without Principle," 363. As many critics have noticed, attention is a central problem in Thoreau's work. See especially Theo Davis, *Ornamental Aesthetics*. My account draws also from Sherman Paul, *Shores of America: Thoreau's Inward Exploration* (Champaign, IL: University of Illinois Press, 1958); Cavell, *Senses of Walden*; Cameron, *Writing Nature*; H. Daniel Peck, *Thoreau's Morning Work* (New Haven, CT: Yale University Press, 1990); Jane Bennett, *Thoreau's Nature: Ethics, Politics, and the Wild* (Lanham, MD: Rowman and Littlefield, 2002); and Arsić, *Bird Relics*.

14. Thoreau, *Walden*, 2. On the tradition of spiritual exercises, see Pierre Hadot, *Philosophy as a Way of Life*, ed. Arnold I. Davidson (Hoboken, NJ: Blackwell, 1995). Hadot connects Thoreau to the tradition of spiritual exercises in a brief essay, "There Are Nowadays Professors of Philosophy, but not Philosophers," trans. J. Aaron Simmons, *Journal of Speculative Philosophy* 19, no. 3 (2005). See also Arnold I. Davidson, "Spiritual Exercises and Ancient Philosophy: An Introduction to Pierre Hadot," *Critical Inquiry* 16, no. 3 (1990): 475–482; and Michel Foucault, *The History of Sexuality*, trans. Robert Hurley, vol. 3, *The Care of the Self* (New York: Vintage, 1988). Foucault analyzes the ancient tradition of ascetic exercises in which "one is called to take oneself as an object of knowledge and a field of action, so as to transform, correct, and purify oneself, and find salvation." Foucault, *The History of Sexuality*, 42.

15. Thoreau, *Walden*, 108, 99. Michael Warner explores Thoreau's weird erotics in two probing essays: Michael Warner, *"Walden's* Erotic Economy," in *Comparative American Identities*, ed. Hortense J. Spillers (New York: Routledge, 1991), 157–174; and Michael Warner, "Thoreau's Bottom," *Raritan* 11 (1992): 53–79. See also Peter Coviello, "The Wild Not Less Than the Good: Thoreau, Sex, Biopower," *GLQ* 23, no. 4 (2017): 509–532.

16. Thoreau, *Walden*, 170.

17. On Thoreau's work as a "disciplined yet eccentric land surveyor" and how it informed his artistry and politics, see Daegan Miller, "At the Boundary with Henry David Thoreau," in *This Radical Land: A Natural History of American Dissent* (Chicago: University of Chicago Press, 2018), 16.

18. The passage from a Massachusetts state legislature committee report is cited and discussed in a classic work of critical education history, Michael B. Katz's *The*

Irony of Early School Reform (Cambridge, MA: Harvard University Press, 1968; re-printed by Teachers College Press, 2001), 190–191. Traditional historiographies of American schools in the nineteenth century emphasized the expansion of education as a public good, opening up knowledge and opportunities for social mobility. Katz and his contemporaries took a darker view. They saw the new schools as disciplinary institutions, designed to shore up social order and prepare students from the lower classes for life and labor under industrial capitalism. In the reformatory, Katz argues, education became a tactic of class warfare. See also Bernard Bailyn, *Education in the Forming of American Society: Needs and Opportunities for Study* (Published for the Institute of Early American History and Culture at Williamsburg, Virginia by the University of North Carolina Press, 1960) and Carl Kaestle, *Pillars of the Republic: Common Schools and American Society, 1780–1860* (New York: Hill and Wang, 1983). On these historiographic debates, see Milton Gaither, *American Educational History Revisited: A Critique of Progress* (New York: Teachers College Press, 2003).

19. My thinking about rehabilitation is informed especially by Kyla M. Schuller, *The Biopolitics of Feeling: Race, Sex, and Science in the Nineteenth Century* (Durham, NC: Duke University Press, 2018). On "pastoral" care as a way of exercising power, see Michel Foucault, *Security, Territory, Population: Lectures at the Collège de France, 1977–1978*, trans. Graham Burchell, ed. Arnold I. Davidson (New York: Picador, 2007). On nineteenth-century rehabilitation theories and institutions, see Anthony M. Platt, *The Child Savers: The Invention of Delinquency*, 40th anniversary ed. (New Brunswick, NJ: Rutgers University Press, 2009); Robert S. Pickett, *House of Refuge: Origins of Juvenile Reform in New York State, 1815–1857* (Syracuse, NY: Syracuse University Press, 1969); Joseph M. Hawes, *Children in Urban Society: Juvenile Delinquency in Nineteenth-Century America* (Oxford: Oxford University Press, 1971); Robert M. Mennel, *Thorns and Thistles: Juvenile Delinquents in the United States, 1825–1940* (Lebanon, NH: University Press of New England, 1973); Harold Finestone, *Victims of Change: Juvenile Delinquents in American Society* (Westport, CT: Greenwood Press, 1976); Steven Schlossman, *Love and the American Delinquent: The Theory and Practice of 'Progressive' Juvenile Justice, 1825–1920* (Chicago: University of Chicago Press, 1977); John R. Sutton, *Stubborn Children: Controlling Delinquency in the United States* (Berkeley: University of California Press, 1988); Margaret K. Rosenheim, Franklin E. Zimring, David S. Tanenhaus, and Bernadine Dohrn, eds., *A Century of Juvenile Justice* (Chicago: University of Chicago Press, 2002); and Geoff K. Ward, *The Black Child-Savers: Racial Democracy and Juvenile Justice* (Chicago: University of Chicago Press, 2012).

20. Emory Washburn, *An Address at the Dedication of the Reform School in West-borough, Mass.* (Boston: Dutton and Wentworth, 1849), 17.

21. Erving Goffman, *Asylums: Essays on the Social Situation of Mental Patients and Other Inmates* (New York: Anchor Books, 1961). Michel Foucault, *Discipline and Punish: The Birth of the Prison*, trans. Alan Sheridan (New York: Vintage Books, 1977).

22. Washburn, *An Address at the Dedication of the Reform School*, 18.

23. Karl Marx, *Capital*, trans. Ben Fowkes, vol. 1 (London: Penguin Books, 1990), 284.

24. Marx, *Capital*, 284.

25. W.E.B. Du Bois, *Black Reconstruction in America* (New York: Free Press, 1992), 10.

26. Eric Williams, *Capitalism and Slavery* (Chapel Hill: University of North Carolina Press, 1994), 202.

27. Frederick Douglass, *Narrative of the Life of Frederick Douglass, an American Slave*, ed. David W. Blight (Boston: Bedford, 2003), 81. My thinking about race and vigilance is informed by Simone Brown, *Dark Matters: On the Surveillance of Blackness* (Durham, NC: Duke University Press, 2015).

28. Saidiya Hartman, *Scenes of Subjection: Terror, Slavery, and Self-Making in Nineteenth-Century America* (New York: Oxford University Press, 1997), 5.

29. Andrew Ure, *Philosophy of Manufactures* (London: Charles Knight, 1835), 15–16. My reading is informed by E. P. Thompson, *The Making of the English Working Class* (New York: Vintage, 1966), 360. I import the phrase "nominally free" from Eric Williams, *Capitalism and Slavery*, 29.

30. Jonathan Crary, *Suspensions of Perception: Attention, Spectacle, and Modern Culture* (Cambridge, MA: MIT Press, 1999), 77.

31. Ure, *Philosophy of Manufactures*, 18.

32. See Matthew Stuart, "Locke on attention," *British Journal for the History of Philosophy* 25, no. 3 (2017): 487–505. A similar theory of attention appears in the Scottish philosopher Dugald Stewart's *Elements of the Philosophy of the Human Mind* (Philadelphia: William Young, 1793). Stewart's special focus is the role of attention in memory: "Attention consists partly (perhaps entirely) in the effort of the mind, to detain the idea or the perception, and to exclude the other objects that solicit its notice." Stewart, *Elements of the Philosophy of the Human Mind*, 102.

33. Charles Wellbeloved, *Devotional Exercises, for the Use of Young Persons* (Pittsburgh: S. Engles, 1815), 15, 18.

34. Joshua G. Fitch, *The Art of Securing Attention in a Sunday-School Class* (London, 1850), 27.

35. "Methodism," E. P. Thompson writes, "was the desolate inner landscape of Utilitarianism in an era of transition to the work-discipline of industrial capitalism." Thompson, *The Making of the English Working Class*, 365. Upstate New York's revivals, Paul E. Johnson observes, "provided entrepreneurs with a means of imposing new standards of work discipline and personal comportment upon themselves and the men who worked for them, and thus they functioned as powerful social controls." Paul E. Johnson, *A Shopkeeper's Millennium: Society and Revivals in Rochester, New York, 1815–1837* (New York: Hill and Wang, 1978), 138. Charles Sellers takes the same

view: "Widening revivalism's market by virtually promising salvation to those making the requisite effort, the crypto-New-Light clergy bolstered their influence as ethical arbiters by equating good works with self-repressive capitalist effort." Charles Sellers, *The Market Revolution: Jacksonian America, 1815–1846* (New York: Oxford University Press, 1991), 210. For a collection of revisionary accounts, see Mark A. Noll, *God and Mammon: Protestants, Money, and the Market, 1790–1860* (Oxford: Oxford University Press, 2002).

36. Washburn, "Address at the Dedication of the State Reform School," 18.

37. Eve Kosofksy Sedgwick, "Jane Austen and the Masturbating Girl," *Critical Inquiry* 17, no. 4 (Summer 1991): 830.

38. On the history of the commune, see Ellen Wayland-Smith, *Oneida: From Free Love Utopia to the Well-Set Table* (New York: Picador, 2016).

39. Christopher Lasch, *The Culture of Narcissism: American Life in an Age of Diminishing Expectations* (New York: Norton, 2018), 4.

40. Focusing on a different region, Gabriel Winant provides an illuminating study of American social life in the wake of deindustrialization in *The Next Shift: The Fall of Industry and the Rise of Health Care in Rust-Belt America* (Cambridge, MA: Harvard University Press, 2021).

41. In *The Ruse of Repair: US Neoliberal Empire and the Turn from Critique* (Durham, NC: Duke University Press, 2021), Patricia Stuelke argues forcefully that American activists and intellectuals, especially critics in the academic humanities, have allowed themselves to abandon historical analyses of capitalism and colonialism in favor of affective "coping mechanisms" such as "reparative reading." As a corrective, Stuelke proposes what she calls "a deliberate exercise of attention," focusing on "ever-shifting violent structures whose nuances must be perpetually, collectively apprehended if they are ever to be destroyed." Stuelke, *The Ruse of Repair*, 17. Here, even as Stuelke raises serious questions about reparative reading, she accepts one of its main premises— that critical methods are modalities of attention. Even a critical practice whose final goal is radical, structural change thus begins by adopting a discipline of attention, guarding against ruses and diversions, seeking to apprehend "perpetually" that which it hopes eventually to dismantle.

42. Sianne Ngai, *Our Aesthetic Categories* (Cambridge, MA: Harvard University Press, 2012), 13. On the utopian impulse in popular culture and the arts, see Fredric Jameson, *The Political Unconscious: Narrative as a Socially Symbolic Act* (Ithaca, NY: Cornell University Press, 1981) and Fredric Jameson, "Reification and Utopia in Mass Culture," in *Signatures of the Visible* (New York: Routledge, 1990). Much of my own thinking about distraction and attention is still informed by Jameson's graduate seminar on Walter Benjamin, in which I was a student in the early 2000s. See also José Esteban Muñuz, *Cruising Utopia: The Then and There of Queer Futurity* (New York: NYU Press, 2009).

43. On militant counter-disciplines in American prisons, see Dylan Rodriguez, *Forced Passages: Imprisoned Radical Intellectuals and the U.S. Prison Regime* (Minneapolis: University of Minnesota Press, 2006); Lisa Corrigan, *Prison Power: How Prison Influenced the Movement for Black Liberation* (Jackson: University Press of Mississippi, 2016); and Garrett Felber, *Those Who Know Don't Say: The Nation of Islam, the Black Freedom Movement, and the Carceral State* (Chapel Hill: University of North Carolina Press, 2020).

44. *The Confessions of Nat Turner* (Baltimore: Thomas R. Gray, 1831), 9.

45. In a classic study of Puritanism and its legacies, Sacvan Bercovitch recognized this pattern in early American devotional literature: "The vehemence of the metaphors, the obsessiveness of the theme, the staccato syntax, the sense of clauses recoiling rather than progressing (since every gesture against I-ness contains its own counter-gesture), the interminable-because-unresolved incantations of the 'I' over itself—every aspect of style betrays a consuming involvement with 'me' and 'mine' that resists disintegration." Sacvan Bercovitch, *The Puritan Origins of the American Self* (New Haven, CT: Yale University Press, 2011), 18. The nineteenth-century theorists of attention who revised devotional practice for modern economic conditions also revived this way of writing about self-discipline.

Part One: From the Devil to Distraction

1. "The painful conflict of body and soul," according to Peter Brown, is fundamental here—"the body's physical frailty, its liability to death and the undeniable penchant of its instincts toward sin served Paul as a synecdoche for the state of humankind pitted against the spirit of God." Peter Brown, *The Body and Society: Men, Women, and Sexual Renunciation in Early Christianity* (New York: Columbia University Press, 1988), 48. For a critique of this reading, see Dale Martin, *The Corinthian Body* (New Haven, CT: Yale University Press, 1995). Martin shows how modern dualism differs from ancient understandings of the body and its counterparts (soul, spirit, mind); modern readers, he argues, have distorted Paul's text by interpreting it through the lens of our own dualism. Martin's argument is compelling and opens up the possibility of reimagining and reclaiming Paul's legacy. For my purposes, though, the crucial matter is not Paul's original meaning but the modern reception of his prescriptions, shaped (or misshaped) by the English terms of the King James translation and by a stark division between the body and the soul, the worldly and the divine.

2. Julia A. J. Foote, *A Brand Plucked from the Fire: An Autobiographical Sketch* (New York: George Hughes, 1879), 28. Foote's story here echoes a catechism from the 1689 text of the *Book of Common Prayer*, where new church members vow, before they are confirmed, to "renounce the devil and all his works, the pomps and vanities of this wicked world with all covetous desires of the same, and all the sinful lusts of

the flesh." For a nineteenth-century edition of this 1689 text, see *The Revised Liturgy of 1689: Being the Book of Common Prayer, Interleaved with the Alterations Prepared for Convocation by the Royal Commissioners, in the First Year of the Reign of William and Mary*, ed. John Taylor (London: Samuel Bagster and Sons, 1855). For the catechism and "pomps and vanities," see page 62.

3. The novelist and cultural theorist Sylvia Wynter has tracked how a Christian notion of natural depravity was refashioned into a "religio-secular" scheme of racial inferiority in the era of settler colonialism and plantation slavery. In the colonization of the Americas, Wynter does not recognize the settlers' democratic emancipation from the theocratic past; instead, she sees them displacing stigma and shame onto nonwhite populations: "While the 'significant ill' of mankind's enslavement [to sin] was no longer projected as being to the negative legacy of Adamic Original Sin, the concept of enslavement was carried over and redescribed as being, now, to the irrational aspects of mankind's human nature." These "aspects" of an unruly nature, governable only by violence, were then projected onto nonwhite populations classified "as 'irrational' because 'savage' Indians, and as 'subrational' Negroes." Sylvia Wynter, "Unsettling the Coloniality of Being/Power/Truth/Freedom," *The New Centennial Review* 3, no. 3 (Fall 2003): 288, 296.

4. I develop this argument about nineteenth-century American religious dissenters and rebels in *The Oracle and the Curse: A Poetics of Justice from the Revolution to the Civil War* (Cambridge, MA: Harvard University Press, 2013). On the dialectics of submission and authority in American conversion narratives, see also Eileen Razzari Elrod, *Piety and Dissent: Race, Gender, and Biblical Rhetoric in Early American Autobiography* (Amherst: University of Massachusetts Press, 2008).

5. Paul North, *The Problem of Distraction* (Stanford, CA: Stanford University Press, 2012), 2.

6. Edgar Allan Poe, "The Man of the Crowd," in *Collected Works of Edgar Allan Poe*, ed. Thomas Ollive Mabbott, vol. 2, *Tales and Sketches, 1831–1842* (Cambridge, MA: Belknap Press of Harvard University Press, 1978), 510.

7. Thomas Clayton, *Seriousness of Attention at the Time of Divine Worship* (London: Richard Sare, 1712), 16.

8. On Clayton's contribution to the discourse of attention in eighteenth-century Britain, see Robert DeMaria Jr., "Attention," in *British Literature 1640–1789: Keywords* (Hoboken, NJ: Wiley-Blackwell, 2018), 21–24.

9. Jarena Lee, *Religious Experience and Journal* (Philadelphia: printed for the author, 1849), 9–10.

10. J. H. McIlvaine, *A Discourse upon the Power of Voluntary Attention* (Rochester, NY: Rochester Daily Advertiser, 1849), 7–8.

11. Frederick Douglass, *Narrative of the Life of Frederick Douglass, an American Slave*, ed. David W. Blight (Boston: Bedford, 2003), 81–82.

12. Donald B. Gibson, examining the rhetoric of these passages, suggests that "Douglass conceives of Covey as the devil." Donald Gibson, "Reconciling Public and Private in Frederick Douglass's *Narrative,*" *American Literature* 57, no. 4 (1985): 557.

13. Herman Melville, *Moby-Dick*, ed. Hershel Parker and Harrison Hayford (New York: Norton, 2002), 136.

14. Federico Bellini, "Driving off the Spleen: *Moby-Dick* and Healing from Melancholy Reverie," *Leviathan* 19, no. 2 (2017): 29. According to Bellini, the images Ishmael sees from the masthead "correspond to the Transcendentalist idea that the world is nothing but the most external layer of the self. This idea is dangerous, Melville seems to imply, because even though one can pretend that everything visible on the horizon is nothing but a projection of one's own mind, there is still much that is not visible beyond it, and much more below the surface of water demarcated by the horizon. Eventually, the disregarded invisible world comes back with a vengeance." Bellini, "Driving off the Spleen," 28. See also Michael J. Hoffman, arguing that for Melville "the prime virtue is the ability to perceive the world as object and to survive in it on the basis of one's clear perceptions"; the deeper "problem" menacing a dreamer like Ishmael "is that this mystical sense of oneness makes you relax just a bit too much." Michael J. Hoffman, "The Anti-Transcendentalism of *Moby-Dick,*" *The Georgia Review* 23, no. 1 (Spring 1969): 14.

15. Ralph Waldo Emerson, "The Transcendentalist," in *The Complete Works of Ralph Waldo Emerson*, vol. 1, *Nature, Addresses, and Lectures* (Boston: Houghton, Mifflin, 1903–1904), 341.

16. Emerson, "The Transcendentalist," 359.

17. The Biblical and Shakespearean sources I mention were identified by Eric C. Brown in "Shakespeare's *Richard III* and the Masthead in Melville's *Moby-Dick,*" *ANQ* 14, no. 1 (2001): 3–5.

18. Edgar Allan Poe, "Berenice," in *Collected Works of Edgar Allan Poe*, ed. Thomas Ollive Mabbott, vol. 2, *Tales and Sketches, 1831–1842* (Cambridge, MA: Belknap Press of Harvard University Press, 1978), 211–212.

19. Poe to T. W. White, April 30, 1835, cited by Thomas Ollive Mabbott in Poe, *Collected Works*, 207.

20. Colin Dayan, "The Identity of Berenice, Poe's Idol of the Mind," *Studies in Romanticism* 23, no. 4 (Winter 1984): 491–513.

21. Joel Porte, *Romance in America: Studies in Cooper, Poe, Hawthorne, Melville, and James* (Middletown, CT: Wesleyan University Press, 1969), 80.

22. Porte, *Romance in America*, 83.

23. Porte, *Romance in America*, 83.

24. William James, *The Principles of Psychology*, ed. Frederick H. Burkhardt (Cambridge, MA: Harvard University Press, 1983), volume 1, 382.

Part Two: Reform

1. See N. Katherine Hayles, "Hyper and Deep Attention: The Generational Gap in Cognitive Modes," *Profession* (2007): 187–199.

2. Jennifer L. Roberts, "The Power of Patience: Teaching Students the Value of Deceleration and Immersive Attention," *Harvard Magazine*, November/ December 2013.

3. Margaret Koehler, *Poetry of Attention in the Eighteenth Century* (New York: Palgrave Macmillan, 2012), 3.

4. Bernard Stiegler, *Taking Care of Youth and the Generations*, trans. Stephen Barker (Stanford, CA: Stanford University Press, 2010), 184.

5. Warren Burton, "The Best Mode of Fixing the Attention of the Young," in *Lectures Delivered before the American Institute of Instruction* (Boston, 1834), 64.

6. Richard Brodhead, "Sparing the Rod: Discipline and Fiction in Antebellum America," *Representations* 21 (Winter 1988): 67–96.

7. *Hints to Parents*, (Salem, MA: Whipple and Lawrence, 1825), 46, 71.

8. Burton, "Best Mode," 61.

9. Harriet Beecher Stowe, "Catharine Beecher," in *Our Famous Women: An Authorized Record of their Lives and Deeds*, ed. Elizabeth Stuart Phelps (Hartford, CT: Worthington, 1884), 89.

10. Harriet Beecher Stowe, *Uncle Tom's Cabin*, ed. Elizabeth Ammons (New York: Norton, 1994), 212, 207, 273, 208.

11. Stowe, *Uncle Tom's Cabin*, 259. On *Uncle Tom's Cabin*, missionary Christianity, and nineteenth-century education reform, see Molly Farrell, "Dying Instruction: Puritan Pedagogy in *Uncle Tom's Cabin*," *American Literature* 82, no. 2 (June 2010): 243–269.

12. Geoff K. Ward, *The Black Child-Savers: Racial Democracy and Juvenile Justice* (Chicago: University of Chicago Press, 2012), 41. On the history of African American education in a context of hostility and repression, see also Jarvis Givens, *Fugitive Pedagogy: Carter G. Woodson and the Art of Black Teaching* (Cambridge, MA: Harvard University Press, 2021).

13. Curtis J. Evans, *The Burden of Black Religion* (New York: Oxford University Press, 2008), viii.

14. Stowe, *Uncle Tom's Cabin*, 385. Stowe goes on to describe the program of missionary education this way: "Let the church of the North receive these poor sufferers in the spirit of Christ; receive them to the educating advantages of Christian republican society and schools, until they have attained to somewhat of a moral and intellectual maturity, and then assist them in their passage to those shores, where they may put in practice the lessons they have learned in America." Stowe, *Uncle Tom's Cabin*, 386. On the New York African Free School and the question of colonization, see Anna

Mae Duane, *Educated for Freedom: The Incredible Story of Two Fugitive Schoolboys Who Grew Up to Change a Nation* (New York: NYU Press, 2020).

15. Susan Paul, *Memoir of James Jackson, the Attentive and Obedient Scholar*, ed. Lois Brown (Cambridge, MA: Harvard University Press, 2000), 67, 87.

16. Saidiya Hartman, *Scenes of Subjection: Terror, Slavery, and Self-Making in Nineteenth-Century America* (New York: Oxford University Press, 1997), 5, 4.

17. Lydia Maria Child, "Conversation on Attention," *Juvenile Miscellany* 1, no. 1 (1826): 72–87.

18. Elizabeth Palmer Peabody, "Method of Spiritual Culture: Being an Explanatory Preface to the Second Edition of *Record of a School*," *Record of a School: Exemplifying the General Principles of Spiritual Culture*, 2nd ed. (Boston: James Munroe, 1836), xx.

19. On Peabody's life and advocacy, see Bruce A. Ronda, *Elizabeth Palmer Peabody: A Reformer on Her Own Terms* (Cambridge, MA: Harvard University Press, 1999).

20. Elizabeth Palmer Peabody, *Record of a School: Exemplifying the General Principles of Spiritual Culture* (Boston: James Munroe, 1835), 1.

21. Peabody, *Record of a School*, 34.

22. Peabody, *Record of a School*, 9.

23. Peabody, *Record of a School*, 145.

24. William Watkins, *An Address Delivered before the Moral Reform Society* (Philadelphia: Merrihew and Gunn, 1836), 5. My thanks to Kyla Schuller for pointing me toward this important document of nineteenth-century thought about race, attention, and the cultivation of sensibility.

25. Susan Paul, *Memoir of James Jackson, the Attentive and Obedient Scholar*, ed. Lois Brown (Cambridge, MA: Harvard University Press, 2000), 74. My treatment of Susan Paul and her milieu draws from Brown's research and editorial work, as presented in this edition.

26. William D. Kelley, *Address Delivered at the Colored Department of the House of Refuge* (Philadelphia: T. K. and P. G. Collins, 1850), 24.

27. My thinking about prisons, religion, and the secular has been informed especially by John Lardas Modern, *Secularism in Antebellum America* (Chicago: University of Chicago Press, 2011). On American Protestantism and prison reform, see also Winnifred Fallers Sullivan, *Prison Religion: Faith-Based Reform and the Constitution* (Princeton, NJ: Princeton University Press, 2009) and Jennifer Graber, *The Furnace of Affliction: Prisons and Religion in Antebellum America* (Chapel Hill: University of North Carolina Press, 2011).

28. A. D. Eddy, *"Black Jacob," A Monument of Grace* (Philadelphia: American Sunday School Union, 1842), 35–36.

29. Austin Reed, *The Life and the Adventures of a Haunted Convict*, ed. Caleb Smith (New York: Random House, 2016), 173–174.

Part Three: Revival

1. On spirituality in the contemporary United States, see Courtney Bender, *The New Metaphysicals: Spirituality and the American Religious Imagination* (Chicago: University of Chicago Press, 2010). On American evangelicalism's rise to power in the late twentieth and early twenty-first centuries, see Steven Patrick Miller, *The Age of Evangelicalism: America's Born-Again Years* (New York: Oxford University Press, 2014). On the long history of racism in evangelicalism, including both segregationist and assimilationist missions, see Anthea Butler, *White Evangelical Racism: The Politics of Morality in America* (Chapel Hill: University of North Carolina Press, 2021). On the evangelical movement's alignment with "tough-on-crime" politics, see Aaron Griffith, *God's Law and Order: The Politics of Punishment in Evangelical America* (Cambridge, MA: Harvard University Press, 2021).

2. Christian Wiman, "All My Friends Are Finding New Beliefs," *Poetry Magazine*, January 2020.

3. Christian Wiman, *My Bright Abyss: Meditations of a Modern Believer* (New York: Farrar, Strauss, and Giroux, 2013), ix–x.

4. David Paul Nord, "Benevolent Capital: Financing Evangelical Book Publishing in Early Nineteenth-century America," in *God and Mammon: Protestants, Money, and the Market, 1790–1860*, ed. Mark A. Noll (Oxford: Oxford University Press, 2002), 162.

5. On the populist and radical tendencies in eighteenth- and nineteenth-century evangelical movements, see Gary B. Nash, *The Urban Crucible: Social Change, Political Consciousness, and the Origins of the American Revolution* (Cambridge, MA: Harvard University Press, 1979); William L. Andrews, ed., *Sisters of the Spirit: Three Black Women's Autobiographies of the Nineteenth Century* (Bloomington: Indiana University Press, 1986); Nathan O. Hatch, *The Democratization of American Christianity* (New Haven, CT: Yale University Press, 1989); Susan Juster, *Disorderly Women: Sexual Politics and Evangelicalism in Revolutionary New England* (Ithaca, NY: Cornell University Press, 1994); Nancy Ruttenberg, *Democratic Personality: Popular Voice and the Trial of American Authorship* (Stanford, CA: Stanford University Press, 1998); Ann Taves, *Fits, Trances, and Visions: Experiencing Religion and Explaining Experience from Wesley to James* (Princeton, NJ: Princeton University Press, 1999); Mark A. Noll, ed., *God and Mammon: Protestants, Money, and the Market, 1790–1860* (Oxford: Oxford University Press, 2002); and Ashon T. Crawley, *Blackpentecostal Breath: The Aesthetics of Possibility* (New York: Fordham University Press, 2017).

6. Robert Baird, *Religion in America: Or, An Account of the Origin, Progress, Relation to the State, and Present Condition of the Evangelical Churches in the United States, with Notices of the Unevangelical Denominations* (New York: Harper and Brothers, 1844), 210.

7. Baird, *Religion in America*, 210–211.

8. Karl Marx, "A Contribution to the Critique of Hegel's Philosophy of Law," in *Collected Works*, by Karl Marx and Frederick Engels, vol. 3, *Marx and Engels, 1843–1844* (London: Lawrence and Wishart, 1975), 175.

9. See, for example, Frances Wright, "Religion," in *Course of Popular Lectures* (New York: The Free Enquirer, 1829), 104.

10. See Christopher Cannon, *Black Freethinkers: A History of African American Secularism* (Evanston, IL: Northwestern University Press, 2019).

11. Paul E. Johnson, *A Shopkeeper's Millennium: Society and Revivals in Rochester, New York, 1815–1837* (New York: Hill and Wang, 1978), 138.

12. Charles Sellers, *The Market Revolution: Jacksonian America, 1815–1846* (New York: Oxford University Press, 1991), 210. See also John Corrigan, *Business of the Heart: Religion and Emotion in the Nineteenth Century* (Berkeley: University of California Press, 2001).

13. Tracy Fessenden, *Culture and Redemption: Religion, the Secular, and American Literature* (Princeton, NJ: Princeton University Press, 2007), 63. On crypto-Protestantism in debates over religious liberty, see also Tisa Wenger, *Religious Freedom: The Contested History of an American Ideal* (Chapel Hill: University of North Carolina Press, 2016).

14. On mesmerism, see Emily Ogden, *Credulity: A Cultural History of U.S. Mesmerism* (Chicago: University of Chicago Press, 2018). On Mormonism, see John L. Brooke, *The Refiner's Fire: Making Mormon Cosmology, 1644–1844* (Cambridge: Cambridge University Press, 1996); and Peter Coviello, *Make Yourselves Gods: Mormons and the Unfinished Business of American Secularism* (Chicago: University of Chicago Press, 2019). On spiritualism, see Dana Luciano, *Arranging Grief: Sacred Time and the Body in Nineteenth-Century America* (New York: NYU Press, 2007); and Molly McGarry, *Ghosts of Futures Past: Spiritualism and the Cultural Politics of Nineteenth-Century America* (Berkeley: University of California Press, 2012).

15. Walt Whitman, *Leaves of Grass* (Brooklyn, NY, 1855), xi.

16. Whitman, *Leaves of Grass*, 48.

17. On religion, the secular, and "buffering," see Charles Taylor, *A Secular Age* (Cambridge, MA: Harvard University Press, 2007) and Charles Taylor, "Buffered and Porous Selves," *The Immanent Frame*, September 2, 2008.

18. James Dana, *The Intent of Capital Punishment: A Discourse Delivered in the City of New-Haven, October 20, 1790. Being the Day of the Execution of Joseph Mountain, for a Rape* (New Haven, CT: T. and S. Green, 1790), 5.

19. [David Daggett], *Sketches of the Life of Joseph Mountain, A Negro* (New Haven, CT: T. Green, 1790). On Mountain's life and trial, see Louis P. Masur, *Rites of Execution: Capital Punishment and the Transformation of American Culture, 1776–1865* (New York: Oxford University Press, 1991); Steven Wilf, *Law's Imagined Republic: Popular Politics and Criminal Justice in Revolutionary America* (Cambridge: Cambridge University Press, 2010); Lawrence B. Goodheart and Peter P. Hinks, "'See the Jails Open

and the Thieves Arise': Joseph Mountain's Revolutionary Atlantic and Consolidating Early National Connecticut," *Atlantic Studies* 10, no. 4 (2013): 497–527; and Greta Lafleur, "'Egyptian Lusts' at the Gallows," in *The Natural History of Sexuality in Early America* (Baltimore, MD: Johns Hopkins University Press, 2018). My treatment of gallows literature is also informed by Jeannine Marie DeLombard, *In the Shadow of the Gallows: Race, Crime, and American Civic Identity* (Philadelphia: University of Pennsylvania Press, 2014). I offer an extended treatment of the legal, religious, and literary aspects of Joseph Mountain's case in Caleb Smith, *The Oracle and the Curse: A Poetics of Justice from the Revolution to the Civil War* (Cambridge, MA: Harvard University Press, 2013).

20. *Sketches of the Life of Joseph Mountain*, 3.

21. *Sketches of the Life of Joseph Mountain*, 10. The version of Mountain represented in the biography, as Lawrence B. Goodheart and Peter P. Hinks have argued, steps out of the nightmares of New England's Federalist elites: "All that a rapacious monarchism, an uncertain patchwork of black freedom . . . , and a disruptive capitalism and democracy had launched in the Atlantic world" had shaped Mountain into "a monster of appetite and tumult." Goodheart and Hinks, "'See the Jails Open and the Thieves Arise,'" 512.

22. Dana is preaching in an era when, as Michael Meranze shows, "critics condemned public punishments for their uncontrollable and contradictory meanings." Michael Meranze, "A Criminal Is Being Beaten: The Politics of Punishment and the History of the Body," in *Possible Pasts: Becoming Colonial in Early America*, ed. Robert Blair St. George (Ithaca, NY: Cornell University Press, 2000), 307. On Mountain's case and the death penalty debates, see Masur, *Rites of Execution*; Wilf, *Law's Imagined Republic*; and Smith, *The Oracle and the Curse*.

23. "Blackness here," as Greta LaFleur explains, "appears as the very monument to habit, denoting a lack of self-governance and a lack of capacity for improvement or sovereignty." Greta LaFleur, *The Natural History of Sexuality in Early America*, 125.

24. Baird, *Religion in America*, 210.

25. Through the formal separation of church and state, Perry Miller writes, "Not only was the state relieved forever of the terrible duty of suppressing heresy and subduing dissent, but the churches so prospered that there was virtually no real heresy in the country, and dissent only strengthened Truth." Perry Miller, *The Life of the Mind in America: From the Revolution to the Civil War* (New York: Harcourt, Brace & World, 1965), 45.

26. Baird, quoted in Miller, *The Life of the Mind in America*, 41.

27. "To consider the career of secularization in American culture," as Tracy Fessenden has argued, is to reckon with "the consolidation of a Protestant ideology that has grown more entrenched and controlling even as its manifestations have often become less visibly religious." Fessenden, *Culture and Redemption*, 5.

28. Henry Clay Fish, *Primitive Piety Revived* (Boston: Congregational Board of Publication, 1855), 61–62, iii.

29. William Apes[s], *A Son of the Forest*, 2nd ed. (New York, 1831), 80. On Apess's life and work, see Philip F. Gura, *The Life of William Apess, Pequot* (Chapel Hill: University of North Carolina Press, 2015) and Drew Lopenzina, *Through an Indian's Looking-Glass: A Cultural Biography of William Apess, Pequot* (Amherst: University of Massachusetts Press, 2017).

30. *The Confessions of Nat Turner* (Baltimore: Thomas R. Gray, 1831), 9.

31. Pioneering historical studies of the Southampton insurrection include Herbert Aptheker, *Nat Turner's Slave Rebellion* (New York: Grove Press, 1966); Henry Irving Tragle, *The Southampton Slave Revolt of 1831: A Compilation of Source Material* (Amherst: University of Massachusetts Press, 1971); Stephen B. Oates, *The Fires of Jubilee: Nat Turner's Fierce Rebellion* (New York: Harper & Row, 1975); and Thomas C. Parramore, *Southampton County, Virginia* (Charlottesville: University of Virginia Press, 1978). On cultural memory and the meaning of the *Confessions*, see Eric J. Sundquist, *To Wake the Nations: Race in the Making of American Literature* (Cambridge, MA: Harvard University Press, 1993); Mary Kempt Davis, *Nat Turner Before the Bar of Justice: Fictional Treatments of the Southampton Slave Insurrection* (Baton Rouge: Louisiana State University Press, 1999); and Kenneth S Greenberg, *Nat Turner: A Slave Rebellion in History and Memory* (Oxford: Oxford University Press, 2002). On religion in Turner's life, world, and rebellion, see Randolph Ferguson Scully, *Religion and the Making of Nat Turner's Virginia: Baptist Community and Conflict, 1740–1840* (Charlottesville: University of Virginia Press, 2008); and John Mac Kilgore, "Nat Turner and the Work of Enthusiasm," *PMLA* 130, no. 5 (2015): 1347–1362. I elaborate my own arguments about religion, law, and expression in the *Confessions* in Smith, *The Oracle and the Curse*.

32. *Richmond Enquirer*, August 26, 1831, quoted in Kilgore, "Nat Turner and the Work of Enthusiasm," 1356. Kilgore offers this gloss on the lines: "Thus black enthusiasm, defined as a religious culture linked to the miscalculating passions, now begins to delineate the character of slave rebellion."

33. Toni Morrison, *Beloved* (New York: Vintage, 2004), 103–104.

34. Morrison writes in her preface that she wanted the novel to be "historically true in essence, but not strictly factual." Morrison, *Beloved*, xvii. Recently, Saidiya Hartman has elaborated a similar method, "critical fabulation," to reimagine the experiences of the criminalized, pathologized, and stigmatized. See Hartman, *Wayward Lives, Beautiful Experiments: Intimate Histories of Social Upheaval* (New York: Norton, 2019). On religion in Morrison's work, there is a rich secondary literature. Recent examples include M. Shawn Copeland, "Enfleshing Love: A Decolonial Theological Reading of *Beloved*," in *Beyond the Doctrine of Man: Decolonial Visions of the Human*, ed. Joseph Drexler-Dreis and Kristien Justaert (New York: Fordham University Press, 2020); Christina Bieber Lake, "The Demonic in Service of the Divine: Toni Morrison's *Beloved*," *South Atlantic Review* 69, no. 4 (Fall 2004): 51–80; Matthew Smalley, "The Unchurched

Preacher and the Circulated Sermon: Literary Preaching in Toni Morrison's *Beloved*," *MELUS* 43, no. 2 (Summer 2018): 29–52; and Emily Griesinger, "Why Baby Suggs, Holy, Quit Preaching the Word: Redemption and Holiness in Toni Morrison's *Beloved*," *Christianity and Literature* 50, no. 4 (Summer 2001): 689–702.

35. Walt Whitman, *Leaves of Grass* (Brooklyn, NY, 1855), v–vi.

36. David Kuebrich, *Minor Prophecy: Walt Whitman's New American Religion* (Bloomington: Indiana University Press, 1989).

37. Reflecting on this passage and others like it, Michael Warner proposes that Whitman understands his writing as continuous with an ancient tradition of spiritual exercises, making his leaves less suited to criticism than to devotional reading. The poet imagines his reception by people who "read with their bodies, and with the full range of faculties, in a project of cultivating not just good heart but its radical possession and habit." Michael Warner, "Whitmaniac Reading," unpublished manuscript. I am grateful to Warner for sharing this text with me, and for our many good talks about Whitman.

38. Edmond Holmes, *Walt Whitman's Poetry: A Study and a Selection* (London: John Lane, 1902), 72–73.

39. Holmes, *Walt Whitman's Poetry*, 73.

40. Holmes, *Walt Whitman's Poetry*, 75, 1.

41. Holmes, *Walt Whitman's Poetry*, 72.

42. Holmes, *Walt Whitman's Poetry*, 74.

Part Four: Devotion

1. Simone Weil, *Gravity and Grace*, trans. Emma Crawford (London: Routledge, 1952), 69.

2. Weil, *Gravity and Grace*, 70.

3. On Weil and attention, see Mario von der Ruhr, *Simone Weil: An Apprenticeship in Attention* (New York: Continuum, 2006); and Robert Chenavier, *Simone Weil: Attention to the Real*, trans. Bernard E. Doering (Notre Dame, IN: University of Notre Dame Press, 2012).

4. Susan Sontag, "Simone Weil" (1963) in *Against Interpretation and Other Essays* (New York: Picador, 1966), 51.

5. Patti Smith, *Devotion* (New Haven, CT: Yale University Press, 2017), 25–26.

6. Saint Augustine, *Confessions*, trans. Henry Chadwick (Oxford: Oxford World Classics, 1991), 5.

7. Elizabeth Palmer Peabody, "Preface to American Edition," *The Confessions of St. Augustine* (Boston: E. P. Peabody, 1843), iii–iv.

8. Constance M. Furey, Sarah Hammerschlag, and Amy Hollywood, *Devotion: Three Inquiries in Religion, Literature, and Political Imagination* (Chicago: University of Chicago Press, 2021), 228.

9. Rita Felski, *The Limits of Critique* (Chicago: University of Chicago Press, 2015), 107. See also Rita Felski and Elizabeth S. Anker, eds., *Critique and Postcritique* (Durham, NC: Duke University Press, 2017).

10. Stephen Best and Sharon Marcus, "Surface Reading: An Introduction," *Representations* 108, no. 1 (Fall 2009): 18.

11. Heather Love, "Close but not Deep: Literary Ethics and the Descriptive Turn," *New Literary History* 41, no. 2 (2010): 375.

12. David Kurnick, "A Few Lies: Queer Theory and Our Method Melodramas," *ELH* 87, no. 2 (Summer 2020): 369.

13. Ann Plato, "A Residence in the Country," in *Essays: Including Biographies and Miscellaneous Pieces, in Poetry and Prose* (Hartford: Printed for the Author), 65–66.

14. Joseph Stevens Buckminster, "Sermon XXII: The Circumstances of the Situation of Our Country, Favorable to Moral and Religious Eminence" (1807), in *The Works of Joseph Stevens Buckminster: With Memoirs of His Life*, vol. 1: Sermons (Boston: J. Munroe, 1839), 374–388.

15. On Buckminster's career and reception, see Lawrence Buell, "Joseph Stevens Buckminster: The Making of a New England Saint," *Canadian Review of American Studies* 10, no. 1 (March 1979), 1–30.

16. Versions of Buckminster's passage appear in Noah Worcester, *Friend of Youth; Or, New Selection of Lessons, in Prose and Verse, for Schools and Families, to Imbue the Young with Sentiments of Piety, Humanity, and Universal Benevolence* (Boston: Cummings and Hilliard, 1822), 150–151 and Samuel Putnam, *The Analytical Reader, Containing Lessons in Simultaneous Reading and Defining* (New York: Jonathan Leavitt, 1831), 70–74.

17. The question of Plato's racial identity is in dispute among scholars. Following the suggestion of Pennington's preface, most readers have assumed that Plato came from a free Black family. Ron Welburn in *Hartford's Ann Plato and the Native Borders of Identity* (Albany: SUNY Press, 2015) draws from government records and other archival sources to offer a "profile of her enigmatic identity as linked to the Algonquian peoples of Long Island Sound." Welburn, *Hartford's Ann Plato*, xi.

18. On Wheatley and her reception, see Paula Bennett, "Phyllis Wheatley's Vocation and the Paradox of the 'Afric Muse,'" *PMLA* 113:1 (January 1998), 64–76; Henry Louis Gates, Jr., *The Trials of Phyllis Wheatley* (New York: Basic Books, 2003); and Joanna Brooks, "Our Phyllis, Ourselves, *American Literature* 82:1 (March 2010), 1–28.

19. Adrien Rouquette, *La Thébaïde en Amérique, ou Apologie de la Vie Solitaire et Contemplative* (New Orleans, LA: Méridier, 1852), 46.

20. An early biographer recalled Rouquette's own impatience in the schoolhouse: "How could the prosy rules of grammar fix the child's attention when the thrill of a mocking bird, or a perfume-laden breeze from the woodland reminded him of the delights his forest friends were enjoying while he was imprisoned and had to undergo the penance of study[?]" Susan Blanchard Elder, *Life of the Abbé Adrien Rouquette* (New Orleans, LA: L. Graham Co., 1913), 24. On Rouquette's life, see also Dagmar Renshaw

LeBreton, *Chahta-Ima: The Life of Adrien-Emmanuel Rouquette* (Baton Rouge: Louisiana State University Press, 1947).

21. Adrien Rouquette, *Wild Flowers, Sacred Poetry* (New Orleans: O'Donnell, 1848), 2.

22. See Tom Mould, ed., *Choctaw Tales* (Jackson: University Press of Mississippi, 2004), xlv.

23. Abraham Jacobs, *Spiritual Meditations, Written in Verse, on Passages Selected from the Sacred Scriptures* (Harrisburg, PA: Wm. Henlock, Printer, 1848), n.p. At least four copies have survived; the one I consulted is held by the Huntington Library in San Marino, California.

24. Henry David Thoreau, journal entry for September 13, 1852, in *The Writings of Henry David Thoreau*, ed. Bradford Torrey, vol. 4, *Journal* (Boston: Houghton Mifflin, 1906), 351. For an extended discussion of this passage and its implications for reading Thoreau's work, see Scott Slovic, "The Inner Life and the Outer World: Thoreau's 'Habit of Attention' in His Private Journal," in *Seeking Awareness in American Nature Writing* (Salt Lake City: University of Utah Press, 1992), 21–60.

25. Hannah More, *The Book of Private Devotion* (Boston: Crocker and Brewster, 1832), 22.

26. The essential account of Brackett's case and its context in nineteenth-century debates about religious and secular truth is Emily Ogden, *Credulity: A Cultural History of US Mesmerism* (Chicago: University of Chicago Press, 2018), 102–158.

27. Thomas C. Hartshorn, "Appendix," in *Practical Instruction in Animal Magnetism*, by J.P.F. Deleuze, trans. Thomas C. Hartshorn (Providence, RI: B. Cranston and Company, 1837), 87.

28. Emily Dickinson, #409 ["The Soul selects her own Society"], in *The Poems of Emily Dickinson: Variorum Edition*, ed. R. W. Franklin (Cambridge, MA: The Belknap Press of Harvard University Press, 1998).

29. I discuss the poem in the opening pages of my first book, *The Prison and the American Imagination* (New Haven, CT: Yale University Press, 2009). My revised thoughts about it have been shaped by ongoing conversations with Virginia Jackson, and by Jackson's great study, *Dickinson's Misery: A Theory of Lyric Reading* (Princeton, NJ: Princeton University Press, 2005).

30. Walt Whitman, *Leaves of Grass* (Brooklyn, NY, 1855), 29.

31. Ezra Pound, "What I Feel about Walt Whitman," in *Selected Prose, 1909–1965*, ed. William Cookson (New York: New Directions, 1973), 145.

Afterword

1. Edgar Allan Poe, "The Man of the Crowd," in *Collected Works of Edgar Allan Poe*, ed. Thomas Ollive Mabbott, vol. 2, *Tales and Sketches, 1831–1842* (Cambridge, MA: Belknap Press of Harvard University Press, 1978), 505–516. Emily Ogden writes

about this tale's special resonance during the coronavirus pandemic in "On Going Outside," *Yale Review*, December 13, 2021.

2. Walter Benjamin, "On Some Motifs in Baudelaire," in *Illuminations: Essays and Reflections*, trans. Harry Zohn, ed. Hannah Arendt (New York: Schocken Books, 1968), 166.

3. Benjamin, "Motifs," 171, 174.

4. Benjamin, "Motifs," 176.

5. Benjamin, "Motifs," 176, 175.

6. Paul North, *The Problem of Distraction* (Stanford, CA: Stanford University Press, 2012), 157. All my thinking about Poe, Benjamin, and the ambivalences of attention has been enriched by reading, talking, and teaching with Paul North.

7. Walter Benjamin, "The Work of Art in the Age of Mechanical Reproduction," in *Illuminations: Essays and Reflections*, trans. Harry Zohn, ed. Hannah Arendt (New York: Schocken Books, 1968), 217–251.

8. Benjamin, "Work of Art," 239.

9. Benjamin, "Work of Art," 218, 238, 240–241.

10. Benjamin's work, with its interest in the aesthetic and political possibilities of modern distraction, belongs to a critical tradition that treats literature and other works of art as historical artifacts, indelibly marked by economic and political forces. Benjamin's essays on attention and distraction also share affinities with other critiques of discipline, including Michel Foucault's. Jonathan Crary's *Suspensions of Perception*, for example, synthesizes a Marxian history of labor management with an analysis of power in the style of Foucault. Though Crary's book deals with a later period and focuses on the visual arts, rather than literature, the critical problem that Crary describes is close to the one that I have taken up in this book. It is to understand "the paradoxical intersection . . . between an imperative of a concentrated attentiveness within the disciplinary organization of labor, education, and mass consumption and an ideal of sustained attentiveness as a constitutive element of a creative and free subjectivity." Jonathan Crary, *Suspensions of Perception* (Cambridge, MA: MIT Press, 1999), 1–2.

11. The idea of the attention economy entered popular culture with the publication of Michael Goldhaber's provocative essay, "Attention Shoppers!" *Wired*, December 1, 1997.

12. Tim Wu, *The Attention Merchants: The Epic Scramble to Get Inside Our Heads* (New York: Vintage Books, 2016), 11–14. Nineteenth-century evangelical publishing houses took a similar approach, selling their pamphlets at a discount or giving them away for free. These enterprises got their funding from churches and Christian philanthropists, not advertisers. In both cases, though, the funding model depended on cultivating a big, persuadable audience.

13. See Shoshana Zuboff, *The Age of Surveillance Capitalism: The Fight for a Human Future at the New Frontier of Power* (New York: PublicAffairs, 2018); Nick Couldry and Ulises A. Mejias, *The Costs of Connection: How Data Is Colonizing Human Life and Appropriating It for Capitalism* (Stanford, CA: Stanford University Press,

2019); and Justin E. H. Smith, *The Internet Is Not What You Think It Is: A History, A Philosophy, a Warning* (Princeton, NJ: Princeton University Press, 2022).

14. Zadie Smith, "Fascinated to Presume," *New York Review of Books*, October 24, 2019.

15. Yves Citton, *The Ecology of Attention*, trans. Barnaby Norman (Malden, MA: Polity Press, 2017).

16. On Poe's difficult relationship to his reading public, see Perry Miller, *The Raven and the Whale: Poe, Melville, and the New York Literary Scene* (Baltimore, MD: Johns Hopkins University Press, 1997); Meredith McGill, *American Literature and the Culture of Reprinting, 1834–1853* (Philadelphia: University of Pennsylvania Press, 2003); and Michael Cohen, "Peddling Authorship in the Age of Jackson," *ELH* 79, no. 2 (Summer 2012): 369–388.

17. Henry David Thoreau, *Walden: A Fully Annotated Edition*, ed. Jeffrey S. Cramer (New Haven, CT: Yale University Press, 2004), 273–274.

INDEX

African American children: Pennington on intellectual and moral capacities of, 161; reformers' attitudes toward, 71, 73–74; Watkins as teacher of, 86–89

African American men, capacity for reform, 99–105, 123, 224n23

African colonization by Black Americans, 74, 87

African Methodist Episcopal Church, 30, 41–42, 87

Alcott, Bronson, 80–85

Allen, Richard, 41

American Tract Society, 113

animal magnetism, 116, 184–87

anti-slavery advocates: Dana as, 121, 123; Peabody as, 81; personal solutions envisioned by, 205; Susan Paul's alliances with, 91; Watkins as, 87, 88

Apess, William, 134–38

Arendt, Hannah, 4

asceticism: consumerism in today's versions of, 112; of devotional practices, 154; of Dickinson's life, 189; Foucault on, 213n14; Melville's references to, 57–58; preparing dissenters for resistance, 27; race and, 145; of Rouquette, 165; solitary prison cells and, 104; of Thomas à Kempis, 150; Thoreau's critique of, 176, 177; Turner's self-discipline and, 140; unacceptable to nineteenth-century Protestants, 173; Weil's studies of,

153; Whitman as counterbalance to, 149–50

attention: of Apess to evangelical revivalism, 135; Baird on religious conversion and, 114–15, 125–30; Benjamin on fascist uses of, 199, 200; blurring line between agency and submission, 196; Buckminster on rural pursuits and, 160; Child's lesson on reading and, 5, 77–79; in *Confessions of Nat Turner*, 140–41; demanded by nineteenth-century life, 31; deterrence by death penalty and, 121–22; devotional practices and, 156; Dickinson's valves of, 188–89; Douglass's call on public to confront slavery and, 53–54; educational philosophy of love and, 71–72; embodied by plantation overseer, 14–15; *The Imitation of Christ* as training in, 150; Jacobs's devotional poetry and, 168, 169, 170, 171–73; of James Jackson, 90–93; labor in Moby-Dick and, 57; Latin root *ad tendere*, 175; literary criticism and, 157–58; Locke on, 17; love in Morrison's *Beloved* and, 144, 145; Marx on, 13–15; McIlvaine on right kind of books and, 43–48; morbid, in Poe's "Berenice," 59–65; More on singleness of, 179, 181, 183; Poe's "Man of the Crowd" and, 195, 196, 198, 204; in prisoners' experiences, 100, 105, 109; ritualized worship and, 191; Rouquette's call

attention (*continued*)
for revival of, 6, 163–64, 166; Sedgwick on elopements of, 18; to sermon
at a hanging, 119–20, 123–24; for
studying the humanities, 69–70;
Thoreau on, 3–4, 5, 174, 176, 177–78;
Whitman's training of readers in, 150;
will and, 35–38, 80, 82; William James's
psychology of, 66–68. *See also*
disciplines of attention
attention ecology, 203
attention economy: digital, 20, 23, 201–4;
More's *Book of Private Devotion* in,
183; nineteenth-century newspaper
and, 202; revivals in, 126, 128; today's
evangelical Christianity in, 111;
twenty-first century seekers in, 111–12
Auburn State Prison: Hodges's time in,
103, 104–5; as model for New York
system, 103–4; Reed's time in, 106–7,
108–10
Augustine's *Confessions*, 81, 140,
154–55, 156

Baby Suggs, 144–45
Baird, Robert, 114–15, 116, 125–30
Beecher, Catharine, 72–73
Bellini, Federico, 219n14
Benjamin, Walter, 197–200, 229n10
Bentham, Jeremy, 16, 97–98
Bercovitch, Sacvan, 217n45
"Berenice" (Poe), 59–65
Best, Stephen, 157
Bible: itinerant hawkers of, 113; Jacobs's
writings based on, 168–69; Jesus's
transformations of traditional scrip-
ture, 148; McIlvaine on reading of,
44; Melville's allusion to, 57; in
prisoner's solitary cell, 105, 106, 107,
109–10; psalm recomposed by Baby
Suggs, 144–45; Thoreau's use of
symbols from, 2, 211n4
body and soul: Clayton on attention
during worship and, 37; McIlvaine's

racist distinctions and, 46; in Paul's
letters, 29–30, 217n11; Poe's psychology
of dissociation and, 65; Whitman's
unsettling of boundary between,
191–92
Book of Common Prayer, 217n2
Book of Private Devotion (More), 155,
179–87
Brackett, Lurena, 184–87
Brown, Peter, 217n1
Buckminster, J. S., 159–62
Burton, Warren, 71, 72
business and religion, 131–33. *See also*
industrial market capitalism

Cameron, Sharon, 3
camp meetings, 111, 113, 116, 127, 135, 138, 142
capitalism: criminal blamed partly on,
224n21; Fish on the business Christian and, 133; Weil as militant critic
of, 153. *See also* industrial market
capitalism
capital punishment, 119–24
Carlyle, Thomas, 174, 177
Cavell, Stanley, 212n8
Chahta-Ima (Rouquette), 164
Child, Lydia Maria, 5, 77–79
Christian morality: industrial market
capitalism and, 16, 17, 18, 22–23,
215n35; juvenile reformatory and,
97–98; repression justified by, 30.
See also conversion, religious;
evangelical Christianity; moral
discipline; Protestantism; Roman
Catholic devotional practices; sin
Citton, Yves, 203
Clayton, Thomas, 35–38
Confessions (Augustine), 81, 140, 154–55,
156
The Confessions of Nat Turner, 139–42
Congregationalists, 161, 104, 121, 129, 131,
133, 155
consumer marketplace: conservative religious discipline and, 23; distraction

at scene of, 13, 16; replaced by trade in attention, 201; Rouquette on shallowness of, 165

conversion, religious: of Apess, 136, 137, 138; Baird on, 114–15, 125–30; encounter with Whitman feeling like, 148; of Hodges, 99–105; mass conversions, 127

Covey, 49–54

Crary, Jonathan, 15–16, 229n10

creeds, 190–91, 192, 193

critical fabulation, 225n34

critical race theory, 200

Curtis, Jared, 104

Dana, James, 119–24, 224n22

Day, Benjamin, 202

Dayan, Colin, 61

daydreams, 16, 31, 56, 57

death penalty, 119–24

deixis, 145

democracy: criminal blamed partly on, 224n21; Holmes on exultant naturalism of, 149–50

devil: Apess's wrestling with, 136, 138; *Book of Common Prayer* and, 217n2; distraction and, 31, 32, 33, 35, 37; Douglass conceiving Covey as, 219n12; Lee's struggle with, 39–42; Poe's "Man of the Crowd" and, 195, 201

devotion: Ann Plato's attitude of, 160, 162; Buckminster on rural life and, 160; as intense desire, 191; Melville's gesture toward, 57–58; New England's deep history of, 9; as nondenominational spiritual discipline, 156; place in modernity of, 204–5; practices referred to as, 154; Turner's plot and, 140, 142. *See also* prayer; spiritual exercises

devotional literature: Christian tradition of, 154–56; genre of, 24; on giving up attachments to worldly things, 175; *The Imitation of Christ*, 149–51,

155; Jacobs's *Spiritual Meditations*, 167–73; modeling discipline for readers, 26; More's *Book of Private Devotion*, 155, 179–87; organized by a plan of days, 169; performance without conviction and, 93; Rouquette's *Thebaid in America*, 163–66; style of, 217n45; Whitman's engagement of the senses and, 191–92

devotional reading: as discipline of attention, 17; by mesmerized Brackett, 184–87; today's renewed scholarly interest in, 156–57; as transformative interconnectedness, 157; Whitman's writing suited to, 226n37. *See also* devotional literature; reading

Dickinson, Emily, 188–89, 204

digital attention economy, 20, 23, 201–4. *See also* attention economy

disciplinary institutions, 18, 26–27, 71, 76. *See also* prisons; reformatories; reformers; schools

disciplinary intimacy, 72

discipline: Holmes on insufficiency of, 149; provided by evangelical revivals, 114–15; in reformatories, 11; to rehabilitate distracted minds, 204; of Thoreau's spiritual transformation, 206; of today's regimens, 19–22, 112–13. *See also* moral discipline

disciplines of attention: Alcott's teaching methods and, 80–85; Ann Plato and, 162; benefits and sacrifices of, 8; Christian morality and, 17; defined, 6; of Dickinson, 189; economic and social transformation and, 22, 216n41; as encounter between two wills, 27; industrial capitalism and, 13; in institutions of reform, 17, 71, 75, 76; Jacobs's devotional practice as, 169; McIlvaine on literary genres and, 43–48; in Philadelphia's House of Refuge for Colored Children, 96; philosophies of the mind and, 16–17;

disciplines of attention (*continued*)
postcritique as, 157–58; radical
analysis emerging from, 205; recasting large-scale problems as private
ones, 7–8, 205; of Reed in Auburn
State Prison, 110; in reformed philosophy of education, 72; as remedy
for distractions of modernity, 6, 33;
study of the arts as, 69–70; Thoreau's
practice of, 9–10; today's escapist or
therapeutic cultivation of, 24; in
Watkins's moral instruction, 88;
Weil's search for, 153; of whale watcher
at masthead, 55; in Whitman's affirmation of desire, 149. *See also* attention; self-discipline
dissociation: defined, 56; of distracted
workers, 13, 31; in Poe's "Berenice,"
64–65; in recital of a creed, 190; of
urban pedestrians, 198; during worship service, 36. *See also* distraction
distraction: in age of new media, 6–7,
200–201; alliance between religion
and economy and, 23; Baird on
difficulty of conversion and, 126, 128;
Benjamin on aesthetic and political
possibilities of, 199–200, 229n10;
as desire for worldly attractions,
29–31; earlier political meaning of,
75–76; eliminated in solitary prison
cell, 105, 109; enslaved workers
making use of, 15, 52; in industrializing market economy, 5, 6, 8, 13; in
marketplace, 13, 16; of modernity, 5,
6–7, 32–33, 47; More on imagination
as, 179–80; personal remedies for,
7–8, 70, 76; Poe's resentment of,
204; in reading, 157–58; reformers
seeing sensational literature as, 110;
reformers' understanding of, 76;
rehabilitating children from, 79;
revivals as solution for, 114–15; as a
sin, 35–38; Thoreau and, 3, 4, 10;
twenty-first century, 23; Watkins's

worries about secular schools and,
89; Webster's dictionary definitions
of, 29, 76; Weil's studies of mystical
and ascetic practices and, 153; in
workplace, 13–14, 15–16. *See also*
dissociation
Douglass, Frederick, 15, 49–54, 115
Du Bois, W. E. B., 14
Dwight, Louis, 104

Eastern State Penitentiary, 103–4
economic and social forces: damaging
distraction caused by, 6–7; disciplines of attention and, 22; isolation
of consoling therapy and, 27;
McIlvaine on stimulation of
appetites by, 47; racial violence and,
145; reformers' views of distraction
and, 76; Thoreau's critique of, 2–5.
See also industrial market capitalism;
modernity
ecstasy, 9, 39, 42, 154, 165
Eddy, A. D., 99–105
Eddy, Thomas, 104
education. *See* schools
Emerson, Ralph Waldo, 56–57
evangelical Christianity: allied with
market economy, 23; American right-
wing nationalists and, 200; Apess's
alignment with, 135; Baird's defense
of, 114–15, 116; conservative anxieties
about, 114; embracing separation of
church and state, 129–30; of industrial
prisons' defenders, 104, 109; in
nineteenth-century attention economy, 183–84; nineteenth-century
growth of, 113–14; opposing economic and social transformation, 22;
on "outward coercion," 130, 147;
publications of, 113, 229n12; in today's
attention economy, 111. *See also*
conversion, religious; Protestantism;
revivalism
Evans, Curtis J., 74

Felski, Rita, 157
Fessenden, Tracy, 116, 224n27
Fish, Henry Clay, 131–33
Foote, Julia A. J., 30
Foucault, Michel, 12, 26, 213n14, 229n10
freedom: of conscience and expression,
    128, 129; revivalism's inward coercion
    and, 130; in student's capacities
    of attention, 80–81; submission
    to reformers' authority and, 71;
    Whitman on willing submission
    and, 148
free labor: industrial prisons and, 103,
    104; juvenile reformatories and, 108;
    reformists disturbed by consequences
    of, 95–96; religion and, 23; social
    control and, 18. See also wage labor
free market, 17, 18, 95, 115
free will, 128, 130, 136
Furey, Constance M., 157

Garrison, William Lloyd, 91
George, Sally, 138
Goffman, Erving, 12
Gray, Thomas Ruffin, 140
Great Awakening, 23, 111

Hammerschlag, Sarah, 157
Hartman, Saidiya, 15, 26, 75, 225n34
Haunted Convict, 106–10
Hawthorne, Nathaniel, 30
Hodges, Jacob, 99–105
Hoffman, Michael J., 219n14
Hollywood, Amy, 157
Holmes, Edmond, 149–51
House of Refuge, in New York City, 108
House of Refuge for Colored
    Children, in Philadelphia, 94–97
humanities: defenses of, 69–70; reac-
    tionary efforts to delegitimate, 200

The Imitation of Christ (Thomas à
    Kempis), 149–51, 155
imperialism, 4, 205

impressions: Apess's susceptibility to,
    134, 135; Baird on, 125–27, 128; moral
    training by reformers and, 76, 88;
    More on soul's development and,
    179, 181–82; Watkins on religious
    education and, 86–87
indentured servitude, 23, 107–8, 115, 135
indigenous people: allegedly ignored
    by Thoreau, 4; Ann Plato's grieving
    poem about, 161; Apess's story, 135,
    136–37, 138; Buckminster's vision of
    America and, 160–61; charitable
    schools for, 71; Child's lesson on
    attention and, 77–79; Christian
    notion of natural depravity and,
    218n3; McIlvaine's racist view of, 46;
    Peabody's activities for benefit of,
    81; punishment of the flesh and, 30
industrial market capitalism: allied with
    conservative religion, 16, 17, 18, 22–23,
    115–16, 215n33; Ann Plato's experience
    of, 161; Benjamin on attention and
    distraction under, 198–99; disciplin-
    ary institutions and, 11–13, 26, 213n18;
    disciplines of attention and, 13;
    distractions of, 5, 6, 7–8, 13, 31–32;
    labor discipline and, 12, 16; Peabody's
    importing of devotional works into,
    156; Rouquette's estrangement from,
    164–65; social and psychological
    dislocations of, 14, 31–32, 95–96;
    Thoreau's effort to free himself from,
    3, 178; Weil's factory experience and,
    153. See also capitalism; consumer
    marketplace
Internet, 200–204
Ishmael, 55–58, 219n14
itinerant ministries, 111, 113, 127

Jackson, James, 74–75, 90–93
Jacobs, Abraham, 167–73, 204
James, William, 66–68
Jefferson, Thomas, 97–98
Johnson, Barbara, 211n4

Johnson, Paul E., 115, 215n35
juvenile reformatories. *See* reformatories

Katz, Michael B., 213n18
Kelley, William D., 94–98
Kilgore, John Mac, 225n32
Koehler, Margaret, 69–70
Kurnick, David, 158

LaFleur, Greta, 224n23
Lasch, Christopher, 21–22
La Thébaïde en Amérique (Rouquette), 163–66
Leaves of Grass (Whitman), 113, 116–18, 146–49, 150–51, 190–93
Lee, Jarena, 39–42
"Life without Principle" (Thoreau), 3, 8–9
literary criticism, 157–58
Locke, John, 16–17
Longfellow, Henry Wadsworth, 165
love: of chaste Rouquette, 165; devotional practices and, 154, 156; disciplines of attention and, 17; Holmes on human need for, 149; in Morrison's *Beloved*, 143–44, 145
Love, Heather, 157

"The Man of the Crowd" (Poe), 32, 194–99, 200–201, 203–4
Marcus, Sharon, 157
Martin, Dale, 217n1
Marx, Karl: on attention, 13–15; Christianity and, 23, 26, 115
Marxism, cultural, 200
Mashpee Revolt, 137
Mason, William, 169
mass incarceration, 23
mass media: American right-wing nationalists and, 200; antebellum sensationalist press, 47; new publishing technologies in nineteenth century and, 23; of nineteenth-century evangelical tracts, 111, 113,

128; today's evangelicals and, 111. *See also* new media
McIlvaine, J. H., 43–48
Melville, Herman, 13, 55–58, 219n14
mesmerism, 116, 184–87
Miller, Perry, 224n25
missionary campaigns, 111, 113–14
Moby-Dick (Melville), 13, 55–58, 219n14
modernity: criminal embodying destructive forces of, 121, 224n21; distractions of, 5, 6–7, 32–33, 47; evangelicals functioning successfully in, 128; reformer's reaction to urban disorder of, 95, 97; Rouquette's primitivist reaction against, 6, 166; Thoreau's diagnosis of, 2–5
moral discipline, 6; in Alcott's experimental school, 82–85; Buckminster's Christian call to, 160; imposed by white Christian nationalism, 22; racist beliefs about, 74, 87. *See also* Christian morality; discipline
moral duty, of cultivating attention, 80, 84–85
moral training: of Black children in free states, 91; at House of Refuge, 108; in industrial prisons, 104; in institutions of reform, 16, 71–73, 76; in Massachusetts reformatory, 12; in schools, 160, 70, 81–82, 86–89; for white, Protestant respectability, 12
More, Hannah, 155, 179–83
Morrison, Toni, 143–45
Mountain, Joseph, 120–21, 122–24, 224n21
mysticism: craving for transformation and, 23; Lee's struggle with the devil and, 41–42; revivalism and, 116; of Rouquette, 164, 165, 166; tradition of masthead-standing and, 57; transcendental, 19, 31; Weil's studies of, 153

nationalists: Benjamin on fascism and, 199, 200; of today's American far right, 200; white Christian, 18, 22, 70, 116, 161, 162

new media: Benjamin on value of distraction and, 199–200; students' drift away from humanities and, 69; television as example of, 70; today's distraction and, 6–7. *See also* mass media

New York system, 103, 104, 109

North, Paul, 31, 199

Oneida Community, 21

outward coercion, 130, 147

Paul, 29, 44, 217n1

Paul, Susan, 74–75, 90–93

Peabody, Elizabeth Palmer, 80–85, 154–56

Pennington, James W. C., 161–62

Pennsylvania system, 103–4

perception: Baby Suggs activating powers of, 145; disciplines of attention and, 6; Thoreau's habits of, 206; Transcendentalism and, 219n14

Plato, Ann, 5–6, 159–62, 204, 227n17

Plumb, Charles, 107

Poe, Edgar Allan: "Berenice," 59–65; "The Man of the Crowd," 32, 194–99, 200–201, 203–4

Porte, Joel, 62

postcritique, 157–58

Pound, Ezra, 192

prayer: as discipline of attention, 17, 182; Lee's experiences of, 39–42; Melville's gesture toward, 57–58; More's essay on, 179–83; Puritans' houses with chamber for, 154; Weil on attentiveness as, 153

The Prison and the American Imagination (Smith), 18–19

prisons: contrast between two types of, 102–5; conversion to Christian

virtue in, 99–105; as disciplinary institutions, 26; discipline in, 106–10; industrial economy and, 18, 23; original systems of, 71; white Christian nationalism and, 22

Protestantism: disciplinary institutions and, 75; in modernizing attention economy, 183; requiring labor and trade, 173; simple literary style and, 168. *See also* evangelical Christianity

Puritans: Cavell on Thoreau's relationship with, 212n8; desire in devotions of, 191; devotional practices of, 9; encounter between two wills and, 217n45; prayer closet in houses of, 154

Putnam, Samuel, 160

race: Child's teaching on inborn equality and, 77–79; death penalty and, 123; punishment of the flesh and, 30, 145

racial integration, 74–75, 87, 88

racism: Ann Plato's stand against, 162; Black children's fitness for moral discipline and, 87; cognitive hierarchy fixed in nature and, 91; in McIlvaine's moralized aesthetics, 45–46, 48; notion of natural depravity and, 100, 218n3; of prison guards encountered by Black Jacob, 103; romantic racialism associated with, 74; of today's American right-wing nationalists, 200. *See also* race

reading: Alcott's teaching about attention and, 82; Child's teaching about attention and, 77–79; critical detachment disarmed by Whitman, 192–93; critics of modern civilization and, 205; McIlvaine on sensational literature and, 43–48; More's teaching on art of, 181, 184, 187; reformers seeing two modes of, 110; writing in relation to, 158. *See also* devotional reading

Reed, Austin, 106–10

reformatories, 10–13, 213n18; disciplines
of attention in, 13, 71, 75; exclusion
of African American children from,
73; industrial capitalism and, 12–13,
18; in Massachusetts, 10–13, 18;
New York's House of Refuge, 108;
Philadelphia's House of Refuge for
Colored Children, 94–97; Thoreau's
self-discipline and, 12–13; violent
punishments in, 108; white Christian
supervision in, 12, 96
reformers: beliefs and goals of, 70–71,
76; calling for end to death penalty,
121; conservative social order and, 19;
disavowing the exercise of power,
76; disturbed by urban temptations,
95–96; replacing punishment with
moral instruction, 96–97. See also
disciplinary institutions
Religion in America (Baird), 114–15, 116,
125–30
religious liberty: Mashpee Revolt and,
137; Protestant definition of, 130
reparative reading, 157, 216n41
revivalism, 19; Apess's organization of
revivals, 138; Baird on, 114–15, 116,
127–28; conservative morality
in, 118; economic conditions and,
118; economic realities and, 215n35;
Morrison's fabulation of, 144–45; recasting disciplines as self-disciplines,
130; regimens and new beliefs in, 116,
118; as social control, 215n35; today's
seekers and, 111–12; in upstate New
York, 30, 44, 215n35; volatile politics
of, 27; Whitman's speech acts and,
149. See also evangelical Christianity
Roberts, Jennifer, 69
Roman Catholic devotional practices,
6, 156. See also Rouquette, Adrien
Romanticism: Melville's treatment of,
56, 57; More's alarmed reaction to,
180; of Patti Smith, 154; Rouquette's
mysticism and, 165

Rouquette, Adrien, 6, 116, 163–66, 204,
212n12, 227n20
Rush, Benjamin, 97–98

The Scarlet Letter (Hawthorne), 30, 191
schools: Alcott's experimental school,
80–85; Baird's work in modernizing,
127; Buckminster's influence on,
161–62; as disciplinary institutions,
18, 26, 213n18, 214n18; disciplines of
attention in, 71, 75; industrial capitalism and, 213n18; for the poor,
indigenous, and children of color,
71; reformers' nurturing style in,
70–73; Watkins's Academy for Negro
Youth, 86–89
secular worldview: Baird's Religion in
America and, 129; capital punishment
and, 121; of industrial capitalism, 164;
McIlvaine on evils of modernity and,
47; Melville's treatment of attention
and, 57, 58; politics of, 97–98;
Watkins on threat to education from,
88, 89
Sedgwick, Eve Kosofsky, 18
self-care industry, 21–22
self-control: authorities training delinquents in, 27; group antagonisms
recast as problems of, 75; McIlvaine's
racist view of, 46; philosophy
of education and, 72; prisoners'
capacity for, 105. See also self-
discipline
self-denial: business Christian excused
from, 133; in Turner's early life, 142;
Whitman as counterbalance to,
149–50
self-discipline: devotional practice and,
182, 217n45; Holmes on Whitman's
lack of, 150; Jacobs on fear of God
and, 171; Paul on attending to the
Lord and, 29; to reawaken powers
of attention, 5; revivalism and, 130;
of Rouquette, 165; of Thoreau, 5, 10,

12–13, 177–78; of Turner, 140. *See also* disciplines of attention; self-control

Sellers, Charles, 115–16, 215n35

separation of church and state, 128–30, 224n25

serpent, biblical, 2, 29, 31, 211n4. *See also* snake

sin: Christian notion of natural depravity and, 218n3; Clayton on willful distraction as, 35–38; Covey's deceptions and, 49, 52; devotional literature with confessions of, 154; Jacobs on God's detection of, 170; Lee's progress from sense of, 39–42; McIlvaine's descriptions of, 46–47

slave rebellion, 142, 225n32

slavery: Ann Plato's knowledge of, 161; Buckminster's vision of agriculture and, 161; denial of education to the enslaved, 91; fears of Black freedom and, 123, 224n21; giving way to free labor, 23; Nat Turner and, 27, 139–42; Pennington on capacities of Black children and, 161; prison discipline and, 104; resistance in, 14, 15, 49–54; Southern evangelicals and, 115; Thoreau's protesting of, 4; urban youth as legacy of, 96; violent discipline in, 14–15. *See also* anti-slavery advocates

Smith, Patti, 154

Smith, Zadie, 203

snake: as Covey's nickname, 50, 52, 53; serpent in the Bible, 2, 29, 31, 211n4; Thoreau's ideas suggested by, 1–2, 11, 211n4

social forces. *See* economic and social forces

social hierarchies: evangelical Christianity and, 115; reformers' views of, 76

social media, 203

solitary confinement cell: at Auburn State Prison, 107; in mind of industrial prisoner, 104; reformers' use of, 76

solitary system, 103–4

solitude: devotional practices and, 154, 158; Dickinson's poetry and, 189; Rouquette's manifesto for life of, 165–66

"Song of Myself" (Whitman), 150–51, 192

Sontag, Susan, 153

spiritual exercises: compulsory for solitary prisoners, 104; Dickinson's belonging to tradition of, 189; economic system and, 12–13, 27; of *Imitation of Christ*, 150–51; nineteenth-century practices adapted from, 26; Peabody's exploration of traditions of, 81; Protestant suspicions about, 173; reformers replacing punishment with, 98; of Rouquette, 164, 165, 166; Thoreau's interest in, 9–10; of today's seekers, 112; in Turner's return to earthly master, 142; Whitman's writing in tradition of, 150–51, 226n37. *See also* devotion

Spiritual Exercises of Saint Ignatius, 155

Stewart, Dugald, 215n32

Stiegler, Bernard, 70

Stowe, Harriet Beecher, 72–73, 74, 220n14

Stuelke, Patricia, 216n41

surface reading, 157

Thebaid in America (Rouquette), 163–66

Thomas à Kempis, 150–51, 155

Thompson, E. P., 215n35

Thompson, Eunice, 120

Thoreau, Henry David: critics of, 4–5; diagnosis of modernity, 2–5, 31–32; distracted by locomotive, 3, 204, 206; revered for writings on attention, 153; Rouquette and, 165; on seeing without looking, 174–78; self-discipline of, 5, 10, 12–13, 177–78; self-reproach of, 3, 4; *Walden*, 2, 3, 5, 9, 203, 205–6; work of self-recovery, 8–10

Thoreau's axe, 1–2, 3, 4, 13, 206, 211n1

Transcendentalists: Buckminster and, 160; Emerson's defense of, 56–57; Melville's critique of, 56, 57, 219n14; Peabody as, 81; revivalism and, 116

transcendental mystics, 19, 31

Turner, Nat, 27, 139–42

Uncle Tom's Cabin (Stowe), 73, 220n14

Ure, Andrew, 15, 16

utopianism, 22, 23, 24

violence: clearing the way for white civilization, 161, 162; death penalty and, 122–23; of prison authorities, 106–10; racial, 145; revivalism potentially devolving into, 116

wage labor, 15, 95, 115. *See also* free labor

Walden (Thoreau), 2, 3, 5, 9, 203, 205–6

Walden video game, 4

Ward, Geoff K., 73

Warner, Michael, 226n37

Watkins, William, 86–89

Weber, Max, 17, 23, 26

Weil, Simone, 153–54

white Christian nationalism, 18, 22, 70, 116, 161, 162

white supremacy, 75

Whitman, Walt: Holmes and, 149–51; *Leaves of Grass*, 113, 116–18, 146–49, 150–51, 190–93; Rouquette and, 165

Wild Flowers: Sacred Poetry (Rouquette), 165

will: attention during worship and, 35–38; attention of students and, 80, 82; freedom of, 128, 130, 136; McIlvaine on struggle between nature and, 48; More's theory of impressibility and, 182; Rouquette on *attendre* as act of, 166; sinful distraction and, 35, 37; Thoreau on seeing and, 174–75, 176–77

Williams, Eric, 14

Wiman, Christian, 112–13, 117

Winnemuca, Sarah, 81

women, church's role in subjugation of, 115

Worcester, Noah, 160

"The Work of Art in the Age of Mechanical Reproduction" (Benjamin), 199

Wright, Frances, 115

Wu, Tim, 202

Wynter, Sylvia, 218n3

A NOTE ON THE TYPE

This book has been composed in Arno, an Old-style serif typeface in the classic Venetian tradition, designed by Robert Slimbach at Adobe.

Printed in the USA
CPSIA information can be obtained
at www.ICGtesting.com
JSHW021113060824
67650JS00003B/4

9 780691 256023